DATE			

FAT
OF THE
LAND

Fred Powledge

SIMON AND SCHUSTER   NEW YORK

Copyright © 1984 by Fred Powledge
All rights reserved
including the right of reproduction
in whole or in part in any form
Published by Simon and Schuster
A Division of Simon & Schuster, Inc.
Simon & Schuster Building
Rockefeller Center
1230 Avenue of the Americas
New York, New York 10020
SIMON AND SCHUSTER and colophon are registered trademarks of
Simon & Schuster, Inc.
Designed by Eve Kirch
Manufactured in the United States of America

1   3   5   7   9   10   8   6   4   2

Library of Congress Cataloging in Publication Data
Powledge, Fred.
Fat of the land.
Includes index.
1. Food industry and trade—United States.
2. Agricultural processing industries—United States.
3. Grocery trade—United States.   4. Agriculture—
Economic aspects—United States.   I. Title.
HD9005.P66   1984   338.4'76413'00973   83–27136
ISBN 0-671-42435-1

I am very grateful to dozens of people, both within the food business and outside it, for taking the time to explain their seemingly unfathomable industry to an outsider. Most of them are named and quoted in the pages that follow. I owe special debts of gratitude to Larry Hamm of Michigan State University, and to his colleagues in the U.S. Department of Agriculture's Economic Research Service, who demonstrate regularly that economics is not the dismal science after all.

For Grace Stearns Bingham

Contents

FAT
OF THE
LAND

1

We Have Lost Touch

There is something wrong with the American food system.

Most of us feel it, but few of us can put our fingers on the problem. Despite constant assurances to the contrary from the food industry itself and from many in government whom we pay to protect and inform us about food, there is the nagging feeling that things are not right.

Of course, "wrong" and "not right" are highly relative terms. Compared to how the majority of the rest of the world's people grow, get, buy, and eat their food, Americans are quite well off. We spend a smaller portion of our family budgets on food (around 22 percent); our food is plentiful and available in great variety, regardless of the season; and we devote little effort to wondering about the safety of what we eat. Compared with the developing nations and even with many of those that are highly developed, America has a strong, safe food system.

And yet the nagging feeling persists—the feeling that maybe things could be even cheaper, even better, even safer.

There are many among us in this well-endowed land who suspect that the system is being operated in ways that are inefficient, wasteful, and manipulative of the consumer who is at the end of the American food chain. We speak darkly of the *middleman* even though we don't know who he (or she, or they, or it) may be. The middle people are out there someplace, standing between us and the rest of the food system, and we don't know what they do for or to our food, or whether they perform tasks that are really necessary.

The nagging feeling surfaces every time we go to the supermarket. We are surrounded by what appears to be a great variety of foods, but if we look closely, we see that most of the cans and boxes that line the shelves are simply variations on the same product. And we feel it again when we are exposed to advertising for food: If it's "100% Natural!" then why does the list of ingredients sound so *un*natural? And would the government let them say something if it wasn't true?

And what about the new forms of packaging? It used to be that the metal can, the cardboard box, and the glass bottle were the standard packaging materials for most of the non-fresh foods we bought. But now there are technologies with which we may be much less familiar—ones with names like "aseptic packaging" and "retort pouching" and "irradiation." Chances are we've already been exposed to the technology of the electronic scanner, the device that adds up our purchases at the checkout counter. We wonder (if we think about it at all) who benefits from all this change. Will the consumer get anything out of it except higher food bills?

Occasionally we wonder about what is happening to the *definitions* of foods we once knew. We have filed away in our minds a very precise definition of what a tomato or ear of corn should taste like, and we know that when we bite into a wintertime import that this is not a tomato. It is an impostor wearing a tomato suit—a marvel of technological achievement, perhaps, but not the sort of thing you'd want to eat. What can we do about this?

Although we are told, and maybe believe, that food in our country is as safe as it is anywhere in the world, we may be concerned that it isn't safe enough. We hear reports that government isn't enforcing the far-reaching laws it has on the books; we read about PBBs in cattle feed in Michigan, about people who get sick after eating clams from the waters of New York's Long Island.

Beyond the question of safety, how faithful *are* our various governments to us on food issues? Why do the important economic decisions, the ones concerning labeling and antitrust, for example, always seem to be made in favor of the sellers of the food business, and not the consumers?

The most persistently nagging feeling of them all is that we simply don't know very much about food anymore. We have lost track of the food system. While we weren't looking, food stopped being something that grows, rather simply and straightforwardly, out of the ground and became a complicated technology.

We are, in short, very frustrated about our ignorance of the food system, and the frustration is made all the more vexing by the fact that we cannot ignore the system. Like water and air, food is something we have to keep consuming in order to stay alive.

All this ignorance should not be surprising. For while the practitioners of the food business have been busily turning it into a cold, predictable technology, most of us who are consumers have gone right on thinking of food in warm, emotional terms. Our history and upbringing have made food an almost sacred thing: It, along with water, is the stuff that keeps us alive and gives us the strength and longevity to perpetuate the human race. Food is a ritual item: We celebrate our births, weddings, deaths, and other special occasions with it. Some people put on evening clothes for it. Some religions use food to symbolize their leader's body, and one of the more memorable of the legends of the Christian faith has to do with a "last supper."

Food, then, is a very emotional matter, and we may be forgiven if we tend to forget that it is also a business. But such forgetfulness is a very big error, for food is a very large business indeed, and to those who run the business, there is no room for warmth or emotion. As long as we fail to recognize that obvious but easily overlooked fact, we are doomed to be the victims of the food system rather than its beneficiaries.

This brief journey through the system spends a little time at each of the major way stations that most of our food touches as it moves from the farm to the consumer's table. It concentrates almost exclusively on food that ends its trip by being sold at the retail level and cooked and served at home. This is an enormous amount of food, and it costs an enormous amount of money.

In 1982, according to the U.S. Department of Agriculture, American consumers spent about $298 billion at the retail level for food produced by U.S. farms. That was food for home use, and that was for domestically produced farm foods alone. The bill didn't include alcoholic beverages, bottled soft drinks, fishery products, or imported foods. Food is the nation's largest business—and, needless to say, it surely is one of our most important enterprises. If the food system were to take even a one-day holiday, the nation would be in chaos, as would be many other nations that depend on American foodstuffs.

While food eaten in restaurants, fast-food places, school cafeterias, and similar settings is very much a part of the system and also a very important part—Americans spent $96.5 billion for food away from home in 1982—it is discussed here (in Chapter 10) only in general terms. What the industry calls the food service business deserves its own volume or two.

Before the journey begins, we would do well to consider some definitions, figures, and assumptions that are important to the industry and ought to be important to the consumer. All of them should be taken with a few vigorous shakes of the salt cellar; not everybody agrees on all the definitions, a lot of the statistics are scarcely more than good guesses, and in a dynamic system like food, one that is almost totally predicated on what people want and are willing to do to get it, the assumptions may change quickly.

Food marketing is what happens to food between the producer and the consumer. It does not include the vital functions performed by the producers—the farmers and fishers who grow or catch it. It does include processing, manufacturing, transportation, wholesaling, and retailing.

Marketing does a lot to food. Sometimes it merely moves a fresh vegetable from the farm to the consumer as quickly as possible, and with a minimum of change in the product being transported. But oftentimes it alters the nature of the basic commodity drastically.

Marketing is where the middlemen make their livelihoods. It is where food gets almost all of its additives—not only the often controversial chemicals that are added to food, but also what might be called the "economic additives." These are the charges imposed by the middlemen at each stage of the food marketing process as they perform whatever job it is that they do. It is these economic additives, more than anything else, that make food cost what it costs, and it is these that fuel the controversy that ought to be at the heart of the food system today. For many of these economic additives are unnecessary. All raise the cost of the food to the consumer, in some cases exorbitantly and in many cases deceptively. And many do actual damage to the quality of the food as it moves through the system.

It is on these economic additives, these frequently hidden and inflated increases in cost, that the consumer should focus attention if he wishes to comprehend and cope with the business of food. It is these additives that must be dealt with, changed, and in some cases eliminated if the system is to change for the better, if the nagging feelings of suspicion are to be minimized. And it is to these economic additives that this book pays most attention.

Government economists devote a lot of time and effort to determining how the total food bill is divided up. Most of them work for the Department of Agriculture's Economic Research Service, the department's most recent name for the agency responsible for assembling social science information on food and agriculture.

Harry Harp, one of the ERS economists, presented some of the latest statistics in a recent issue of the service's quarterly publication, *National Food Review*.

Of the approximately $298 billion that Americans spent for domestic foods in 1982, wrote Harp, farmers got $84 billion, or 28 cents from each food dollar. The remaining $214 billion, or 72 cents per dollar, went to pay the costs of marketing the food. Economists call this the "marketing spread," and they define it as the difference between the retail price of food and the food's equivalent farm value—in other words, the cost of processing, packaging, transporting, and distributing. The spread has been expanding steadily in recent years; farmers have been getting less of the total pie, and the middlemen have been getting more.

Where does the $214 billion go?

Economists have broken the spread down into a number of categories, all of which help to show who the middleman is and what he gets for his additives. The biggest middleman is labor; more than 7 million workers in the food business account for 45 percent of the marketing bill.

Packaging is the second-largest cost, with 11 percent of the marketing bill, or almost a third as much as farmers got for producing the food. Transportation of food by truck and rail accounted for 7 percent (local delivery costs were not included here). Corporate profits took about 6 percent. Energy costs, excluding those for transportation, ate up almost 5 percent. The remaining 26 percent was attributed to "other" costs, including business taxes, depreciation, rent, advertising, and interest.

And where does the food go that is purchased with all those billions?

Most of it goes into our stomachs, although an alarming portion is wasted in one way or another. The Department of Agriculture's most recent estimate of per capita food consumption in the United States, determined by dividing the amount of food by the number of people, is that in 1982 the average American consumed 1,393 pounds of food. The average has hovered around 1,400 pounds for several years.

Of that estimated total, 577 pounds came from animals— 149 pounds of red meats, 64 pounds of poultry, 34 pounds of eggs, 306 pounds of dairy products, and 24 pounds of "other," including animal fats and fishery items. Crop products made up the remaining 816 pounds: 151 pounds of cereals and bakery products, 49 pounds of vegetable oils, 159 pounds of fruits and melons, 287 pounds of vegetables, 135 pounds of sugar and sweeteners, and 35 pounds of "other," including beverages such as coffee, soft drinks, and alcohol.

The amounts consumed per person may remain fairly constant, but the ways, shapes, and forms in which food is consumed are constantly changing as a result of shifts in the natures of the population and of the industry. At one time, the marketing spread in America was quite low, because people ate food that was only minimally processed, packaged, advertised, and transported. The middleman had few chances to tack on his additives. But as the nation changed, so did the ways of presenting food to the people. Foods became more highly processed, more elaborately packaged—and, inevitably, more expensive.

It is not only the food itself that is changing. Another shift that is occurring now, and that holds the food industry's fascinated attention, is the one that is generally referred to as the "changing American family." Partly because of economic conditions, partly because of better recognition of the rights of women, the consumer is changing, and the changes are affecting what gets sold and who buys it. Because divorce and separation are not viewed by as many people as the catastrophic events they once were, there are more people living alone and there are more one-parent families today; because of attitudes toward and means for controlling birth, there are fewer children in those households. Most important from the viewpoint of the food industry, there are more two-income families—families in which both husband and wife work at jobs outside the home and bring income into the household.

Women who called themselves "housewives" before did plenty of work, of course—it was the sort of employment that was, as the saying goes, "never done"—but working outside the home means in some cases more disposable income, more need and desire for foods that do not take half a day to prepare, more willingness to eat meals away from home.

Advertising people love to talk about these trends, because changing population means more opportunities to sell things. "Working women have increased the number of two-earner households and paved the way to a life of even greater abundance," advertising executive Patricia Greenwald told a meeting of food marketing executives a few years ago. "The kitchen is almost obsolete in this modern household." Lest her audience of food sellers grow despondent, though, she added that "there will still be a need for shopping, and Mom probably will be too busy to do it herself. She'll have help from the kids, Dad, and anybody else she can collar to do the job.

That means more shopping will be done by unskilled shoppers, putting a greater emphasis on brand-name products."

Some in the business see the trend in a somewhat more serious light. Joseph Sullivan is the president of Swift & Company, manufacturers of everything from Peter Pan peanut butter to Butterball turkeys. Sullivan, a thoughtful executive who has tried to look beyond the immediate future of his industry, feels what he calls a "churning" in food manufacturing, and in farming as well, that is founded on troublesome economic trends—energy costs, inflation, the costs of borrowing money—and that is affecting consumers profoundly.

Speaking of the two-breadwinner trend, Sullivan said in an interview, "I think we have greatly overdone the idea that this is a fundamental change in life-style and that this is a *choice* that people make. Many family units have two breadwinners today because they *have* to have two breadwinners. Which leads to the point that if two people are working, there is a greater need for convenience in foods. Convenience foods, in a two-family household, become a necessity—more convenience foods, more processed foods, and the tremendous increase in eating out.

"But I think that doesn't tell the whole story. I think what we are seeing is a more bipolar approach, where people are looking for radically different answers which produce rather significantly different outcomes. On the one hand you have the increase in eating out, an increase in looking for more and more convenience foods. On the other hand, I think you have a return to basics, too. People are more and more interested in nutrition, not only because of an increased awareness and interest in health; but ultimately, I think, they're going to be looking at the basics because there are going to be some very volatile periods in food costs that we have very little control over in the next ten to fifteen or twenty years."

Sullivan was asked to rate the industry's performance in reacting to the challenges that grew from the trends.

"I would rate the industry's efforts in the convenience area as probably about a B or B-plus. With respect to how to deliver basic foods more efficiently, I would rate that about a C-minus. I don't think there's been a *terrible* job done; I just don't think there's been the same kind of excitement that there has been in developing the convenience food market."

The executive said he was concerned that in the coming ten or fifteen years the issue of food supply would become a serious one. "We're operating on a very thin edge in terms of food inventory," he said, "and we're operating with a highly sophisticated system of transportation and distribution that could break down very quickly. I think the Northeast, for example, is very vulnerable to severe food dislocations simply because of the distances required to move food there and the very short inventories that that particular area of the country has. It sort of gives me a *déjà vu* feeling about some of the other parts of the world I've been in. There are precisely the same sorts of problems: You have a deteriorating infrastructure. In many of those countries there's an infrastructure that never existed. You have a very short supply of food, and that makes one very vulnerable. I think that in the next fifteen or twenty years, many people in America will have a better feeling of how people in developing countries feel. I hope to God it won't be as bad, quite obviously. But I think that they'll recognize how critical an issue the whole area of food supply is in a much more meaningful way than they do today."

The problems that Sullivan discussed—the cost of transporting food, the vulnerability of the system as it now exists, the possibly shocking adaptations American consumers may have to make—are ones that are obvious to anyone in the food system who takes the trouble to look at what is happening. Few do take the trouble, though, and even less effort is given to informing the consumer—who pays for the whole system—about what is going on. Few of us have more than a vague idea about what happens to food during its circuitous journey from the farmer to the consumer. It is not that the journey is too complex for us to understand. It is just that we have taken food, like water and clean air and plentiful energy and most of the other resources we depend on, for granted. In our rush to embrace whatever is advertised as "modern," whatever smacks of "technology," whatever claims to be "New!," we have managed to lose touch with many of the substances that keep us alive, and that is a very dangerous thing to do indeed.

2

Becoming Food

Once upon a time, and not really all that long ago, "food" was something edible that sprang from the soil, or that walked upon it until we slaughtered it, or that swam in Earth's waters until we captured it with spear, hook, or net. American citizens, whether they were residents of the countryside, suburbia, or city, had a close relationship with the food they ate.

Now it's not nearly that simple. The industry has decreed that food must be *processed*, must be *manufactured*, before we can take it home and eat it. And the decree applies not only to the breakfast cereal factories and entrée-freezing emporiums, but also to the very essence of food production itself, the American farm. The result is that the idea of the independent family farmer has just about become a nostalgia item of its own.

The farmer and fisher are just as indispensable as they always were—for no matter what happens, someone must plant the seeds and work the land and fight the weeds and cope with the weather and harvest the crop, must catch the fish and at least connect the automatic milker to the cows at five o'clock in the morning—but the power the producers once had to make basic decisions about the nature and quality of their work has been deeply eroded. In the minds of much of the rest of the food industry, the farmer has become just another processor who occupies a slot along a very lengthy line (and a minor slot at that), and who conducts business in an archaic way and complains a lot. The farmer, like the consumer, is thought of as little more than a necessary evil.

The depressing story of the American family farmer's present situation has been told often, and the details are familiar to many of us. They are rooted in the history not only of agriculture in this nation, but also of urban and technological change.

During its early years, American agriculture was a matter of self-sustenance, as was most everything else. But then the population changed. People moved to the cities and earned money at jobs far removed from agriculture, and they spent some of their money to buy food that others grew, food that came from increasingly greater distances. In the meantime, farmers used specialization and the technology that was available to grow far more than the population needed. One result was that farmers tended to overproduce, and that brought them low prices and lower incomes. So in the thirties Congress enacted a number of farm programs designed to control the amount of production and to protect the farmer— who was invariably described in political rhetoric, then as now, as the "small family farmer." The principal food issue before the government, as one federal agency put it, was "managing what seemed to be a perpetual surplus."

The issue grew in intensity after World War II, when technology encouraged farm production to expand while simultaneously the importance of farm labor declined. Capital, in the form of newly developed synthetic agricultural chemicals

and more complex and useful machinery, replaced labor as
the thing a farmer had to have more of. Production soared,
and although government programs were expanded and altered to try to keep a lid on it, the Agriculture Department
had to rent warehouses all over the nation to store the wheat,
cheese, eggs, and other constituents of the surplus. Because
there was so much of everything, the prices of commodities
stayed low.

The situation was so serious, USDA economist J. P. Penn
wrote in a 1979 department overview of structural issues in
American agriculture, that by the beginning of 1972 all the
government's grain storehouses were full and one-fifth of the
nation's cropland was lying idle, unplanted and unharvested,
as part of federal programs to lower the surplus. But then,
says Penn, there was a series of events that changed things
dramatically: "Crops were poor in many parts of the world
(notably the Soviet Union), some countries made major shifts
in policy, the value of the dollar was allowed to float (un-
pegging it from the value of gold) in world currency markets,
and demand soared for U.S. agricultural produce." There followed a period of "relative equilibrium" in U.S. agriculture.

What the situation has evolved into now is difficult to say,
since farming has been affected as much as any other calling
by the worldwide economic recession, but it is clear that
"agriculture" in the United States no longer means the "small
family farmer." Nor does it mean the farmer who feeds America. Agriculture now is a part of the global scheme of things,
just as are automobiles and textiles and oil stocks and instruments of war. President Ronald Reagan's Secretary of Agriculture spoke, not long after taking office, of using food as a
weapon in our international dealings, and hardly anyone
batted an eye. In the meantime, farms have decreased in
number and grown in size, making it less likely that the traditional farm family will be in charge of the land and the way it
is used and more likely that a distant corporation, possibly a

foreign-owned one, will make the decisions. In the middle thirties, according to USDA economist Lyle P. Schertz, there were more than 7 million farms in the nation. By 1950 the number had fallen to 5.6 million, and in 1981 it was 2.4 million. That land didn't disappear; much of it was absorbed into other farms, with the result that the size of the average U.S. farm has doubled since the fifties.

This may be explained (and it is, by many observers) as a logical extension of the same process that is going on everywhere. There are fewer examples of independent or family-operated *anything* now than a generation or so ago, from movie theaters to department stores to book publishers. As for foreign investment, just look at where we get many of our automobiles and television sets. And yet there are many who see all the signs as being especially ominous, even dangerous, when they apply to food and farming.

One of the most ominous is the fact that the recent changes in the industry have removed farmers from their traditional positions at the beginning of the food processing chain and installed them as what some see as almost incidental, trifling elements of it. No longer do farmers own a little machinery, buy a little seed, and collect much of their fertilizer from their own animals and then get down to the business of growing the food. Now they are very much at the mercy of what the economists call the "input sector" for the raw materials of seed, chemicals, machinery, money, land, energy, and labor.

The cost of borrowing money is one input that is easily overlooked but that farmers are intensely aware of. Traditionally producers have obtained operating funds by borrowing against the proceeds of the coming season's crop, and while that system has had its tricky moments—as when a late spring or a plague of locusts damages the crop—their effects were minimal when compared to the outrageous interest rates of the early 1980s. Mary Kay Quinlan, writing in the *Omaha World Herald* in November, 1981, noted that in the three

previous decades the amount of money farmers paid in interest had increased from $598 million to $15.8 billion, or by
more than twenty-six times.

And technology, even the kind that expands production,
is not inexpensive. As farmers have decreased their expenditures for labor, their costs have risen sharply for machinery
and chemicals. One result of all this is that the "small" and
"independent" family farmer is quite likely either to have sold
his farm to a large agribusiness corporation or to have become
more "businesslike" himself, more oriented toward that bottom line even if it means growing soybeans in a way that
promotes soil erosion, a deplorable practice which is currently
widespread. It also may be that in order to survive as a
farmer, the tiller of the soil has signed a production contract
with a major packer—a company that puts its nationally
recognized label on a can of green beans, or perhaps a firm
that packs for several brands, some well known and some not.
In entering such an agreement, the farmer gains a measure of
security but gives up a measure of control over what is
planted and how it is harvested.

The freedom that is signed away, both on high-interest
loans and on production contracts, disturbs some observers of
the agriculture scene. One of them is Elizabeth J. Martin, the
executive director of the California Agrarian Action Project.
The project is headquartered at Davis, California, near the
campus of the branch of the University of California that
specializes in agricultural research. One of the project's con-
tinuing efforts is to examine the issues involved in university
research that benefits private industry. Another concerns disseminating information about the health effects of pesticides
used in agriculture. And much of its work is aimed at preserving and improving the lot of the small, noncorporate farmer.

Farmers in California, said Martin in an interview in Davis,
"won't plant until they have a contract, many of them, and
this puts them at the mercy of the big packers.

"Again and again you see this. Somehow we've got to break that chain where small farmers are totally at the mercy of the Bank of America [the nation's largest bank, which has its headquarters in San Francisco and which is omnipresent in California] to give them lines of credit and of Hunt's Tomatoes to buy their produce. It puts them in an awkward market situation where whatever those people tell them they're going to buy the produce for is the price they have to sell it for. They have no choices. I think everybody might be happier with an alternative scheme."

If an alternative is developed, it will take a lot of effort and probably a great deal of time. The system as it currently functions is the product of many forces that are closely interrelated now, but that were not directly related before and whose effects could not easily have been predicted.

Three agricultural economists have studied those forces and have presented their findings in a paper published by USDA's Economics and Statistics Service. The researchers are Donn A. Reimund and J. Rod Martin, of the ESS staff, and Charles V. Moore, of Texas A&M University. Their findings illustrate what is happening throughout the food business.

They examined three areas of agricultural production, called "subsectors" by economists—the raising of chickens for sale as broilers, the fattening of cattle on feed lots, and the production of vegetables for canning and other forms of processing—and found that significant change occurred in each of the industries in the two decades following the end of World War II. The change was caused by a number of forces, including new technology, market conditions, and various governmental policies, and as a result operations in each of the subsectors became less like "small family farms" and more like real businesses.

In the beginning, the three subsectors shared several characteristics. They were populated by large numbers of farmers in various parts of the nation, and each was a sideline to something else. Broilers were not the low-cost alternative to meat that they are today, because few farmers were raising them as broilers. The chickens were just the young male offspring of the hens that produced the *real* crop, eggs. Stuffing corn into cattle was a more lucrative way to sell grain than marketing it directly. And farmers who sold vegetables for processing were disposing largely of off-grade and surplus produce from the fresh market.

But by the late sixties all that had changed. Technology arrived and operations became more specialized and highly capitalized, fewer in number, greater in size, and more concentrated regionally. As the operations became more economically stable, bankers started showing more interest, as did the suppliers of chemicals, seeds, and other "inputs."

Farmers made concessions to these forces. They bred vegetables to withstand the rigors of mechanical harvesting and long-distance shipment, and taste and quality were the inevitable losers. The producers gave up a large portion of their decision-making powers to the newly interested suppliers and bankers. It started to make sense logistically that broilers should be raised in factory buildings along Maryland's Eastern Shore rather than in henhouses scattered through the countryside, that cattle feeding should be centered in the Southern Plains, and that the growing of vegetables should become a California operation. Farmers started signing production contracts.

Along with greater efficiency, and partly because of it, the three subsectors became more concentrated—that is, a smaller number of producers gained a larger share of the market. In some cases this fostered a phenomenon that is at the heart of the food business today: an attempt to take a commodity—a generic product, like a plucked and eviscerated chicken, a butchered cow, or a quantity of lima beans—and turn it into a branded item. Nowhere has this been seen more clearly than in the broiler business, where, on the East

Coast, television viewers are entertained frequently by the spectacle of a man named Frank Perdue, who has a look about him that is not unreminiscent of live poultry, offering the following advice:

"*Don't* buy a chicken! A whole chicken that has meaty legs could have measly wings. One with plump wings could have puny breasts. The only way to make sure all the parts are perfect is to buy *my* prime parts to begin with. . . . If you want to make sure you're buying the best-quality chicken you can, *don't buy a chicken.* Buy Perdue's prime parts. . . ."

With concentration has come what the economists refer to as higher "barriers to entry," which means that it's more difficult for a farmer, particularly a small farmer, to get into these fields than it used to be. And this is the trend not only in the three specialties studied, but in many areas of American agriculture.

One product of the change has been that American consumers get chicken any day of the week, not just Sunday, and they can get high-quality vegetables from a can. But another effect has been to further move the once independent American farmer toward the status of the middleman's hired hand.

In some cases farmers who produce the same commodities have gathered together for self-protection and promotion, and this adds another stratum of control to the lengthy chain between the earth and the consumer. One form that this takes is the agricultural marketing cooperative. In 1979 there were about 3,800 such co-ops, and they accounted for around 30 percent of the farm products sold. Another is the marketing order.

Among the agricultural legislation passed during the post-depression era was a law authorizing the Secretary of Agriculture to establish federal marketing orders to regulate the handling and selling of fresh vegetables, milk, fresh and dried fruits, and nuts. The aim of the orders was to bring some harmony to the market by allowing producers to obtain fair prices for their products.

In the case of vegetables, nuts, and fruits, fair prices were supposed to be assured by allowing producers to control the flow of their products to the market. In milk, the law allowed the establishment of minimum prices to be paid to producers by processors, the theory being that a fair price would guarantee a steady and adequate supply. What was fair was termed "parity," and parity was determined by a complex set of formulas that took into consideration the prices of other components of the general economy. Along with protection for the producers, marketing orders were designed to protect the consumer and the nation in general by maintaining markets that were economically healthy and therefore more stable. Although controls are ultimately in the hands of the agriculture secretary, the real work of the marketing orders is done by industry groups—by the growers and dairymen themselves. Such groups have immense power, not the least of which is that what they decide affects *all* growers of the regulated commodity, whether those growers agree with the market order or not. And agreements struck under the orders are specifically exempt from the nation's antitrust laws.

Currently there are forty-seven such market orders in effect in vegetables, fruits, and nuts, regulating produce with a farm value of more than $5 billion a year, along with forty-seven others in milk production that has a value of more than $11 billion. Milk marketing orders are spread all over the nation, but the others are concentrated in Washington, Florida, Idaho, Texas, and especially California, where regulation is carried out by dozens of organizations ranging from the Artichoke Advisory Board to the California Celery Research Advisory Board, the California Prune Board, and the California Kiwifruit Commission.

Some marketing orders seek to impose quality standards on

produce, such as minimum sizes for California oranges, that also have the effect of reducing the supply available to the public and, not coincidentally, holding prices up. A clear advantage to proponents of the orders is that they eliminate any possibility that competing growers can undercut them on price. One distinct problem with this is what to do with a surplus.

In the case of fruit grown under the California-Arizona Navel Orange Marketing Order, to cite a typical example, quantity and economics are dealt with by sending the better-looking oranges to the fresh market and reserving the others, which might taste perfectly good but might be blemished or smaller than the growers' standard allows, for the "by-product market." This could mean they are processed for concentrated orange juice—or, if the growers feel the price of juice isn't high enough, ground up and used for cattle feed. In other cases, surpluses have been handled by dumping fruit on the desert floor to rot, actions which have justifiably enraged antipoverty and pro-nutrition groups. In 1981, California navel orange growers were holding an estimated 3.5 billion oranges off the market in order to keep prices from dropping, according to United Press International.

Under most marketing orders, growers combine efforts at controlling the volume and price with elaborate campaigns to promote their products as quality food—or, in some cases, as with prunes and kiwi fruit, to help consumers overcome a reluctance to buy the stuff or simply to inform them of its existence. These campaigns usually involve a lot of national advertising that is expensive but that apparently works. The ideal situation here, as in chicken farming, is not only to convince the public that it's a quality item but also to stick a brand label on something that is patently a commodity— "Sunkist" oranges, pineapples with little tags attached, bananas that bear brand-name stickers. The nation's best such success story, however, involves not a sweet-tasting tropical fruit but a bland, brown, unphotogenic tuber, the Russet Burbank, better known as the Idaho potato.

Since 1936 the potato farmers of Idaho have been working, with great success, to see that a considerable portion of the 118 pounds of potatoes consumed annually by the average American comes from their potato fields. Nature is on their side, as it is said that the Burbank grows exceptionally well in Idaho's volcanic soil and its climate of warm days and cool nights. Promotion does the rest. Since soon after the depression, Idaho farmers have been represented by the Idaho Potato Commission, a quasi–state agency that has the power to tax them and to advertise their product nationally.

In the beginning, explained Gordon Randal, the commission's executive director, the farmers faced a dilemma. The growers, he said in an interview in Boise, "knew they couldn't sit in Idaho and ship potatoes to the East and Midwest without paying a lot for freight. So they had to have something going for them. Which was, *We've got the best potatoes.* Ever since then, the Idaho industry has advertised itself, promoted itself, made itself known to consumers. And frankly, the product is better. It tastes better, in my view, and it's drier and mealier. And everytime I go someplace else in the country and get another kind of potato, it just doesn't taste the same.

"And it's nutritious. It's got a lot of fiber. Fiber's a big deal now. Everybody needs fiber. I know in my own case, if I eat a potato, my whole digestive system just works beautifully. Whereas if I go have a pizza or something else, for a day or so everything plugs up. Anyway, people are realizing that it's a good value.

"We have a branded product. For one thing, the Idaho potato is a registered trademark, and it's the only commodity in the country that is registered. We have to continually police it to make sure other people don't erode it. Four or five years ago we sued the State of Washington. They got kind of cute in their advertising and said 'an Idaho potato grows better in Washington.' "

A prime reason for what Randal likes to call the Idaho potato "mystique" is the serious campaign of advertising and promotion that the Idaho Potato Commission wages on behalf of its product. Advertisements are placed in magazines aimed at homemakers and food lovers; grocers are supplied with posters and selling tips; the editors of newspaper food sections are besieged not only with recipes but also with photographs (black and white and color), some of which they run, as often is the habit with food sections, with no hint of their origin. As part of its "Consumer Education Campaign" for 1981–82, the commission dispatched a "specially prepared Idaho potato lunch" to "the desks of food editors of national publications." It is little wonder that the Idaho potato has become a branded item, and that the farmers who grow it are considerably more secure than American food processors in general.

At first glance, the reasonably skeptical consumer—the consumer who knows there's something wrong with the American food system—might easily assume that the federal marketing orders protect and enrich the producer far more than they do the supermarket shopper. In some cases, that is a valid assumption. The western orange growers clearly have demonstrated unacceptable levels of greed, and dairy cooperatives in some places have held the cost of milk artificially high. But on the whole, the orders may be doing more good than harm. They provide an important element of protection against even greater control of specific foodstuffs and of farmland by a single corporation.

Whatever approach modern U.S. farmers have taken, it has become obvious that if they want to continue farming, then they have had to become a real business, as have almost any individual entrepreneurs who hope to survive these days. It is an unfortunate fact that in many cases in the food and other businesses, from automobiles to postal service, becoming "more businesslike" means lowering quality. With specialization and technology, as a government document puts it, "agriculture, now part of the industrial age, becomes part of a large economic complex—the Nation's food and fiber system. . . . The farmer's function has become that of transforming inputs, which come more and more from other industries, into agricultural products. These basic raw materials, in turn, become inputs for the food and fiber processors."

3

The Process of Processing

And what happens now to these things we used to think of as "food," but that we now are told are just "inputs" to an elaborate process?

For some of the products that leave the farm gate, there will be minimal processing. The fruits and vegetables that are headed toward the fresh market will quickly enter the distribution system and soon be in the customer's hand (they *must* move quickly, or they will spoil), as will such items as eggs and fish and the foods that are processed but that retain their essential character, such as milk and the denuded products of the broiler factories. These foods are already "food," by anyone's definition, and consumers would feel cheated if they underwent too much processing and ceased being what they are supposed to be.

They may be considerably more "processed" than the typical consumer knows, however. The chickens are in a sense man-made, since they hatch, live, and die by mass-production timetables. Their feet never touch the ground, and some of

them never experience darkness, since they are urged to stay
awake and eat day and night. Tranquilizers and red-hued
contact lenses keep them from fighting (chickens, someone
discovered, get excited at the sight of each other's blood; the
lenses change red into just a shade of gray), and a hormone
called estradiol palmitate makes them fat.

Oranges can be eaten right off the tree, and many are, but
those that are shipped to the fresh market from California,
Arizona, and Florida are put through several procedures before the public gets them: presizing, pregrading, washing,
brushing, drying, waxing to replace oils lost in washing, dye-
ing (in some areas at some times of the year, but not in
California and Arizona), hand sorting, machine sizing, packing, and storage or shipment.

Even the vegetables that are sold as "farm-fresh" at supermarkets and produce stands a few days after picking must
undergo some processing. One of the first steps after harvest
is precooling, or the rapid removal of field heat to slow deterioration. This can be done with rapidly moving air, crushed
ice placed on the vegetables, or cooling by water or vacuum.
Hydrocooling, which is used on peaches, sweet corn, celery,
asparagus, and other vegetables, involves immersing the food
in water that is close to the freezing point. Almost all the lettuce shipped from western states is cooled by placing it in huge
steel chambers and then subjecting it to a partial vacuum.

These processes change the food little, however, and the
basic definition of "food"—or "corn" or "radishes" or "oranges"
—remains pretty much inviolate. The definition may even be
extended to include produce that undergoes traumatic
change, as when it is frozen and packaged in rectangular
blocks and sold in supermarket freezers, or when it is put
inside metal cans, sealed, and then cooked rapidly. The essential nature of the food has been maintained.

For another, and growing, portion of the food that America
eats, the route to the consumer is a circuitous one, and the

farm gate is just the beginning of a very long journey. Most of what comes from the fields and grasslands and oceans is not considered "food" by the industry until it is processed—or, to use the depressing term that is employed by much of the industry, until it has been "manufactured." The result of this manufacturing procedure is a careful blend (and an expensive one, in terms of the manufacturer's investment in time, money, research, and packaging) of attempts to determine what the public wants, what the retailer will put on his shelves, and what will move easily through the channels of distribution and capture for its backers a comfortable share of the dollars the public invests in that particular category of product, be it children's breakfast cereal, tuna-flavored cat-food, or canned chile con carne. It is interesting to note that somewhere along this process, people in the business stop referring to the object of all their work as "food" and start calling it "product."

There are distinctions between "manufacturing" and "processing." Both manufacturers and processors, according to one definition, take the raw or nearly raw product and turn it into something else. But manufacturers then put it through another process that gets it to the market—"branding" it, which includes naming and labeling it, advertising it, and moving it into the retail stores. So a *manufacturer*, the Quaker Oats Company, takes several ingredients, including corn and corn bran flour, sugar, oat flour, salt, oil, and a number of chemicals—among them artificial colors for blue, red, and yellow—and turns it all into Quaker Corn Bran. A number of *processors* may be responsible for getting the corn, oats, and sugar into the necessary shape for Quaker to use them, as well as for blending the chemicals that make the colors. The result of all the operations is a breakfast cereal, a food product which in America is usually about as far removed from the actual, basic food as could be imagined.

It doesn't have to be this way. Quaker also sells Quaker

Oats, the ingredients label of which lists only "100% oats." But in most cases the process involves wreaking elaborate changes on the basic commodity. Only then does it become what much of the food industry is willing to acknowledge as "food."

To some people, the term "processed food" whips up visions of food that has been bent hopelessly out of shape by some greedy middleman, food that is "laced" with "chemical additives." A lot of food does fall into that category, but the term also has a more general meaning. The Office of Technology Assessment, an agency formed in 1972 to help Congress "anticipate, and plan for, the consequences of uses of technology," as a government description puts it, has defined the word as "one of the series of operations performed on a product that aids preservation, makes it more convenient to use, produces a new food form, produces an ingredient for use in further processing, or produces a more palatable food." This definition easily includes one of the older and more accepted forms of processing, the canning of foods, particularly of fruits and vegetables soon after they are harvested.

More than half the nation's acreage devoted to fruits and vegetables goes for processing. Many vegetables have been genetically engineered to lend themselves better to the canning process; tomatoes, nine-tenths of which are raised for processing, lead the list here. Half the peach crop, seven-tenths of the apricots, and 99 percent of the tuna go into cans, according to the National Food Processors Association. There are about 1,700 canning plants in the nation. Most are situated as close to their raw materials as possible, and many are mechanized marvels. The NFPA boasts that in the case of peas, human hands never touch the produce.

In a typical process, the food is washed and trimmed; sorted for size and maturity; trimmed again; mechanically pitted, seeded, cut, diced, halved or peeled; blanched (in some cases) in hot water or steam; poured into tin-plated steel cans or glass containers; subjected to partial vacuum and then sealed; processed under pressure and at high heat long enough to sterilize and cook the contents; cooled; labeled; and packed—all in the same plant. The mechanical processes are quite precise: When whole kernel corn is being canned, knives are set to slice off the kernels close to the cob as it goes by; for creamed corn, only the tops of the kernels are sliced off, then the cob moves on to a device which scrapes off the rest of the kernels. The resulting substance is what provides the creamy texture of creamed corn.

Canned and frozen produce is among those foods whose definitions are not unduly damaged by processing (although the frozen foods industry likes to stretch a point well past the boundaries of truth by trying to make people believe its products are "at the peak of freshness"). But unless we pay a great deal of attention to what we eat, a vast portion of our food will be far removed from the reality of the grainfield or vegetable garden or apple orchard. It is food that is truly manufactured, as surely as a pair of tennis shoes or a ball-point pen is manufactured. It is painstakingly fabricated out of ingredients that may or may not be organic—that is, that had some direct connection with a living plant or animal—or, to use a word that the business has abused to death, that may or may not be "natural." The Office of Technology Assessment definition of these "new and modified foods" is much less reassuring than its definition of processing:

> These products generally have been designed, engineered, or formulated from various ingredients including additives. They are made by structuring, texturing, shaping, or blending ingredients and in most instances use a combination of technologies. They may be made to resemble traditional items, they may be new forms of snack foods, diet foods, or other

products, or they may be a new substance used as one ingredient in an otherwise traditional food product, such as
non-caloric sweeteners.

"Structuring," "texturing," and "shaping" may sound like
strange words to apply to food (another one that the business
sometimes uses in private, "extruding," sounds even worse),
but they epitomize much of what is happening nowadays in
the food industry. Although advertising dwells on such con-
cepts as freshness and naturalness, back in the food factories
the trend is toward grinding a lot of things up and forcing
them into food shapes. This is a trend in the rest of society,
too, it should be remembered: Clothing is rarely "natural,"
but rather a mixture of chemicals; much of what goes by the
name of lumber is extruded and reformed, as in plywood and
flakeboard. The list is endless, and few seem to mourn the fact
that in many cases the fabrication has become the commodity
—that plywood has become "wood" and nylon has become
"cloth." Whether it is right for this to happen with food,
though, is another question.

And very few people would be willing to argue that it is
right for this to happen without the knowledge of those who
will eat the fabrication. Yet that is what is happening, and
happening more and more, in the United States. An inquisi-
tive consumer still can learn a lot about what she or he is
buying by studying the label of a package of food at the
supermarket, and can, therefore, avoid the more horribly
manufactured items. But much of the food we eat does not
come with labels: It is served to us in fancy restaurants, fast-
food joints, takeout delis, commercial airliners, school cafeterias, mess halls, and the burgeoning hybrids of fast-food and
white-tablecloth eating places known as "family restaurants."
Without barging into the kitchens and inspecting the labels
on the food *there*, we might have no idea that we are consuming fabrications such as these:

■ Dress-All, which Durkee makes, is an oil the restaurateur pours on top of mashed potatoes (which squirt out of a portion-controlling machine known as the Tater-Jet), corn on the cob, and anything else he wants to coat with a substance that "tastes and looks just like butter."

■ "50/50 Blend Cream Cheese Substitute" goes into manufactured "cheesecake"; or, perhaps, "Pizza-loaf Mozzarella Cheese Substitute"; or, maybe, "Product-21 Process Cheese Spread Substitute," which promises "maximum economy." These fabrications come from Borden's, a brand name which used to be associated with real dairy products.

■ Fake food flavors save manufacturers and "chefs" time and money and don't have any of the real thing's pesky problems of perishability or market fluctuation. The Food and Drug Administration has reported that the average number of flavors used in a processed food, excluding meat, poultry, and egg products, is about forty. Advertising for fabricated flavors in trade publications tries hard to associate them with the term "natural," although they are not natural at all. Firmernich International makes "new orange flavors" that are "nature-identical" (meaning that they share the real orange's chemical formula) and that have "all the good things found in nature" but "none of the bad." "Obtaining a typical fried onion note is no easy task," advises Naarden International. "Our savory group has succeeded in creating such a distinct note." Not to be outdone, Givaudan makes Naturalseal Flavors (Chicken Type) RD-10605-B, RD-10606-B, and RD-10607-B, which are Fatty, Brothy; Meaty, Gravy Drippings; and Roasted, Dark Meat Notes, respectively.

■ Artificial cheese flavors are big items, since manufacturers can use them in all sorts of snack, bakery, and sauce products. A Cincinnati firm makes a "natural cheese flavor" named, naturally, F-1046-2, which has "15–20 times the strength of spray-dried cheddar cheese on a flavor basis."

There are also spray-dried "natural identical" tomato flavors that can be used as "extenders or full flavoring agents" in sauces and frozen pizzas. And the firm of Alex Fries reminds potential industry customers of what everybody knows, which is that these fake foods are rarely identified as such to the consuming public: "It's surprising how many food producers (and consumers too) just can't tell the difference between our flavors and the natural ones."

■ The Ralston Purina Company has marketed a "Gourm-Egg," which is a 13-inch-long frozen object that resembles an elongated egg and that its inventors referred to as "the hard-cooked egg roll product we've created from USDA inspected processed eggs." A spokesman for Ralston explained that Gourm-Egg was "approximately 95 percent real egg" and that the item was sold all over the food service business. "Fancy restaurants buy it," he added. But why? It's easy to use, and its obscene length means more uniform slices can be gotten for salads and garnishes. Gourm-Egg has a shelf life of one year.

■ Basic Foods of Englewood, New Jersey, produces "the finest, freshest, most flavorful tasting Hard Roll Concentrate in the industry" ("Nature Creates," advises the firm, while "Basic Foods Perfects").

■ Onions are pulverized and extruded into onion-ring shapes, which then are coated with breading, cooked, frozen, and shipped to restaurants, which heat them and serve them, often, as "our famous onion rings." The strange-looking hashbrown potatoes that accompany many coffee-shop breakfasts might be Redi-Shred Hashbrowns that are "pre-conditioned and pre-cooked" and that require grilling for one and a half minutes before serving.

■ Meat and seafood are extruded, too. Clams of varying shapes, sizes, and appearances are ground up and formed into clam shapes, and similar shaping occurs with shrimp and fish, usually preparatory to breading and partially cooking, then freezing, them. Steak Tonight is billed as "USDA Choice flaked and formed beef steak," and a chicken sandwich is likely to contain an amalgam of chemicals, skin, broth, and soybeans. Real effort goes into making machine-formed products look as if human beings had some hand in making them; Ship Ahoy Breaded Fish Cutlets "have the taste and appearance of being 'made-on-site,'" says their creator, because they are "irregular shaped."

The big trend in seafood these days is toward minced fish, which is a sort of extrusion process applied to species that might otherwise be hard to sell because they are too small or are what the fisheries business calls, officially, "underutilized," and, unofficially, "trash fish." (Sometimes a species' name is partly responsible for this. Sand lances and dogfish are certainly edible, but they lack the name appeal of flounder and red snapper. Ratfish, stumpknockers, and viperfish have an even more upstream battle to fight.) Paul Earl, the chief of the export and domestic market development branch of the National Marine Fisheries Service in Gloucester, Massachusetts, explained in an interview what happens to the fish after they have been caught, landed, deboned, and skinned. Some are then minced, while others are filleted.

"They're processed into what is called fish blocks," he said. "The fish are placed into regularly shaped frames and they're compressed when the freezing process begins. They're molded into a regularly shaped block."

After this shaping, he was asked, could someone detect individual fish among the frozen mass?

"You can *sort* of detect the individual fillets," he said. "But it doesn't really make any difference, because generally the way they're processed is that these blocks are then sawed or cut, sometimes with a bandsaw, into what are called 'shims,' and the 'shims' are then cut into 'sticks' and 'portions.' You go to McDonald's to buy a fish sandwich, you get a nice square

—a two- or two-and-a-half-ounce portion of fish, usually cod-fish, that's been battered and fried. It's all been preprocessed."

Fish processed in this manner are also used extensively in the frozen "fish sticks" and "fish dinners" that are sold in supermarkets. One brand of "Heat & Serve Cod Filets," for example, contains (in order of predominance) cod, wheat, flour, water, corn flour, cornstarch, salt, nonfat dry milk, spice, spice extractives, baking powder, monosodium glutumate, dry egg, cellulose gum, and paprika to color the breading. It was fried in vegetable oil.

Having invented blocks of fish, the industry and government are trying to think of other ways to use marine animals. Extruded fish have been made into sausage, and hot dogs containing 10 percent pollack and 90 percent beef were tried out on schoolchildren, with no apparent problems. There is some talk of manufacturing "imitation canned tuna," and some West Coast packers have experimented with selling pilchard, a member of the sardine family that has been thought of as a "trash" fish, as "chunk light sardine." In the meantime, research continues to find ways to decrease the amount of "fish" that is lost when minced blocks are sawed into smaller quantities. The waste sawdust that remains is called "kerf" in the fish-construction business.

Everyone connected with the fisheries industry who was interviewed said, frequently voluntarily, that he found nothing wrong with these new methods of processing and selling fish, as long as consumers were made aware of what they were getting—a condition that is rarely met. Sometimes even the experts have trouble getting the straight information.

Anthony E. Klos helps to operate Oceanside Fisheries International, at Gloucester, where fish from the local fleet are deboned, minced, made into 5-pound blocks, frozen, and shipped to domestic and export markets. Klos clearly sees processing as playing a heavy role in the future of seafood, although, he said, some people will always want and be willing to pay for fresh fish of the highest quality. Most people, he said, aren't very good judges of fish. "Everyone has an obligation to know what they're eating," he said.

One day Klos was in New York, and he decided to eat at a fancy, expensive, highly praised restaurant. "Known to be one of the best restaurants in the country," said Klos, and he named the place. "Ordered broiled scrod.* I asked the waiter what it was, cod or haddock. 'I don't know. I'll go talk to the chef.' Came back: 'The chef guarantees it's a baby haddock.'

"I ordered it. That came off a grown cod; it had to be a three-inch-thick fillet. And yet they called it 'scrod haddock'! People don't know what they're buying."

The processors and fabricators not only are alert to new and more economical ways to manufacture food, they also stay tuned to what they feel the public wants, and when a trend blossoms they are ready to judge its intensity and durability and to exploit it if they think it will last. Hardly had a mild mania for quiche Lorraine swept the nation a few years ago when a food service supplier unveiled its Coronet Quiche Stabilizer, which allows a cook to whip up a fluid "quiche" which can be frozen, shipped, stored, thawed, poured into shells, mixed with other ingredients, cooked, frozen, stored and thawed again, then reheated for serving. At about the same time, the nation developed a taste for Mexican-type foods. Dell Food Specialties quickly came up with spray-dried Mexican flavorings, including picante, jalapeno, nacho, enchilada, taco, and hot taco.

When concern about the amount of salt in foods became a general one, and not confined to "consumer activists" and other troublemakers, the canning industry started bringing

---

* The designation "scrod" refers to the age, or size, of a fish. A young cod or haddock can properly be sold as "scrod." Scrod is a prestige dish among fish lovers, however, and "substitutions" are often made.

out low-salt and no-salt-added products. Del Monte proudly announced its creation of lower-salt-content cut green beans, corn, peas, and tomatoes. "Finally," said the bold headline on Del Monte's advertisement: "Vegetables with No Salt Added." As if Del Monte had discovered, all on its own, that vegetables could be cooked without adding a lot of salt. This, of course, is something millions of consumers who eat fresh produce have known for centuries.

4

Only So Many Stomachs

There are several motives behind all this fabrication, manufacturing, and assorted processing. One concerns the economics of the food service business. Restaurants, from the fast-
food stores to quite a few of the "fancy" eating places that
make much of their "gourmet" images, are unwilling to pay
the wages of professional chefs, or even short-order cooks. So
food preparation is geared to the talents and experience of
teenagers and others willing to work for the minimum wage.
One result is food that has all its basic decisions made for it
back at the factory: food that is preformed, precooked, and
"portion-controlled," that needs only to be dropped in a pot of
boiling water or run through a microwave oven on its way
from the freezer to the unsuspecting customer. It is not
stretching the truth to state that most American eating places
now are hardly more than final-assembly and warming-up stations for processed, fabricated foods.

Another motive—and this applies to foods manufactured
for the supermarket shopper as well as for the restaurant

trade—is to make money where money was not being made before. And the best way to do that, the American food industry has discovered, is to make something that somebody else doesn't make: to manufacture a product that is *differentiated*. Similar foods are made to appear different from others, with the anticipation that the public will buy more of them. In some situations, there are attempts to differentiate commodities; as we have seen, some marketing orders seem to have this as their main mission.

The consumer is most likely, however, to encounter differentiation (also known as "product proliferation") on the supermarket shelf and in advertising behind the word "new"—or, more likely, "new" with several exclamation marks after it.

Thousands of "new" food products are released to the market each year, but only a handful are really new. John M. Connor, until recently an economist at the USDA Economic Research Service in Washington, has studied proliferation, among other fields, and he has unearthed estimates that from 70 to 100 percent of all "new" food items are actually imitations of things that were already there, extensions of a manufacturer's present line, reformulations, or "repositionings" of existing products. Since it is clear that the great bulk of differentiation is the result not of processing but rather of merchandising strategies, the techniques involved will be explored in the later section of this book that is devoted to the selling of food. But differentiation is so vital to the manufacturer of food that it must be introduced here.

Manufacturers have developed several rationales for differentiation. Most claim it gives the consumer greater choice, but few add the obvious comment that if they didn't differentiate they might not make as much money. One food manufacturer who is in the business of proliferation recently discussed that important other reason: survival. Preston (Pete) Townley is the executive vice-president of General Mills' new business division. When Townley was asked in Minneapolis why manufacturers are interested in new foods, he replied:

"I think the primary reason has to do with looking at the facts of the food business. It's sort of a mundane way of putting it, but there are only so many stomachs in the country. And though as a people we're probably heavily overfed, and using even *that* as a growth drive, there isn't a lot of apparent growth in selling food in the United States."

There was a small underlying growth rate, said Townley. "But just in caloric terms we're consuming less calories, and we have been on almost a continuous basis since the turn of the century. And as the population slows in growth there just is a kind of finite universe out there. And most, if not all, food companies are growth-oriented, just as our country is growth-oriented. So we're all looking for new areas to get growth for our individual companies. And that says 'New and better ways of presenting food.'"

Townley recalled a few of the new and better ways of the past. One of them flourished in the days after World War II, and it was epitomized by the development and widespread acceptance of cake mixes—some of the most successful ones made by General Mills. "That was a period of convenience," he said. "You could add value to products and have a new product area if you delivered something that the consumer was already eating, but if you could deliver it in a more convenient way."

Sometimes the attempts at injecting convenience into foods backfired. "We went through a period where everybody was looking at manufacturing foods that were going to deliver more and better of everything," said the executive. "You just had to rip the package open and eat. Nobody was going to have to eat three meals a day again. There was pretty real consumer resistance to those things." He named some of the memorable "new" foods, such as Tang and Kool-Whip.

"And we did Breakfast Squares. They were going to be one of those products where 'Here's everything in a square; you eat two of these and get everything you could possibly need in life'—except that it didn't taste too good and it certainly wasn't a very exciting experience to sit there and eat one of them. I remember this well; I was the general manager of our cereal-breakfast division then, and I had Breakfast Squares under me.

"I remember going to dinner one night with a bunch of our sales guys. We had a regional meeting, and there was a very nice dinner all set up—silver covers on the plates and everything. I looked around and saw that I was the last guy being served, and I wondered about that, since I was the senior executive.

"Finally I was served mine and the guys removed their covers. Everybody had steak and whatever. And I had two butterscotch-flavored Breakfast Squares in the middle of the plate. And the guys said, 'Now tell us how good it is!' "

Another phase that America and the food manufacturers have gone through, and that is not yet over, either, is the period of demand for, and supply of, foods that are said to be "natural." "It's still a very important area," said Townley. "It's an intensified concern on the parts of consumers—most of the time it's a perceived problem rather than a real one—that additives and things like that are a negative. And hence if you could deliver really good stuff that was natural or so positioned, that would be a hot button."

The trend that seems to be growing as the eighties head toward their midpoint, said the manufacturer, is an elaboration of the "natural" period. "A lot of us feel there is a growing sophistication out there," he said, motioning in the direction of the consuming public, "and it's growing from 'natural' to getting fresh, close-to-the-field kind of stuff. If you can *deliver* that in our distribution system in some way, through improved processing or improved packaging or in some way being closer to the marketplace, and still get the mass economies of the distribution system, then you've got a very hot button."

*   *   *

When Preston Townley speaks of differentiation and proliferation of food products, he speaks (as might be expected)
of industry's meeting the changing needs of the consumer.
One of General Mills' best-known products, Bisquick, probably does this as well as any manufactured foods. Bisquick
is a baking mix, a prepared combination of the things that go
into biscuits, pancakes, muffins, pie crusts, and the like:
bleached wheat flour, shortening, preservatives, leavening,
dried buttermilk, salt, and whey.

The formula is quite close to one a cook might choose to
make quick breads "from scratch," although the preservatives
would be omitted and the forms of some of the ingredients
would be liquid rather than dry. Bisquick is a manufactured
food that promises, and delivers, convenience and a saving in
time, and for that reason the product has been around for
more than half a century and consumers have been willing to
pay extra for the work General Mills has done for them. The
mix sold for about 85 cents a pound, in the 20-ounce box, in
1983. Furthermore, the product's packaging is filled with information of use to the consumer—a dozen recipes on a box
that is about 5 by 7 by 2 inches in size. Bisquick represents
one of the few cases in which a commodity was turned into a
branded item and then the branded item got so popular that
it became a virtual commodity.

Many other manufactured foods, however, are quite obviously differentiated for the sake of differentiation. Breakfast
cereals, especially those aimed at children, are examples of
this, and General Mills is well represented here. Some other
examples:

■ A supermarket's freezer section is a cornucopia of
processed variations on the theme of the basic white potato:
Tater Tots, Tiny Taters, Shoe Strings, Cottage Fries, Deep
Fries, Tasti-Fries, Crispers!, Stuffed Potatoes with Sour
Cream and Chives, Stuffed Potatoes with Cheddar Cheese
and Microwave or Ovenproof Container, Stuffed Potatoes

with Onions. Some packages claim to contain "100 percent fresh potatoes," although they clearly are frozen and could not possibly be "fresh."

■ A New York company unveiled a bottled soft drink for dogs. The founder of the firm was interviewed on the Canadian Broadcasting Company's weekly radio program *The Food Show*, and he commented, "If *we* had to drink nothing but water, many of us would be malnourished in terms of liquid intake, too." The implication was that neither dogs nor people like to drink plain, unadulterated water. His product, which is "beef-flavored," costs about $1 a quart.

■ Campbell's, the soup company, started selling "Campbell's All Natural Mushrooms" in a semirigid plastic box. In some stores the branded mushrooms were placed right next to loose, unbranded mushrooms that were also "all natural" but that cost less, inasmuch as they were not differentiated brand labels.

The chief motive behind differentiation is to capture a larger *share* of the market. The word "share" is heard almost constantly in the food business, where it means a portion of the total money spent by the public on a product category. Or it could mean a portion of the physical space allotted by a supermarket to an item in a product category. A product category could be as broad as "canned vegetables," but more often it is narrowly defined, as, for example, "canned baked beans" or "packaged dried prunes."

The notion of share is not exclusive to the food business, by any means. Increasingly, the other elements of our lives are affected by decisions based on "share." Television offers perhaps the most grotesque examples, with its self-destructive contests among and within networks to control segments of the evening viewing hours—contests that frequently lead to the destruction of popular and attractive programs simply because they are scheduled in competition with others that pull a greater "share." More and more now, we see success in many fields measured not by overall popularity or income (forget about quality, reliability, and workmanship) but by popularity or income within a narrow sociodemographic segment of what is called "the market"—another way of expressing the idea of "share."

Thus a manufacturer of grain products could feel good about capturing the leading share of the breakfast cereals sold to grownups who worry about the regularity of their bowels and who are drawn to products advertising fiber and bran, while simultaneously deploring its abysmally low share of the much more lucrative market for children's cereals, with its emphasis on cartoon characters and use of artificial colors and sugar.

One way to get share, to obtain the all-important winning segment of a particular market or submarket, might be to make a better, more honest-to-goodness product and to make it consistently, and some manufacturers still try to do that. Bisquick serves again as a good example. But there aren't many Bisquicks being invented or even sold these days. What *is* being invented is a mass of imitations of successful products (products that already have a large share) and extensions of successful products (the next step for the manufacturer of a successful creamy peanut butter is to bring out a crunchy version, and after that a New! Extra-Crunchy! version, and after that maybe a version that mixes, but maintains the visual separation of, both peanut butter and jelly in the same jar). Or, if you're the Iceland Seafood Corporation, which sells precooked, individually quick-frozen, breaded "cod and pollack wedges," you invent a seafood called Crunchies. "America loves to crunch," an Iceland ad advises the food service business: "Peanut butter, cereals, candy bars, fried chicken—all broadened their sales appeal by adding 'crunch' to their lines. Your customers will like having an alternative style of breaded fish, and you'll love the increased dollars from seafood sales."

Many differentiated products at least try to meet what their inventors see as a public need. After Swift & Company brought out Sizzlean, a bacon look-alike, not long ago, it reported on the invention to its stockholders. In one paragraph of its annual report the company managed to put its finger on much of what the food industry has become. The description went this way:

> Sizzlean breakfast strips gained market share in the last year [1980] and represent an example of Swift's recent progress in developing and marketing new products designed to meet a number of consumer needs and wants. For example, Sizzlean is 50 percent leaner than bacon. At a time when consumers are attempting to limit the amount of fat in their diet, Sizzlean represents a unique and differentiated product which satisfies this desire. Because it is a value-added product, Sizzlean commands a premium price and higher profit margins.

Larry G. Hamm is a USDA agricultural economist who sees differentiation as a manifestation of competition. "The very top food manufacturers are very sophisticated," he said in an interview at Michigan State University in East Lansing, where he teaches (the federal agency traditionally has supplied staff for the state land grant colleges). "Tide, which is one of the leading brands of laundry soap, has been reformulated some fifty-four times in its existence. Seventeen of those have been very basic chemical changes. So if you had boxes of Tide that you purchased every two years since 1940 or whenever it was brought out, you'd find that those products were not chemically identical."

Hamm said he suspected that if the manufacturers of Tide were asked about this, they would reply that the reformulations were responses to consumer needs and demands. But he said he felt another important reason was the manufacturer's need to stay competitive with other participants in the laundry soap market. "What keeps those companies honest is the fact that there is competition," he said.

John Connor approaches the matter of competition in the food business from a slightly different angle. "There are a lot of different brands out there," said the economist, "and a lot of different products, and everyone's trying to shift the consumer to buy his brand rather than the other guy's brand.

"But the *focus* of competition is at a much finer level. It's 'Who's going to be big in the pourable dressing market?' 'Who's going to be big in the mayonnaise market?' 'Who's going to be big in the breakfast cereal market?' Those are the segments, or parts of the market, that are most relevant to the people who are planning marketing strategies.

"In general, the people in the industry are trying to increase their share of the commodity, on the assumption that the category is not going to grow very much anyway. The real amounts of food consumed in this country are going up roughly at the same rate as the population. The human stomach is limited. We consume 1,400 pounds of food per capita per year on average, and for the last forty years it hasn't changed.

"Now, the *composition* of what we buy has changed. There are a few more sweeteners in the diet, a little more oil than there used to be; more fish, less beef. But in terms of total poundage it's not much different.

"So in terms of real growth, it's population growth and the ability to *add value*, which is what the manufacturers call it—to add something to it: to add convenience, add storability, add variety, add something that people are willing to pay for. The real price, or value, of food rises faster than population. Because people are willing to pay for what they regard as, or have been convinced to believe is, a more convenient, novel, tastier, or whatever product, a product with some advantage in it for them."

*   *   *

Since differentiation is such a helpful tool in helping a manufacturer gain a larger share of the market, the economists are interested in seeing what happens after that. A larger share means a greater measure of control over that market. Sometimes a manufacturer's share is so large that he virtually runs the market—Gerber's in canned and bottled baby foods is one example, and Campbell's in canned soups is another—but more often control is apportioned among several manufacturers, each with large shares. This leads almost inevitably to the condition known as market *concentration*. It is of great importance to consumers, since it has a lot to do with the price of the food they eat.

Market concentration, as was seen in the earlier discussion of agricultural production, is the domination of a market by its leading members. The General Accounting Office, the agency of Congress that gathers information and makes recommendations "designed to provide for more efficient and effective government operations," has found that firms in a strongly concentrated market "tend to avoid those actions most likely to produce competitive reactions—especially price rivalry—which could lead to reduced profits for all."

By itself, the term provides little in the way of information, but when it is expressed in terms of the share of the total market controlled by a number of participants, it starts to mean a lot. Economists generally are most interested in the market share possessed by the four leading firms. It is widely believed that when four-firm concentration reaches 40 percent of the market, oligopoly, or the condition known as "partial monopoly," is starting to occur. Concentration is important not only in food manufacturing, but in all other segments of the industry, particularly in retailing. People who live in areas where there is a high degree of supermarket concentration can expect to pay more for their food. There are several areas of high as well as low concentration in the United States, and they will be discussed later in the section on the selling of food. Concentration is not by any means confined to the food business, but rather is becoming a distinguishing characteristic of much of the American "free enterprise system."

The GAO, in a report on food costs, addressed itself to concentration in food manufacturing. The report was compiled in 1978, but much of what the agency discovered is as true, if not truer, today. There was, said the GAO, a "growing amount of evidence that market concentration is high enough in certain market areas or commodity groups to limit the amount of price competition."

In those circumstances, wrote the agency, there *was* competition, but it was competition "in terms of product variations, package design, promotions, and other advertising," not in terms of the price the public pays. "Such competition increases the costs incurred by the food marketing industry," the report continued, "and thus decreases the possibility that a drop in a commodity's farm price will be passed on to the consumer."

Former Congressman Fred Richmond of New York, who served on the House Agriculture Committee and was considered an articulate spokesman for the consumer in food and agriculture matters (and who since has served time in federal prison for income tax evasion, marijuana possession, and making an illegal payment to a government employee), gathered figures for a hearing in 1979 that showed which areas of the food business are highly concentrated. The top four corporations controlled about 54 percent of the market in flour milling, reported Richmond, along with 49 percent of baked foods, 90 percent of the cold breakfast cereal market, 59 percent of the breweries, 72 percent of soft drinks, 49 percent of winemaking, 57 percent of distilled liquors, 68 percent of coffee, and 63 percent of pet food.

It is axiomatic that the more highly differentiated the foods, the more likely it is that their market will be highly concentrated, as can be seen from a list of individual food items presented by Richmond. The numbers represent the percentage of the market controlled by the top *three* brands, as calculated by *Progressive Grocer* magazine:

Table salt	92 percent
Flour	80
Catsup	86
Mustard	76
Peanut butter	79
Salad and cooking oil	86
Vinegar	84
Gelatin desserts	98
Whipped toppings	86
Canned evaporated milk	82
Marshmallows	98
Instant puddings	96
Shortening	81
Jams and jellies	75
Nuts	81
Honey	82
Frostings	98
Spaghetti sauce	86
Pickle relish	79
Instant tea	86
Frozen dinners	93

In some of the product categories, the leaders come instantly to mind. More people would recognize the name "Jell-O" than "gelatin desserts," for instance.

Concentration is on the rise in American food manufacturing, particularly among the manufacturers of the more differentiated foods. In 1963, USDA calculated that the largest two hundred of the food manufacturing companies held 68 percent of all the manufacturers' assets. By 1975, the largest two hundred held 81 percent of the assets.

Increased concentration brings with it a number of trends and events that affect the price and availability of food—or perhaps it is that the events and trends bring on concentration —or, even more likely, that all are too closely interrelated to be separated as to cause and effect.

In any event, the factors usually associated with concentration include a high volume of advertising, greater difficulties for other firms that want to get into the marketplace, more dominance by conglomerates, and, most important, higher prices for consumers.

Bruce Marion is a professor in the University of Wisconsin's agricultural economics department and the head of its Food Systems Research Group. He has calculated that in 1975 the largest two hundred manufacturers did 85 percent of all the food business's media advertising and 100 percent of the network television advertising done by food manufacturers. In a 1980 study of the future organization of the U.S. food system, the researcher wrote:

> Advertising obviously has a role in a market economy in providing information to potential buyers about alternative products and services. However, advertising can also be used to restructure markets and to encourage consumers to live in an illusory world in which products are sold on the basis of their "image." It is hard for me to rationalize that consumers are better off because they spend 30 to 50 percent more for Realemon than for identical concentrated lemon juice under another brand; or that they have realized $500 million in benefits because 70 percent will buy premium or super-premium beer in 1980 compared to 30 percent in 1970—when blind taste tests reveal they are unable to distinguish between brands. Such rationale defies common sense.

Concentration isolates the "share" available in a market, putting it in the hands of the leading firms, and thus makes it more difficult for outsiders—brand-new contenders who think they have a better mousetrap, or perhaps regional firms that want to go national—to enter that particular segment of the marketplace. The economists call these difficulties "barriers to entry." To think of an illustration, one needs only consider what it would take for a small firm (or a big one, for that matter) to get past the well-guarded gates of the canned soup business. Not all segments of the market are dominated by firms as powerful as Campbell, but in many of them substantial barriers to entry exist.

The domination of industries by conglomerates is one of the most pronounced characteristics of the seventies and eighties, so no one should be surprised to discover that conglomerates are active in the food industry as well. What might be worth noting, though, is that while many of us might be unperturbed about buying, say, fire insurance from the same conglomerate that makes telephones, since it's all business, we might not be emotionally prepared for the shock of buying our daily bread from the same outfit. Bread, after all, is what we put peanut butter and jelly on, or liverwurst and mustard; bread, we have been told (and really believe), is the very staff of life. The sanctity of food is one of the last myths that we are prepared to abandon, even in this era of unrestrained cynicism.

For most of us, food is an elemental, ritualistic, almost holy thing, and we have difficulty remembering or comprehending that for the people who sell it, it is nothing but a *business*. Food is a necessity for human life, and it brings us joy as well as occasional heartburn, and our feelings about much of it are grounded in experiences, many of them satisfying ones, that we had when we were very young. Anyone who doubts this should spend ten minutes observing customers in an ice-cream parlor: Adult people come in and stare at the lists posted on the wall, and then they look at the small icy barrels of the various flavors, with bits of strawberry and chocolate randomly dotting the temptingly cold substance, and sometimes they indulge in a little ritual of deciding which cone they want. They have, even the most ancient of them, the faces of kids. And then, when they place their order, amazingly often they speak almost in the language of the children they used to be back when they first learned to love ice cream: "I wanna Rocky Road, please, with sprinkles. Lots and lots of sprinkles."

Conglomerates care nothing for these subterranean memories, unless it is discovered that they lend themselves to exploitation, in which case they will be exploited to a fare-thee-well. Nor, amazingly, do they appear to care much for the loyalties consumers develop toward foods and food makers in the years from childhood forward. Conglomerates seem to work more efficiently when they confine their interests to only one thing, and that is the much-celebrated bottom line.

Economist John Connor, in a series of articles in the *National Food Review*, examined the role of these firms in food processing in 1979 and found them well entrenched in the business. About thirty of them that had assets of over $1 billion were engaged in processing.

It is not surprising that conglomerates that are shopping for firms in the food business are attracted to those that are more highly differentiated—frozen foods, bakery items, candy, oils, canned fish, and snack foods. They also buy into industries, according to some studies, in which substantial barriers to entry exist. "Thus," wrote Connor, "it appears that target industries are those in which a firm is most likely to be able to establish a monopolistic position. . . ."

A result of all this is bigness breeding bigger bigness. James D. Shaffer, a Michigan State agricultural economist, once pointed out "an intriguing example of vertical control" involving the Cargill Company, the multinational grain conglomerate which is a privately held U.S. corporation. "Cargill," said Shaffer at an international seminar on food pricing, "is the largest private grain handler in the world and operates the largest beef-feeding organization in the U.S. . . . which sells to a wholly owned subsidiary of Cargill, which is the second-largest beef processor in the U.S., which in turn sells under contract to McDonald's, the largest fast-food chain in the world. This certainly represents a drastic change in the organization of the U.S. food system." Furthermore, conglomerates demonstrate little in the way of sentimentality about the firms they buy and sell, although their public relations departments are capable of very eloquent statements and their annual reports are marvels of handsome graphics that can almost conjure up the smell of hot bread in an aerial photo of a highly mechanized bakery plant. If a division doesn't make enough money for the conglomerate's "profit center," it's out on its ear.

In such an atmosphere, steady, repeat customer patronage means little, and it becomes questionable whether shoppers should invest their loyalty in any food product. Why cultivate a friendship for a particular brand of margarine when it is likely (and increasingly likely) that the firms that manufacture it are being swapped about like bubble-gum trading cards, that the formula is thus unlikely to remain the same, and that the name is the only thing about the product that is consistent?

Conglomerate activity in the food business offers big outfits an opportunity to engage in what John Connor calls "special forms of strategic business conduct not open to single-product firms . . . even those with strong market positions." These include, among others, what economists refer to as forbearance and cross-subsidization, terms that will be explained below. One of the others has been identified as a loss of information to the public, since conglomerates function in ways that are simply less open to public, or even stockholder, scrutiny. Another is the tendency by conglomerates to acquire firms that are the leaders in their markets. Thus conglomerates automatically "are eliminating the companies most likely to be their competitors," says Connor. And conglomerates rarely *earn* their successes; they don't start from the bottom and work up, in the best Horatio Alger technique, but rather buy out the winners after they've become winners. And far too often the conglomerates don't know how to manage their acquisitions properly and the winners quickly become losers. This has happened more than once in fast-food and family-restaurant chains that have been purchased by conglomerates that then set out to run them like shoe factories or South American hardwood plantations and were surprised when the customers started eating elsewhere.

"Corporate forbearance" is the name for the phenomenon that occurs when big, diversified firms have several "contact points" with one another—points at which they meet to sell or buy something, to engage in competition. The more diverse a conglomerate's holdings, the more likely it is to have a number of such meeting points with other conglomerates. With an increase in contact points there comes a decrease in a firm's desires to compete in terms of the prices it charges. Why, Conglomerate A might well wonder, should we engage in a yogurt price war with Conglomerate B if we suspect Conglomerate B is going to retaliate by undercutting us next summer in the power lawnmower market? The tendency to forgo price competition is intensified by interlocking directorates and stock holdings—a sort of conglomerate "old-boy network" that means that prices that might normally have come down won't.

"Cross-subsidization" occurs when a conglomerate uses the profits of one money-making line to support another line that isn't doing so well—something the smaller competition cannot do. One of the more notorious recent examples of cross-subsidization is the Miller Beer case of the early seventies.

Willard Mueller, who is a professor in both agricultural economics and law at the University of Wisconsin, has traced the developments from 1969 and 1970, when Philip Morris, a huge conglomerate, bought Miller, a respectably well-off but unspectacular brewer, for $229 million. At the time Miller was fourth largest of the four national beer brands.

Philip Morris soon started using its conglomerate treasury to subsidize Miller's expansion. A Chicago brand, Lite beer, was purchased and bottled under the Miller label, then promoted with enormous advertising outlays. There had been previous attempts to sell the nation's beer drinkers on a "light" beer, or one that promised fewer calories, but they had met with resistance, perhaps from those who suspected, accurately, that "light" beer is beer with a greater proportion of water.*

But Philip Morris's efforts succeeded, probably due to the sheer number of dollars it put behind its "new" product as much as to anything else. Ad expenditures shot from $525,000 in 1973 to $27.7 million in 1979, said Mueller in a paper on conglomerates published by an association of seventeen university agricultural experiment stations. The professor wrote: "The Lite success story represents the ultimate achievement of advertising-created product differentiation—being able to sell a lower-cost product at a higher price."

Having gotten more money for less product, Philip Morris then started advertising blitzes for Lowenbrau, which had been a reasonably good German beer but now was being manufactured in the United States without any inordinate fuss over the fact that it was no longer an import.

So, in a relatively short period of time, a conglomerate had

* According to James D. Robertson, in *The Connoisseur's Guide to Beer* (Aurora, Ill.: Caroline Publishers, 1982), "some brewers simply dilute their regular beer" to produce a "light" label. In other cases, he writes, the process used to lower calories has the effect of producing an alcohol that is absorbed more rapidly in the drinker's bloodstream, and that thus is more intoxicating. Brewers then adjust the intoxication level by adding water.

managed to do several things: It created a market for "light" beer that sells for more than "non-light" beer; it elevated an ordinary domestic beer to the status of "super-premium"; and, more important, it made it much more difficult for other brewers to compete. As Philip Morris and its leading competitor, Anheuser-Busch, follow similar patterns of drowning the market in national advertising and "new" brands, competitors who can't do the same, including the previously important regional brewers, may be forced out.

In addition, any competitors that want to compete must do so with the money they have on hand, while Miller can always dip into the Philip Morris conglomerate treasury. "Thus," concluded Mueller, "the PM-Miller conglomerate merger triggered an inexorable trend toward shared monopoly in which price competition is replaced by promotional competition and higher prices; an environment in which survival and success often depend on market power, not efficiency."

One possible and potential result of all this action in the marketplace is *monopoly*, which can be defined as a condition that allows a seller to have single control over the total supply of a product. Power utilities, to the rue of many of their customers, usually have monopolies over their product within specific geographical areas; until recently, the Bell System had a monopoly over the legal sale and installation of telephones in most places. The dangers of monopoly power are great, and the practice was outlawed in 1890 by the Sherman Antitrust Act. Which is not to say that monopoly isn't still practiced, or that—to a far greater degree—partial monopoly isn't attempted and achieved in many businesses and industries, including the food system.

Monopoly occupies the opposite extreme from what economists call "perfect competition," which is a situation in which there are so many buyers and sellers dealing in the same product that no one of them can control the price of that product. Markets in the United States operate somewhere between monopoly and perfect competition. In the view of economists (but probably not of lay persons), attempts to sell a product by advertising and other forms of promotion are influences leading away from perfect competition.

Through the years, efforts have been made to gauge the amount of money consumers have to pay for the products of certain industries because of what is called "monopoly overcharge," or the "taxes" that are imposed by imperfect competition. Russell C. Parker and John Connor in 1979 gathered studies estimating the monopoly-inspired consumer loss in U.S. food manufacturing industries, and they came up with a shocking total.

The economists said their estimates were "conservative," and they warned that because of the techniques that had to be used in arriving at them, there were ample possibilities for error. But they concluded that losses to consumers because of monopoly overcharge in 1975 amounted to 1.1 percent of the U.S. personal disposable income that year, or 5.7 percent of the nation's household expenditures for food. In other words, they wrote, consumer loss was "at least $10 billion, but possibly as high as $15 billion."

That is an enormous amount of money. The lower figure works out to about $50 that year for every female and male, adult and child, living in the United States at the time. An obvious question is, What is society doing about this? Or, as social scientists prefer to put it, What are the implications here for public policy? Parker and Connor found "significant implications." They wrote, in conclusion, that "the annual loss to consumers in food manufacturing alone is 250 times the combined antitrust budgets of both U.S. antitrust agencies and several times that part of federal antitrust expenditures," and they raised some issues that, if pursued by the government, would be extremely controversial. One suggested that "consideration be given to limiting advertising in industries where it is already intense," and another posed the possibility of "direct restructuring" of noncompetitive food manufacturing by government action.

That was strong language even for the late 1970s, and only a few years later, with virtually no aspect of the nation's life untouched by the hands of Ronald Reagan and the pro-business philosophy that put him in power, it is language that sounds almost like science fiction. Washington, as will be seen later in the section dealing with government and the food business, has no intention of regulating advertising, discouraging conglomerate mergers, restructuring businesses, fostering anything close to "perfect" competition, or even enforcing the antitrust laws. American consumers are very much on their own when they venture out into the marketplace to buy food.

5

Delivering It

If Americans consume 1,400 pounds of food per capita each
year, and if there are about 226 million Americans, then that
is a great deal of eating indeed. It is 316.4 trillion pounds of
food a year, or 26.4 billion pounds a month, or almost 867
million pounds a day, or more than 36 million pounds an
hour, or around 600,000 pounds a minute. And, like water and
clothing, spare parts for automobiles, and doctors who make
house calls, the food we want does not magically appear in
front of us at the moment we want it. Our food has to be
delivered, and delivered it is.

Baby cows are born in Texas, trucked to California or
Colorado for fattening, moved to Nebraska for slaughter, then
shipped all over the country (including Texas and California
and Colorado) for sale and consumption. Fresh fruits and
vegetables roll out of California, Arizona, and Florida by
truck and train virtually year-round with better-than-military
precision, and during the lulls in those states' growing seasons
they are augmented by produce from Mexico and the semi-

tropical Lower Rio Grande Valley of Texas. (The scenario has some odd scenes: At certain times of the year, supermarket chains in Florida buy their produce from California. It is shipped by way of Atlanta. When the Mediterranean fruit fly attacked California in July 1981, one of the states which imposed embargoes on California produce—including oranges—was Florida. The reason was that Florida has oranges growing in July and August, but they aren't ready to be picked and sold.)

Much of what is delivered, be it from the warm, moist fields of the growing states or the precisely humidified, sterilized environment of the canneries of the West or the food manufacturers of Minneapolis, Kankakee, and Battle Creek, is delivered to the East, since the whole point of the delivery system is to get the food to where the people are who will buy it, eat it, and come back for more.

And to buy, eat, and return frequently. One of the basic phrases of the food business, particularly at the retail level, is "turn." It stands for "turnover," and it means just that: the number of times (usually measured in a yearly period) that a product moves through a warehouse or store. Supermarket turn is around twenty times a year for most grocery items. If the average falls much below that the retailer becomes concerned, because turn is a vital component of sales volume, and, with the grocer's relatively low per-item markup, volume is everything.

Turn means a lot to the individual grocery store manager, and it means just as much to the food delivery system. The entire chain is built (if such a term can be used to describe a system that is without much design, one that created itself out of necessity and experience and innovation) on the idea that there will be many fluctuations in both producer and manufacturer supply and in consumer demand, but that the prevailing theme will be one of endlessness—of "turn" writ gigantic and continuous. In theory, and to some extent in

practice, if for some reason consumers suddenly stopped buying, say, Acme Brand canned baked beans, there would be an
almost instant reverse-domino effect throughout the system:
The grocers would notice the change first, of course, and they
would quickly let the wholesalers, brokers, and warehouse-
men know. The Acme Brand people would be immediately
affected, as would their merchandisers and field buyers. It
wouldn't be very long before the bean farmers felt the effects,
and eventually the people who sell them their agricultural
chemicals and hardware would know, too. And all along this
line, the people who transport food would be involved—
although not as much as one might suspect, since Americans
have shown a tendency to go on eating around 1,400 pounds
of food a year no matter what, and if they stop eating Acme
beans they'll probably take up the slack with something else.

     And so the trucks and boxcars roll—and, increasingly, the
cargo planes fly, as more Americans discover the sweet truth
of the fact that when it's winter here there are strawberries
growing in Argentina and nectarines in Chile.

     The distribution system is enormous, but nobody seems to
know quite *how* enormous. Reliable statistics, which are readily available for many of the other components of the food
system, are far less available for delivery. Nor is there as
much on hand describing the system itself, possibly because it
is such a dynamic, changing system, and because some of its
practitioners prefer to keep details of their operations to
themselves for reasons of competition.

     The USDA has estimated that the total costs of bringing
food to market include heavy expenditures for delivery. Of
the total "marketing bill" of $214 billion in 1982, which in-
cluded labor, rail and truck transportation, corporate profits,
and "other," the government found close to $15 billion, or
about 7 percent, went for nonlocal transportation, including

charges for "protective services" and heating and refrigeration. The sum doesn't include local delivery or the wages of people employed in the delivery system who aren't directly involved in transportation.

The consumption of vast amounts of energy in transportation has brought criticism from a number of observers of the food system. And the oil embargo and shortages helped them make their point that the system, with its reliance on growing things on one side of the country and then moving them to the other, had become dangerously vulnerable to disruption. Most of these critics also complain that food shipped across the nation is less fresh than food that could be grown close to home. And, they point out, far-flung distribution networks make food a lot more expensive than it ought to be.

Carol Tucker Foreman was at the Consumer Federation of America before she joined the Carter administration as Assistant Secretary of Agriculture for Food and Consumer Services. More recently she has been working as a consultant in Washington. In an interview not long ago, Foreman articulated the critics' transportation argument:

"Our food system was developed at a time when Americans assumed that energy costs would always be very low," she said. "You went to the filling station and they gave you a set of china or a set of glasses for buying their gas at 25 cents a gallon. That time is gone forever, but I don't think the system has made a lot of those changes. We still grow tomatoes in Florida and Mexico and California and ship them all the way across the country to be sold in New England and Washington, and we develop harvesting systems and plans to kill off pests and diseases in the field that are highly energy-related. . . .

"Farming has gotten to the point where, as more and more land is taken out of production by urbanization, and as more and more production is directed solely at export, we are becoming almost totally dependent on bringing fruits and vegetables from south Texas, California, and Florida. Almost nobody does truck farming anymore. It used to be that New Jersey was called the Garden State. They supplied all their part of the country with produce, and it was reasonably priced. But because we've developed a food system in which people think they can go to the supermarket and buy a tomato in the middle of January, the food system is very expensive."

Robert Rodale agrees, and is trying to do something about it. He is the head of Rodale Press, of Emmaus, Pennsylvania, which is best known for books and magazines on organic gardening and healthful living. A few years ago Rodale and others started what they call the Cornucopia Project as "an effort to encourage thinking and action now" on important food issues, "while there is still time to act." In one of a series of newspaper advertisements encouraging participation in the project, Rodale used the example of broccoli. Residents of the New York area, he said, in the previous year had bought some 24,000 tons of the vegetable, almost all of it shipped from the West Coast at a cost of nearly $6 million. The irony, said Rodale, is that "broccoli prefers cool weather. Except for southern Florida, it could have been grown successfully—and delivered to New Yorkers less expensively—from virtually anywhere else in the continental U.S. Including New York's own backyard gardens." And that was the case, too, with dozens of other fruits and vegetables.

Delivery is not just transportation, but rather transportation from the producer to the consumer and all the steps and stops along the way, which include not only those created by the makers and sellers of food themselves, but also those required by the federal, state, and local governments, which impose thousands of regulations on the business, some of them conflicting. So it should not be surprising that distribution is one of the more complicated, and unfathomed, parts of the food chain. We simply do not have solid information on how food gets to us.

One way to examine the flow of food is to take a look at some of the ways it gets to a specific city. At first glance, New York City might seem a bad place to start—a system that is known to be complex elsewhere is probably going to be unmanageably so in New York, and participants in the food business interviewed for this book all over the nation warned against treating New York as anything but an anomaly, since its stores, its selling and buying techniques, and (many non–New Yorkers are quick to add) its very *people* are atypical to the point of being bizarre.

But New York is a densely packed laboratory of life and commerce, and it is possible to observe at first hand a lot of the distribution process that might be almost invisible in a smaller city or a suburban community. Where else in the United States, for example, is one likely to see a quarter of a slaughtered steer being dragged from the rear of a Chevrolet station wagon and hand-trucked across a busy sidewalk (dotted with dog excreta) into a butcher shop? And in how many other places can one witness a freighter unloading millions of pounds of bananas? Or watch close up during the predawn hours as tons of fish are sold at wholesale to anybody who wants to buy a lot of them, from neighborhood fishmonger to restaurant proprietor?

New York is a hungry place. By one very rough estimate it consumes around 10 billion pounds of food each year. As with most other things, New Yorkers don't just eat food; they *demand* it. And around the city and around the clock, but particularly in the hours of the deepest night, there are thousands of people meeting that demand.

Down near the foot of Manhattan at three o'clock on a cold,

raw morning in February, 1983 (or practically any other day), a somnambulist could have turned a corner from quiet darkness into a raucous, brightly lighted scene that seemed surely to be the set for a Fellini movie: the archaic, anachronistic Fulton Fish Market, somehow still kicking, still moving fish from the catchers to the eaters.

Not far away, at another East River pier, a freighter named the *Tropical Breeze* prepared to unload about 5 million pounds of bananas. Outside the city limits, in Montvale, New Jersey, and in suburban Mt. Kisco, New York, and in Farmingdale, on Long Island, powerful little forklifts scooted about at a dozen grocery warehouses big enough to house pro football contests, plucking cases of canned creamed corn, geriatric dog food, two-ply paper towels, and extra-crunchy peanut butter off 30-foot-high shelves and depositing them in neat piles on wooden pallets. The piles were assembled and checked against the computer printout of the previous night's orders that had been phoned in from the supermarkets, and everything flowed with marvelous efficiency into the cavernous trailers of trucks. By the time the sun rose they would have moved out and begun the resupplying of the city's more than three thousand supermarkets. Similar operations were performing the same early-morning packing routine for an estimated equal number of smaller stores.

It was all very heroic in scale, but most of the drama was reserved for Hunt's Point. The city-operated terminal market in the Bronx was going full-tilt at three in the morning, receiving boxcar and truck loads of fruits and vegetables from around the world and breaking them down into smaller wholesale lots and then reselling them to the supermarkets, bodegas, restaurants, neighborhood co-ops, and institutions of the city.

"New York City is the mirror image of the rest of the nation," says Howard Tisch, a lawyer who is the executive secretary of the Greater New York Metropolitan Food Council. By that he means the *real* mirror image: "It's the exact opposite in almost every category, and for a number of reasons."

Supermarkets in New York, for instance, are generally limited in size by the existing architecture and by the enormous cost of erecting new buildings or renting larger space, while the trend nationwide is to larger stores. "And we are limited by the streets that we have here, particularly in Manhattan," said Tisch in an interview. "The place was built by Peter Stuyvesant, and that's the way it's going to be." Smaller and older stores and nonstop traffic problems mean, in addition to fewer grocery items and no customer parking, that the trucks that deliver food to the stores have no convenient place to stop while unloading and no docks on which to drop their goods.

Another difference is that New York is the home of uncounted thousands of smaller stores, often called "mom and pop" operations but now being identified generically as "bodegas" by the industry, which maintains a lively interest in the city's growing Hispanic market. Like the 7-Elevens and other "convenience stores" of the suburbs, these stores serve as places to buy a limited assortment of food in a hurry without having to go to a supermarket. But in the city they are much more. Their prices are higher than those in the supermarkets, but not outrageously higher, as at their suburban counterparts. Many, if not most, are operated by their owners and offer a number of personal services to their customers, from credit to action in the numbers game.

Delivering the food for 7,071,030 or so people to six thousand retail stores rather than to a relative handful of modern supermarket chains presents logistical problems unlike those of any other American city. And there is a demand for a greater variety of food, because of the city's ethnic and racial variety.

Ben Zdatny is the president of one of the giant food warehouses that serve supermarkets in the New York area. Because of all the human diversity, he finds himself having to stock 6,800 separate items, rather than the usual 4,500 to 5,000.

"I don't *like* to handle 6,800 grocery items," he said. "But I do, because of the ethnic environments in which we deal. We have to have collard greens and black-eyed peas for Harlem and at the same time I have to have gandules for the Spanish trade, and we have to have blintzes and pizza as well. But one of the beauties of that is that we have absorbed each other's tastes. *That's* what makes us different from the rest of the country."

And there is the demand for food on New Yorkers' own terms, which means no once-a-week trips in the station wagon to the supermarket that dominates the shopping center to drop $150 or $200 on a family's rations for the next seven days. New Yorkers have small refrigerators and limited freezer space, and very few station wagons, so they shop on the way home from work, and that often means at the stores they encounter between the subway and the apartment. Food tends to get bought once a day or even more frequently—two potatoes and a head of lettuce from the greengrocer, a pound of coffee beans from the "gourmet" shop, a pound of chopped chuck from the butcher. All this has profound implications for the distribution of food in New York City; not only is food bought in different ways than elsewhere, but the amount that is bought is enormous.

Department of Agriculture "unload" statistics for 1981 in the New York City–Newark, New Jersey, area counted more than 3.8 billion pounds of fresh fruits and vegetables entering the area by truck, rail car, and boat. Of the total, said Mike Pflueger, the officer in charge of the department's Market News Service in New York, around 55 percent arrived at the Hunt's Point terminal. Of the remainder, Pflueger estimated, about 35 percent was shipped in directly by supermarket chains and the rest went to repacking plants. An uncounted amount—not large in the big picture but very important in terms of quality and other factors that often don't find their way into statistics—gets to New York tables from its neighborhood direct marketing centers, called Greenmarkets, and straight from backyard, windowbox, and community gardens.

The totals show that New Yorkers and their neighbors may lead active, hardworking lives, but they also love to eat. If the government's unload figures may be taken as rough indicators of consumption (*very* rough, since an unknown portion is redistributed outside the city and another undetermined quantity is not counted in the official totals), the Big Apple and its environs in 1981 devoured some 108,000 tons of conventional apples, along with 47,000 tons of cucumbers, 29,000 tons of bell peppers, 5,500 tons of spinach, 131,000 tons of oranges, 76,000 tons of tomatoes, 3,300 tons of mangoes, 29,000 tons of plantains, and 450 tons of persimmons. The most-eaten commodities in what is known as the most sophisticated city in the nation are the old, bland standbys, potatoes (248,000 tons a year) and iceberg lettuce (205,000 tons).

Bottled-milk statistics are also fairly reliable. The state department of agriculture and marketing estimates that 63,253,000 quarts of packaged milk were sold in the city in a typical month in 1981. Numbers for other foods may be guessed at by applying federal and industry statistics on per capita food consumption (themselves not much more than educated speculation) to the city's population. That would mean an annual consumption of something like 451 million pounds of poultry, 547 million pounds of beef, 126 million pounds of cheese, 79 million pounds of coffee, tea, and cocoa, 245 million pounds of eggs, and 126 million pounds of ice cream.

Food that is rotten is food that is valueless, so the entire distribution operation, in New York as elsewhere, is geared to moving the stuff in as quickly as possible. Meat gets to the city four or five days after slaughter in the Midwest. Milk,

which is subjected to a lot of abuse by deliverers and shop-
keepers, who often leave it unrefrigerated, must be sold
within ninety-six hours after six o'clock on the morning of the
day it was pasteurized. Eggs are unpredictable: Although
USDA experts say they arrive soon after being laid, city-
bought eggs rarely have the fresh taste of those right off the
farm. Poultry gets to the city one or two days after slaughter,
and there are some live poultry markets where the customer
chooses the bird even before it's killed.

Fish in New York (and elsewhere) are hardly ever as fresh
at retail as advertised. Although some seafoods arrive alive in
the neighborhood markets—lobsters, clams, and oysters—
most fish take at least a day to get to the city after the trawler
docks in Massachusetts or Maine, two days at best by truck
from Florida. And that does not include time spent on the
boat. Some fishers go out for three or more weeks at a time,
and although they are capable of icing their catch expertly,
what they unload is hardly "fresh," although the standard
claim is that it is.

Produce can take three days or less to arrive from Florida,
five or six to come from California by truck (sometimes
longer by train; the experts blame the delay on the fact that
trains are reconfigured along the way, usually in Chicago, and
often a load of lettuce is condemned to rotting in some midwestern switching yard). The Florida Citrus Commission figures that it takes "roughly a week at the earliest" for an
orange to get from the tree to a New York consumer.

As with anything else, those who want what they consider
the best can get it, for a price. In February, 1983, Lew Solo-
mon, a salesman at Hunt's Point for Goodie Brand Packing
Corporation, was offering delicious-looking tomatoes from
Israel at $1.43 a pound wholesale. He figured the mostly rip-
ened tomatoes could be harvested on a Monday, emplaned at
Tel Aviv on Tuesday, arrive at Kennedy Airport on Wednes-
day, then brought to the city—"It can take as much time

getting them from the airport as it took them to get there," he said—and sold to retailers in time to tempt consumers by Friday or, possibly, Thursday.

Each kind of food that enters New York City has its own system of distribution to the retail store, and each kind of store has its own system for obtaining the food it sells. "System" perhaps is too weighty a term to describe what actually takes place. Foods get to consumers in New York, as elsewhere in the nation and world, through an elaborate vein of informal procedures—in industry and the military they are called "standard operating procedures," or SOPs—that have grown up through the years. New York's food SOPs have evolved over time from a lot of give-and-take among management, labor, retailers, and consumers.

Some foods, including the more basic commodities, arrive in a relatively straightforward manner. They are trucked in or brought by rail, deposited at a central point, and then resold by brokers or distributors to smaller members of the food chain. The fruits and vegetables that arrive at Hunt's Point are a clear example of this.

The New York City Terminal Market, as it is officially known, is said to be the largest produce market in the world. Its bigness is measured in money—some $2.5 to $3 million in produce from all over the globe is sold there on a typical day—and in sheer size. Situated on 125 acres in the South Bronx, the market is essentially four narrow buildings, each a third of a mile long. The plan was for shipments to come in on one side by train and large truck, get broken into smaller lots, and then go out the other side to the retail market's smaller trucks and vans. In actuality, incoming and outgoing produce use the same side, creating enormous traffic problems and occasional violence among truck drivers. Around three thousand buyers a year come to the market on a regular basis.

The city's Department of Ports and Terminals Hunt's Point office claims not to know how many trucks deliver food to the market, even though it counts them as they go through the gate.

Downstairs on the broad aprons between sheds, truck tractors (called "horses") move trailers ("pigs") around to disgorge their 40,000-pound cargoes, and Conrail crews bring strings of refrigerated boxcars down from the staging area in Yonkers, a city in Westchester County just north of New York. The prime consideration here, as throughout the food business, is the speed with which produce can be "turned." "If they can walk it from the back door to the front door and onto a truck, they're happy," said Bob Sormani, Ports and Terminals supervising inspector at Hunt's Point. "That's the name of the game. Room is at a premium here."

The Hunt's Point schedule, Sormani explained, provides for the pigs to arrive very early in the morning and unload. Then buyers come and make their purchases, in some cases still before dawn. In the hours before midnight, the city's sanitation department is supposed to clean the complex, and then the trucks start arriving again.

A visit to the market, however, reveals an operation that is overlaid with filth. What covers the terminal market is not just the institutional trash of a busy industry but rather a thick slurry, a congealed *presence* that seems to be made of equal parts of rotten, black ice (some from cooling devices, some left over from a long-departed snowstorm), cast-off shards of trucks and pallets, and rotting vegetables—everything from diseased chestnuts to oddly unround grapefruit that have imploded from rot. The maintenance of the place is like that of some of the city's more neglected subway stations.

In the sheds and on the platforms, though, which are maintained not by the city but by the partnerships, corporations, and individual entrepreneurs who rent the 25-by-60-foot stalls, a higher standard prevails, as it does next door to the market at the meat terminal, which also is owned by the city but operated by a cooperative of packers and distributors who service much of the city's meat demand. Samples of the food itself are attractively displayed beneath spotlights—for retailers are no less susceptible than ordinary consumers to the temptations of impulse shopping.

On that cold February morning there was much to be displayed, and the loading docks looked more like summertime than New York's harshest month. By three o'clock most of the big trucks and refrigerated boxcars had already deposited their loads: broccoli, globe artichokes, spaghetti squash, and strawberries from California; green beans, leeks, Bibb lettuce, sweet corn, and late-blooming mandarins from Florida; collards from Georgia; yams from North Carolina and Colombia; asparagus and green beans from Mexico; bok choy from Arizona; limes and plantains from Ecuador; ginger root from Costa Rica; mangoes from Haiti; nectarines from Chile; individually wrapped hothouse cucumbers from Cleveland, Ohio; rutabaga and carrots from Canada. Very little came from New York: alfalfa and bean sprouts, and some upstate apples.

As they went through the 252 stalls, the carloads of produce got redefined into boxes, pecks, and bushels and resold to the produce managers of small independent supermarkets, chains, Italian greengrocers, and New York's growing corps of hardworking Korean merchants, as well as the purchasing agents for neighborhood co-ops, restaurateurs, and anybody else willing to pay the price of admission (50 cents a car, $2 a truck) and to buy at least a case of something.

Just how many bushels and pecks are resold, and for how many dollars, is determined by the action on the floor of the stalls themselves and in the quieter, better-appointed offices upstairs, where the executives of the wholesale firms tap numbers into their adding machines and cut deals on the telephone with shippers a continent away.

Outsiders are not welcome upstairs, but anybody can enjoy the free show down on the docks. Dave Chubinsky, a salesman for the huge producing and wholesaling firm of D'Arrigo Brothers, has been selling food wholesale for forty-seven years, and he doesn't need an adding machine or telephone. He does make notes on a sixteen-column ledger sheet on the wooden lectern that stands on the dock and serves as his office.

Prices are not posted at Hunt's Point, because they change rapidly. The wholesalers, taking their cost and other factors into consideration, establish an asking price for an item. "Take these green beans here," said Chubinsky. "Say they cost me seventeen dollars for a box. One of these boxes is about twenty-eight pounds. Say I'm asking nineteen or twenty [people in the food business rarely bother to say "dollars" or "cents"], and an hour goes by and I've sold just twelve or fifteen beans. People are walking away. I know I've got the wrong price.

"Now, there are some guys out here, some buyers, who I know and trust, and I can say to one of them when he walks by, 'Hey, Joe, what are they asking for beans?' He'll say to me, 'Well, they're asking eighteen, nineteen.' That's what we call 'getting posted.' So now I know that the others aren't getting twenty. They're not even getting nineteen. Maybe I'd better sell for eighteen."

When someone does buy beans from Chubinsky (or anyone else), the seller makes out a receipt stating the quantity and agreed price. Receipts rarely contain buyers' full names, relying usually on nicknames or "market initials." Once the deal is made, the buyer leaves to do more shopping. At the end of his day at Hunt's Point, which is likely to be before most people have made it to the office, he returns with a truck and claims his purchase.

Lots of factors go into the prices asked by the middlemen at Hunt's Point, and it is impossible to calculate precisely what their markup is. Federal statistics for a few days before that day in February, however, show that when broccoli was leaving California it cost around 29 cents a bunch. That was the average price being paid to farmers in Salinas, minus any commissions they may have paid to sales agents there.

After being shipped across the nation and run through the sheds in the South Bronx, the price had risen to around 55 cents. That is a 90 percent markup, but it's not the outrageous profit that it sounds. The wholesaler in New York must pay freight, which usually runs about 30 percent of the wholesale price (on that day, freight added about 18 cents to the cost of a head of broccoli) and icing and drayage charges (about 2 cents). So the Hunt's Point wholesaler, who was charging 55 cents for his broccoli, had to lay out about 49 cents to get it.

The next step is the retailer, the person who purchases the broccoli at Hunt's Point for 55 cents a head. In New York City the following day, broccoli was observed selling in several retail outlets—both neighborhood greengrocers and super-markets—for 79 cents a bunch. This 44 percent markup is somewhat higher than the average, which USDA's Mike Pflueger estimates at about 35 percent.

Some comparisons of other produce prices showed ba-nanas going from about 26 cents a pound at Hunt's Point to 39 cents in the retail store, celery going from about 40 cents to 69 cents, green beans going from about 65 cents to 98 cents, cabbage rising from 9 cents to 19 cents, and spinach going from 30 cents to 79 cents. These represent markups as high as 163 percent, in the case of spinach, which is some-what unusual for an ordinary, non-fancified produce market. Some consumers might consider the margins high, but they should remember the retailer's investment in time, fuel, and labor. Just coping with the ambiance of Hunt's Point is worth something.

The idea that New York City is an anomaly and an anachronism seems firmly supported by the Fulton Fish Mar-ket. Like Hunt's Point, the city-operated seafood facility is economically important—its merchants turn over an estimated $750 million a year—but in every other sense the market would seem to be a prime candidate for extinction.

Although the market is situated on, and partly hangs over, the East River, the vast majority of the fish and shellfish arrive not by boat but by tractor-trailer truck from shippers in Florida, the Carolinas, and New England.

Diesels throb on the big tractors and dozens of fishy-smelling vans and small trucks maneuver around the stanchions that support the elevated Franklin Delano Roosevelt Drive above. The hook, a device similar to the one used by longshoremen, is everywhere: Workers use it to drag soggy cardboard boxes around, buyers use it to pluck a sample fish from the box for examination. It is all very macho. You half expect to see one of the men (there are few women here) impale a Styrofoam cup of coffee on his pointed, curved hook and hoist it to his mouth.

Inside one of the sheds on a winter morning a giant of a man, dressed like the others in multiple layers of rough clothing to ward off the chill, relieved himself on the concrete floor in the midst of what someone later might declare to be the "Catch of the Day." The urine ran down under a tow sack full of clams. A large rat walked self-assuredly along a wall. Outside, on a muddy parking lot (that is controlled, like most else at the market, by organized crime, according to federal investigators), an oriental woman moved silently between the vans and trucks. She pushed a baby stroller that contained a large plastic bag. She found a discarded fish in the mud, picked it up, and put it carefully into the bag. Then she moved on to the next one.

The fish market may soon be gentrified out of existence by the developers of the South Street Seaport, a fancy commercial project. In the meantime, the market, for all its problems, is one of the few places in the city where a resident can go and actually see food being distributed out in the open, and where the people who handle that food don't refer to it as "product."

A few blocks north of the Fulton market, Pier 42 looks almost sleekly modern by comparison. The pier, another joint operation between the city as landlord and a corporation as tenant, represents a combination of what threatens to become a nostalgia item for New York City—shipping—and the fast, efficient distribution of food. In this case the commodities are the tons of bananas and pineapples that New Yorkers eat and that are funneled through the city to much of the rest of the East Coast.

The tenant in the 78,000-square-foot shed at Pier 42, which used to be the city's unloading terminal for newsprint, is Standard Fruit, a part of the Honolulu-based Castle and Cooke. Each week of the year two or three large refrigerated freighters arrive at Pier 42 with cargoes of bananas and, sometimes, pineapples and coconuts that were loaded at ports in Honduras, Costa Rica, or Ecuador.

It is a very efficient operation, as Nino Pupeti, the firm's East Coast terminal manager, described it in an interview. When the vessel is packed, New York is advised of the cargo and time of arrival. In the three and a half or four days it takes the ship to steam north at 20 knots, the marketing specialists line up their sales. By the time the ship has docked and is ready to unload, at seven o'clock on the morning after its arrival, hundreds of empty tractor-trailers from New York chains and distributors and from as far afield as South Carolina, Detroit, and New Brunswick, Canada, are lined up under the Franklin Delano Roosevelt Drive, waiting to be filled.

The manager said the ships are often more reliable than the trucks, which must contend with traffic and weather conditions. "Our ships, they run quite well on schedule," said

Pupeti, a Genoan who has spent most of his life on water. "The last time we had a shortage of bananas here that I can remember was when the ships were delayed by Hurricane Fifi. That was in 1975."

Gantry cranes reach into the ship's holds and lift the bananas, packed in 40-pound boxes and already bearing Standard Fruit's "Dole" sticker, into the shed, where they enter an intricate and noisy conveyor system that moves them swiftly into the trailers of the trucks parked on the other side. The ubiquitous forklifts scoot about everywhere. Bill Mc-Kinley, Standard Fruit's eastern marketing division vice-president, said that when all is going well the bananas spend no more than one minute inside the shed. "Time is not an ally of ours," he told a visitor.

Much of the food that enters the city isn't as easily categorized as produce, seafood, and bananas. It comes in plain brown cardboard cartons from manufacturers like General Mills and Purina and Del Monte and Heinz. No one knows the total tonnage of dry groceries and frozen foods that descend upon New York, but it is a staggering amount that moves in a continuous stream into the warehouses, then the retail stores of the city, and finally into consumers' homes. "The great thing about food," said one warehouseman, "is that people keep eating it. Tomorrow they want more."

Before it is stacked on the stores' shelves, though, the food must be broken down into lots that not only are manageable in size but also fit the needs of a particular store and its clientele. Canned matzo-ball soup is not a hot item in stores in Harlem, and pork sausage does not do well in Williamsburg, where thousands of Orthodox Jews live.

Many of those knowledgeable about food distribution in New York City believe that the retailer who succeeds in such an intensely competitive environment is the one who can judge his or her customers' needs the best. This is usually cited as one reason why large supermarket chains have less of the total market in New York than in many other places. Howard Tisch, who counts among his retailers' association most of the locally owned supermarkets and homegrown chains, said the nationally run chains are tied to centrally run computers that blindly think of New York as one homogeneous marketing area.

Rocco Lopardo, vice-president for distribution at the Grand Union supermarket chain for the region that includes New York, said if such was the case at one time, it isn't anymore. Lopardo oversees a large distribution system that is similar to those of most chains: Individual managers conduct a quick inventory of their stores several times a week—in busy stores, every day—and record their needs on small hand-held devices that resemble programmable calculators. At the end of the day they clap the machines up against a telephone handset, punch a few buttons, and send their shopping lists electronically to the chain's central distribution computer.

New York City's seventeen Grand Union stores dictate their orders by phone to a computer in Paramus, New Jersey, which relays them to the chain's warehouse in Mt. Kisco. By three or four in the morning, warehouse workers are busy "picking" boxes and bags of everything from sweet peas to Gainesburgers and loading them onto 40- or 45-foot-long trailer trucks backed up to one side of the warehouse. A typical store will receive its order by the middle of the afternoon.

Not all the food warehouses are run by chains. There are thousands of independent food stores in the city, some of them supermarkets and some of them not so super. They all need to buy food in quantities more manageable than boxcar loads. The independent wholesale warehouse meets their needs.

Ben Zdatny's warehouse is typical. It stands on a huge tract of land in suburban Long Island, close to highways and a rail line and to the urban and suburban stores it services. Inside, the simple, rectangular building is a supermarket magnified a hundredfold: Cheerios are stacked twelve cases high, and there are what seem to be eternal supplies of paper towels, tomato sauce, and peanut butter. Forklifts dart about pulling some of the 1.5 million cartons of food down and taking them to trucks waiting at the loading bays. Four hundred people work in the facility. Doors on one side of the building can open and accept shipments from eighteen to twenty boxcars at a time. The place has an area of 600,000 square feet, and, just as in a well-run grocery store, every inch is utilized.

The wholesaler's customers receive magazine-size books periodically, listing thousands of food and household items and their current prices, as well as information on manufacturers' specials and promotional offerings. The customers telephone their orders to the warehouse, where a computer prints an unusual shopping list: It tells the warehouse's "picker" what items to get, but it also identifies the location of the items by aisle and slot and it contains a sheet of numbered stickum labels that contain coded information about the order. Pickers fetch the merchandise, affix the labels to it, and stack it on pallets, which then go into trucks backed up to loading bays. Like many of the operations of the food business, this one is very efficient and quick. The process is a vital one for stores too small to have their own warehouses. "If it were not for the independent wholesaler," said Zdatny, "the independent operator could not exist. Where would he get his food products from?"

Guido Mannarino is in charge of warehouse operations at the Long Island facility. He explained that the way things were shelved had a lot to do with speed and efficiency. "We lay things out in family groupings," he said, pointing to a tall column of Strained Carrots, Oatmeal with Bananas, Zwieback, and other infant delicacies. "And we also have all the fast-moving items and a lot of our bulk items in front, so we have to do as little traveling as possible to get them." Paper goods, he said, are both bulky and fast-moving, and a lot of the warehouse space and effort are devoted to getting them. "One of these days they're going to come out with concentrated turlet paper," said Mannarino, "and it'll make me very happy."

Somewhere between the bodegas and the supermarkets are numerous other channels through which food gets into a large city. Food brokers, for example, are found at the terminal markets if they deal in produce or seafood, or virtually anywhere else if they work in dry groceries. They are practically invisible to the general public but they play important roles in making promotional and delivery arrangements between manufacturers who do not have their own field networks and large independent warehouses and supermarket chains or associations.

A lot of distribution *is* handled directly by the manufacturer. Quite a few items—your Dr Pepper, Charles Chips, Arnold's Bread, Twinkies, Thomas' English Muffins, and most dairy products—traditionally have used their own route salespersons to deliver food and preen the displays inside the store. And throughout New York's boroughs, particularly those outside Manhattan, there are unpretentious-looking buildings that turn out everything from whole-wheat Italian bread to preformed Jamaican meat patties and truck them to stores, restaurants, and institutions. The food service industry, which in New York is a spectrum running from the famed Lutèce to the tiniest storefront pizzeria, has its own distribution system. Tucked into corners of the Bronx are small but energetic enterprises that raise and market fresh herbs, and bean sprouts are grown in darkened Chinatown cellars and delivered to restaurants and produce markets all over the city. New York's many stores that sell fancy foods can't get all the merchandise they want through normal channels, so some have built their own networks of specialty distributors. Similarly, restaurants that want foods that are especially hard to find or out of season, or both, often get them by air, using specialized distributors or making their own arrangements with producers or shippers. Almost anything can be had for a price—white asparagus in January, succulent raspberries in December.

A surprising amount of the food that is sold in New York is manufactured there. The city has dozens of small and large processors and manufacturers and packagers of private-label lines. Sterling Gordon runs one of the latter, the Coffee Holding Company, in a generally neglected section of Brooklyn near the fetid Gowanus Canal.

Gordon buys coffee from around the world, blends it, roasts it, packages it, and ships it out, all to the specifications set by the wholesaler or supermarket chain for which he's packing it, and under whose label it will be sold. In addition, he sells his own brand, Cafe Caribe, which is popular among the city's Hispanic population. Of the "house blends" that appear in some of the city's "gourmet" shops, he said in an interview, "I sell to the people who sell to those stores."

Gordon, an energetic, outgoing man, denied that he was a big frog in a small pond, but he said there are compensations for being in a part of the food distribution business where the competition is fierce and where much depends on world events, but where a small operation can remain lean and flexible and try to outmaneuver the big guys.

It is, he said, "a high-action game. When I went to Vegas one time, I fell asleep in the casino. When I went to Atlantic City two years ago, I took a walk on the boardwalk. I don't have the need for that. When I'm working, the crap table's open, so to speak."

* * *

Fairly recently the moms and pops got a new source for their merchandise. There developed in New York, and in a few other large cities around the nation, a number of warehouses that call themselves cash-and-carry operations (although they may take checks and arrange deliveries for a fee). They have tapped into the important small-store business by promising the store quick service and the ability to fill small orders. This is because the bodega owner, or the mom, or the pop, drives to the warehouse and pulls the merchandise down off the shelves. The middleman, it seems, has managed to cut out some of the middlemen.

The new warehouses are living proof that the industry in New York is a dynamic one, constantly shifting its strategies and trying to find ways to capture more business. Some of the food business's working strategies seem clearly aimed at trying to eliminate competition and to establish monopolies—the breakfast cereal and beer industries are glaring examples—but in many others, such as the cash-and-carrys, they seem to really help the consumer. This sort of dynamism can be found, however, only in places where there is competition. Rivalry for the consumer's food dollar is especially intense in New York City, to the benefit of its citizens. In many other places, particularly suburbia but also some large metropolitan areas, the lack of competition manifests itself in inflated prices.

6

Selling It

No matter how or where it is grown, what processes it endures or avoids as it becomes what the business acknowledges as "food," no matter what system of delivery it is destined to enter, virtually all food is sold: sold and resold, always to someone who, the rules say, must "add value" to it before moving it along the line. (The question that is only rarely explored is, value for whom? Far too often, the beneficiary is the middleman, and his value is received at the expense not only of the consumer but of the quality of the food itself.) The food that leaves the manufacturing plant in canned, boxed, or frozen form has already been sold several times, and even the fresh produce that flows through the terminal markets and chain-store warehouses has been through several brief ownerships. Now come the stages of the final selling, the selling that puts the food into the shopper's hand and onto the consumer's table.

Like most of the other links of the chain, this final one is a lot less simple than it might appear. The selling of food is made up of a number of interrelated processes, several of them only vaguely familiar to the average consumer. What is happening to the food now is that it is being *merchandised.* Some prefer to use the term "marketing" to describe the process, but that is sometimes employed to describe the total system of moving the food from producer to consumer, and here we are concerned with the final steps.

The ultimate, overriding goal of those who merchandise food is to obtain what the business calls a consumer franchise —a strong claim on consumer loyalty for a particular product, along with an assurance that consumers will pay what is asked for it, within reasonable limits. Bisquick has a consumer franchise on the baking mix market. Arm & Hammer baking soda, reports *Advertising Age,* has "unaided recognition among 97 percent of U.S. female heads of households," and at any moment about 95 percent of all the households in the nation have one or more packages of the product in use.

Much, if not all, merchandising is based on the belief that regardless of how little the consumer may know about the food business, the business knows an awesome amount about the consumer. Trade publications are forever revealing the results of "studies" and "surveys" of consumer attitudes and actions, and while some of them are conducted along the most rigorously scientific lines, most are obviously of the seat-of-the-pants variety. Thomas Pierson, a professor of agricultural economics at Michigan State, commented in an interview, "We're in the dark ages on what a consumer wants in comparison with the kinds of technology that industries like RCA and Texas Instruments and the auto industry, for that matter, bring to their decision-making process."

The statistics continue to tumble out, nevertheless, and the food industry continues to give the impression that it knows everything there is to know about the consumer—the better to determine what the consumer wants, as the industry puts it; or the better to manipulate the consumer's want, as the industry's critics put it. Some samples illustrate the trouble and expense the industry is willing to incur in its search for consumer franchise:

■ An ad agency that specializes in affixing advertising to supermarket carts proclaims that the shopper "puts off 65 percent of her brand decisions until she is actually in the store." This admonition, which ran in *Advertising Age*, neatly proves the observation made by Carol Tucker Foreman, a former assistant agriculture secretary, that the people who run the food business "always define customer in the feminine gender. It's always 'The customer *she*.' And they always believe she's stupid. The insult to the intelligence is pretty severe."

■ The trend toward single-person households has caused a flurry of research into the habits of male shoppers as well, and although that half of the human race is probably a lot less knowledgeable about food, on average, than the females, men are rarely depicted as stupid. *Newsweek* did a survey in New York City in 1979 and found that in 30 percent of the families it surveyed, men regularly did the shopping alone. In 20 percent, men shopped with their wives. Two-thirds of the shoppers arrived in the store with shopping lists—bad news for the business, which loves that statistic about 65 percent of the brand decisions being made on impulse—and 10 percent of the lists were prepared, said *Newsweek*, solely by the husbands.

■ *Seafood America*, a trade publication, quotes "national surveys" as revealing that "75 percent of the fish eaten in this country is consumed outside the home in restaurants. People surveyed said that was because they didn't like to cook fish and they didn't like the odor." The sample apparently did not include the same women who read *Glamour*. That magazine reported to the advertising world: "With Americans consuming 10 percent more fish than they did 10 years ago, *Glamour* gives its readers quick-reading seafood recipes for good eating and good entertaining. To catch their interest, put your message where the big ones bite—That's Glamour." Women's magazines routinely conduct elaborate surveys of their present and potential readers to collect facts and suppositions to place before advertisers. Often such survey announcements are accompanied by the claim that the magazine can "deliver" half the population between the ages of eighteen and forty-four, or "deliver" the people in the nation's most affluent zip codes, or whatever—a clear indication of the feedlot attitude some of the industry has toward consumers.

■ Condé Nast Publications, which includes *Vogue,* *Glamour, Mademoiselle, Bride's,* and *Self* magazines, has run ads announcing, "She drinks 679,000 gallons of liquor!" She, it seems, is "The Condé Nast Package of Women," 13 million of whom are said to drink wine, another 13 million of whom pour down the hard sauce, and 12 million of whom chug beer—statistics which may help explain why the modern homemaker is also on the lookout for evening meals that aren't too difficult to prepare.

■ Children between the ages of two and seven, it is said, constitute 30.3 percent of the nation's television audience on Saturday mornings and 18.5 percent on Sunday mornings. This information is in the "so what?" category to a parent who has firsthand knowledge of the high-tension, animated violence that clogs the TV set on weekend mornings, but it is money in the bank to manufacturers who want to sell highly sugared breakfast cereals.

■ A *Progressive Grocer* survey of the supermarket products most used by consumers found toilet soap number one at 97.5 percent, wrapped bread close behind at 97.3 percent, and toilet paper next at 97 percent. Farther down the list, TV dinners drew 38.9 percent, and position number 183 was occupied by canned stews, at 13.2 percent.

An essential—perhaps *the* essential—part of the selling process is promotion, for nobody knows about the products that are available unless they are promoted in some way. Here, the term is defined very broadly, as it is in the industry: to include advertising within the industry itself, long before the food gets to the consumer; advertising both inside and outside the store; cents-off coupons; packaging; and other efforts to influence the public and its representatives through devices that don't directly involve traditional advertising techniques.

A lot of the work of promotion is done long before the food gets before the public. Some of the jobs of matching product with wholesaler and retailer are done by food brokers, whose national trade association defines its typical member as "an independent sales agent acting for and on the account of sellers of food, grocery, or related products," and who doesn't work for or on behalf of a wholesaler's or retailer's food buyer. The broker's pay comes from a commission, which averages around 5 percent of the manufacturer's selling price and is paid by the seller. Brokers never take title to the food but rather make the arrangements to get it, and in many cases its accompanying promotional campaigns and various follow-up activities, from the manufacturer or producer to the wholesale warehouse or supermarket chain. They are, then, the quintessential middlemen.

Henry M. Girodo is the president of the grocery products division of the Ferolie Corporation, a food brokerage with headquarters in Englewood Cliffs, New Jersey. The Ferolie firm's prowess as a middleman is certified by a lobby wall full of plaques and awards from food and allied manufacturers: Universal Foods Corporation has saluted the brokers, for example, for making its National Compressed Yeast "the only refrigerated retail yeast in the New York market," and Alberto Culver's Household/Grocery Division sent a large framed butcher knife for "carving out $1 million in business."

"What do we do for our commission?" said Girodo in an interview. "We represent the manufacturer, we sell the product, we assist in the marketing of the product and the preparation of the plans for the programs they want to put on. We represent the manufacturer at the store level. We visit the store every day of the week, and should there be a damaged product on sale there, we take it off sale. We do a lot of things for a fixed cost that the manufacturer enjoys, and the savings from this are passed along to the consumers."

One of the tasks brokers help with is relaying the details of manufacturers' sales promotions to the retailer and, thus, to the public.

The food business recognizes two major forms of promotional activity: "push" and "pull." The consumer is on intimate terms with the "pull" variety—it is the array of print and broadcast advertisements, trading stamps, cents-off coupons, contests, and other devices designed to get her or him into the store and to get the promoters' products into the shopping cart. Less is known publicly about "push." It is the promotion that goes on inside the industry—for before the manufacturer will be able to sell his product to the consumer, he first must sell the retailer on the idea. USDA economist Anthony E. Gallo has written that push promotion is aimed at getting shelf space. "This includes advertisements in the trade press, direct selling costs, in-store displays, and sales efforts through trade fairs and conventions. In addition, there are also related push promotion allowances to retailers including discounts, rebates, price packs, and reimbursements for local advertising." Two typical forms of push promotion frequently encountered by the consumer, although the shopper may not be aware of their origin, are the supermarket ad offering brand-name items on sale and the end-aisle display.

Gallo's colleague John Connor explained in an interview that manufacturers frequently offer temporary deals to retailers of from 5 to 20 percent off the usual prices. "Retailers

that have a lot of wholesale storage space, such as supermarket chains, can buy a lot during the two or four or six
weeks that the deal is on, and they can store it and sell it for
several months beyond the end of that discount period," he
said. "Now, if they sign up to buy at this special reduced rate,
they agree to give special attention to the product in their
own retail ads that appear in the newspapers. It's called a
'cooperative allowance.' "

The manufacturer may also insist that end-aisle or custom-
built displays be used. "Retailers accept all this because it
gives them a discount on a price-sensitive item and it allows
them to undercut some of the competition," said Connor.
"Any retailer can take advantage of the deal [the federal
Robinson-Patman Act requires manufacturers to give all retailers in a market access to the same offers and prices], but
only those with sufficient storage space can take advantage of
it for a long time, even beyond the end of the deal period.
And the advertising allowances are nice, too. In some studies
done in the sixties—I think they're still true—the retailers'
profit margins are equal to the allowances they get for advertising from manufacturers. In other words, for some retailers
at least, if they *didn't* have manufacturers' allowances, their
profits would be zero.

"The manufacturer gets something out of it," he continued.
"The retailer gets his allowance. And the consumer gets his
discount. So everyone thinks he's gaining from the system.
But the manufacturer who cannot get into the system is the
one who's at a loss, in my opinion, and so is the retailer who
can't take advantage of it because he doesn't have the storage
space. These are the people who, I think, are at a competitive
disadvantage."

Packaging may not commonly be thought of as part of selling, but it is. Packaging carries the manufacturer's message to

the shopper, and since something like 40 percent of all grocery purchases are made on impulse (the 65 percent cited earlier applies only to brand-name purchases), the message is of prime importance. "Out there on the front line your first weapon is the package," readers of the publication *Snack Food* are advised by Hercules Incorporated, which makes Balanced Oriented Polypropylene packaging film.

Packaging comes in all sorts and shapes, with most of it in paperboard cartons, followed by metal cans, flexible materials, and foil containers. The federal government has established very strict and quite helpful rules about what is printed on the labels to guide or tempt the consumer in his or her choice. There is much that falls through the cracks, however, and there is much about packaging that is excessive to the point of deception.

Nowhere is deceptive excess practiced with greater devotion than on the supermarket shelves that are reserved for breakfast cereal. A grocery store's most valuable commodity is its space. Of that, there is only so much, and manufacturers and their package designers know this. They know that a product that cannot get shelf space is by definition a product that cannot be sold. The obvious solution to this problem is for the manufacturers to make their package as large as possible, so that it takes up more shelf space, providing more room for attention-grabbing graphics and words like "NEW!" and, not coincidentally, leaving less shelf space for their competitors.

Anyone who has opened a box of cereal knows that it is never full of the product, and anyone who has read the small print as well as the big letters on the box knows that the manufacturer would have you believe that when the box was filled, it was *filled*, and that if it's not filled when you get it that's because "some settling of contents may have occurred during shipment and handling."

There must be a prodigious amount of settling going on,

then. A fairly scientific survey of the contents of a number of cereal packages, conducted by the author by comparing actual volume of the product with total volume of its package, showed that the amount of dead air inside was quite high. For Nabisco's Team, the box was only 63 percent full. Quaker Corn Bran was 69 percent full in the 16-ounce box and 77 percent full in the 12-ouncer, while Post's Grape-Nuts was 72 percent full. Kellogg's Nutri-Grain, one of the cereals recently formulated to appeal to consumers who are down on additives and too much sugar, hit 74 percent. It was interesting to note that a Kellogg product that comes very close (for a breakfast cereal, at least) to being a commodity, its Corn-flakes, was a whopping 82 percent full—a percentage that would seem attainable for other packagers as well.

All this "settling" of contents is not limited to the highly differentiated breakfast cereals. A box of Near East Precooked Couscous, a grain often found in "health food" stores, measured 68 percent full. The most spectacular example of dead air encountered was found also in a "health" emporium: Golden Harvest Low Sodium Sesame Crackers ("No salt, no sugar added. All natural ingredients") came in a box that was less than 59 percent full.

A lot of food packaging is an obvious and shameless attempt to imitate something else—usually the product with the greatest share of the market—and an unwary consumer can be influenced by this. A new dishwashing detergent appears on the market in a plastic bottle that closely mimics the coloring and labeling graphics of "the leading brand." Another form of imitation is less humorous. Many packages of hot dogs sold in supermarkets weigh in at 16 ounces, but a package of those sold by a regional chain under its own label weighed 12 ounces. The weight was properly stated on the package, as the law requires, but the package—the semi-transparent, tightly clinging plastic that often is used for hot dogs—was constructed so there was more than an inch of superfluous material along one of its sides. The result was that 12-ounce packages of the chain's product looked even larger than the 16-ounce packages of its competitors in the meat case.

Even items that are not usually packaged are promoted. Fruits and vegetables are very important to the supermarket and grocery store business, for they provide a store with its highest percentage of gross profit of any food category (however, because they are so perishable, they also are the most expensive for the store to handle). Every shopper has seen supermarket tomatoes, loaded with all the texture and flavor of well-used major league baseballs, described as "hard ripe, selected for slicing."

The United Fresh Fruit and Vegetable Association has a campaign called Fresh Approach which seeks to inform Americans of the delights of produce, and the trade group has published a handbook of phrases that may be used in advertising and promotion. "Crisp apples," it advises, "cleanse the mouth" and are "better for children than sticky sweets." Many vegetables are promoted as low in calories and rich in vitamins, which a lot of them are, but avocados, which run to about 568 calories a pound, both make "a fine buttery spread without the butter" and are "for the underweight who need to gain." When it comes to cabbage, "the greener it is, the more nutritious," and parsley is "remarkably nutritious." As for tomatoes, the association's Tomato Division has another publication, titled "Handling Tomatoes Profitably," that inadvertently helps to explain why the store-bought fruit is so awful. In a section dealing with "Quality Guides," the association states that consumers are concerned first with the appearance of tomatoes, then their firmness, their flavor, and their nutritive value. Tomato *sellers*, on the other hand, are said to be most concerned with appearance, firmness, and shelf life. Taste isn't even mentioned.

A great portion of the energy spent selling food is devoted to trying to cash in on trends and their shorter-lived cousins, fads, through differentiation of existing products. Partly because of Miller's success with Lite beer, a plethora of "Light" and "Lite" items may be found on the shelves. "People are switching to light fruit and deciding Del Monte Light tastes best," goes a television commercial, cleverly managing to ignore the fact that "light fruit" may be had, more cheaply, by peeling a banana or biting into a peach. There are on the shelves already light spaghetti sauce, pancake mix, and wine, with potato chips and cookies in the pipeline. Campbell's Soups joined the movement by taking some of its products that were fairly low in calories anyway—beef broth, onion soup—and relabeling them as "Light Ones."

Snobbishness and uneducated gourmandism have always been great ways to sell food, and today one of the money-making divisions of trendy department stores is the food section. Bloomingdale's, the New York–based store that appeals to people who are or want to think they are suave, sophisticated, and celebrity material, sells honey for $4.20, jam for $7.16, and dried fennel for $13.54 a pound each, and water for $1.73 a quart. It also sells mayonnaise that comes from France in toothpaste-style tubes and costs $8.23 a pound. Several of the status clothes designers, having learned that there are fortunes to be made from selling blue jeans with their names stitched on the rumps, are getting into designer foods as well. Pierre Cardin, who has rented his name to practically everything that people have been known to buy, recently announced he was getting into "luxury foods," while Bill Blass is designing candy.

When all else fails, it is possible to design a selling strategy based strictly on the customers' gullibility about price. "Why give them 98-cent half-gallons," asks an ice cream packager's advertisement in a trade publication, "when they gladly pay 55 cents for cones?" That was a couple of years ago, before ice cream fanciers started gladly paying $1 or more for their cones.

The selling device that is most familiar to the consumer is advertising—the conveying of information or impressions about specific products by way of printed or broadcast words and pictures. Economist Anthony Gallo calls advertising "any strategy to influence consumer choice among different brands or retail outlets." Advertising is the major way in which products are differentiated.

There is nothing inherently wrong or evil about advertising; it can be and very often is quite helpful. In a world that is increasingly cluttered with events, pseudo-events, information, pseudo-information, and *things*, advertising is a good way to inform people about what is available, what it's made of, what it costs, and where it can be obtained. The Federal Trade Commission staff, in a 1981 report on the issue of advertising aimed at children on television, notes, "Advertising informs consumers as to product availability, price, and performance characteristics. Thus it facilitates consumer purchasing decisions. Moreover, it may stimulate competition among sellers of a product, resulting in lower prices for the consumer." The problem is that advertising doesn't always perform these functions. A lot of it is deliberately uninformative to the point of concealing important information; much appeals only to emotions or fears. And, as the FTC staff went on to point out, "Of course the benefits of advertising, as enumerated above, accrue only to truthful advertising, and do not attach to advertising that is deceptive or misleading."

Many people have long had the assumption that advertising *is* truthful, at least until proven otherwise. Often this assumption is based on the belief that "they wouldn't let them say it if it weren't true." Sadly, this has become a dangerous assumption. A good deal of the advertising that a consumer encounters these days is patently honest, but much of it, whether of the written or spoken variety, has fallen into the category of a game between seller and potential buyer—a contest in which the seller tries to trick the buyer, and in which it becomes the buyer's job to figure out where the trickery lies: where the loaded word is, which phrase has the double meaning; in essence, what is wrong with this picture. An advertising message nowadays is about as tricky a document as a used-car warranty. Lawyers learned to play this game long ago; indeed, many of them make their livings on the imprecision and manipulability of words; but now the problem exists with the language of the marketplace. The identity and integrity of simple, descriptive words have been ravished.

There are several potential remedies for this problem. One would seem to lie in a self-policing effort started more than a decade ago by advertising agencies and their clients. The National Advertising Review Board, as it is called, is based in New York, and it listens to complaints about deceptive, false, or misleading national advertising. When a complaint seems to have merit, the NARB staff asks the advertiser for substantiation. If the reply is satisfactory, the complaint is dropped. If not, the staff tries to negotiate a settlement, which typically means a promise to drop the ad or change it in future presentations. If the advertiser refuses to cooperate, the private agency can turn the matter over to the appropriate federal agency. In the manner of most self-regulatory efforts, this one represents an attempt to ward off governmental regulation.

A relatively low portion of the complaints—only 9 percent in 1982—set before the NARB comes from the consuming public or from those who call themselves the public's advocates. Many come, instead, from other advertisers who see the ads in question as unfair competition for their own products. In 1982, competitors filed 39 percent of the complaints. A like percentage came as a result of the NARB's own monitoring program. In many cases, by the time a disputed advertisement reaches the decision level, its author has finished the campaign and moved on to other advertisements, leaving the deceptive damage done. Since the life of an ad campaign is limited anyway, the result of the self-policing may be to exert no control at all, or perhaps some deterrent influence.

The same may be said for other, more public attempts to regulate false advertising. The Federal Trade Commission in 1981 entered into a consent decree with Standard Brands (now known as Nabisco Brands), which sells such products as Planters peanuts and Chase & Sanborn coffee, after it had accused the food conglomerate of deception in marketing its Fleischmann's margarine. Standard Brands had claimed that doctors recommended the product and that "twice as many" doctors personally used it. The FTC said only about 15 percent of the doctors surveyed recommended Fleischmann's and that most of them named no specific brand. The consent decree settlement, according to a report from United Press International, amounted to little more than a promise by Standard Brands not to lie in the future.

As might be expected, much deception in food advertising concerns the bogus use of the words "fresh" and "freshness," which are words advertisers seem compelled to attach to everything no matter how frozen or ancient it is.

A competitor for the share of the orange juice market enjoyed by Beatrice Foods' Tropicana Products complained to the NARB that one of Tropicana's television commercials misled the public into thinking the juice was squeezed "fresh" into a container, without any sort of processing, such as pasteurization, freezing, concentration, or reconstitution. Tropicana's reply was surely one of the lamest of advertising history: The commercial, it said, was a "symbolic device" to get across the notion of the product's "fresh, fresh taste." While the NARB investigation was going on, the commercials

were changed. Beatrice Foods is a multinational conglomerate that makes, advertises, and sells more than nine thousand
products, many of them foods and fabricated foods ranging
from Clark candy bars to La Choy oriental-type vegetables.
One must wonder how many "symbolic devices" are routinely
employed to get the public to buy all these products.

Evian Waters of France attempted to sell its product,
water, by appealing to more than the usual hydro-snobbish-
ness: It claimed in a series of radio commercials that it had
"a unique mineral balance almost identical to your system's
natural chemistry . . . so Evian helps to improve your diges-
tion and your circulation. Evian helps your body work better
and that helps you look better." When the NARB requested
substantiation for these claims, reminiscent of those made in
the Old West by the hawkers of patent medicines, Evian replied with information on its water's mineral composition and
origin and what *Advertising Age* referred to as "more general
material on the healthful attributes of water."

Many advertising claims appear to be carefully designed
so that they would stand no chance whatever of being supported by serious research, nor could they be disproved—
because they are written on what amounts to puffs of smoke.
Nevertheless, they routinely claim to be unique at whatever it
is they are claiming. The Buitoni Foods Corporation started a
campaign for its boil-in-bag products in 1982 with the promise: "Now only one company gives you 150 years of Italian
know-how in just 15 minutes." And there is the nonclaim
made by "fresh, rich, creamy Peter Pan. One taste and you'll
know why. Nothing spreads a smile like it."

Many people in the industry describe the battle for turf
between "fresh" and "frozen" as a thing of the past. It isn't.
Manufacturers and their advertisers persist in trying to make
the consumer think that something that is frozen can also be
"fresh." The problem is particularly severe with seafood; the
industry apparently feels that consumers would be put off by

the idea of frozen fish, although for many parts of the country (including most of those along the coasts) freezing may be the best way to preserve fish between the time they are caught and the time they are cooked. But supermarkets continue to sell "fresh frozen" rainbow trout from Japan. And a package of Gorton's frozen fish sticks, made from minced and diced seafood, contains "our promise of freshness and high quality," even though the box also says "Keep Frozen" and "Cook While Frozen."

To Paul Earl, of the National Marine Fisheries Service, if an advertiser calls a fish product "fresh frozen, I guess they're saying that the fish was very fresh when it was frozen." The logical alternative, he said in an interview, would be " 'Not-so-fresh frozen' or 'Watch out,' or something. It's just a gimmick. It's not a commonly accepted term on the waterfront; it's either fresh or frozen and there's no in-between."

But the abuses of "fresh" continue. A package of Oh Boy! frozen potatoes stuffed with onion, sour cream, and chives is labeled "100% fresh potatoes," although it reposes in a supermarket freezer. And Buitoni stretches the idea out of all proportion with its advertising claim "We start fresh every morning. You get great taste tonight." A typical consumer, even one who himself starts fresh every morning, might have trouble understanding that Buitoni is speaking of its "twenty delicious frozen entrées."

"Fresh" problems of another sort were visited upon ITT Continental Baking Company, part of an international conglomerate that makes, among other things, Twinkies junk food and Wonder Bread. The Federal Trade Commission in 1979 obtained a consent order against ITT Continental over the way it was selling its Fresh Horizons bread—by claiming, among other things, that Fresh Horizons had five times as much fiber as whole wheat bread. What made this "false, deceptive, and misleading," said the FTC, was the fact that the fiber in Fresh Horizons was "derived from wood, an ingredient not commonly used, nor anticipated by consumers to be commonly used, in bread." Even for those consumers who might actually enjoy eating peanut butter-and-pine-tree sandwiches the FTC had bad news: ITT Continental's claim about the amount of fiber was untrue, as well.

Ten years ago, when the National Advertising Review Board was just getting started, William H. Ewen, its executive director at the time, was asked in an interview for his thoughts on the deceptive practices of the future. He greatly feared, he said, what was about to happen with and to the word "natural." His fears were well founded. The term has been so warped that it has become a dead tipoff that the object being described probably *isn't* natural at all; why else would its fabricators make such a fuss over its "naturalness"? The federal government, which has not hesitated to specify the maximum number of maggots that may infest the grains we eat, has declined to define either "natural" or the penalties for its misuse. The refusal clearly documented the Reagan administration's unwillingness to interfere with the food industry's deception and exploitation of the consumer.

Twisted variations on the theme of "natural" are not at all confined to fly-by-night manufacturers, but appear to be used by virtually everyone in the business. The Kraft Cheese people would seem to be as traditional and trustworthy as they come. For years the firm has tied its name to family-quality theatrical presentations on television, with a mellow-voiced presenter gently extolling the virtues of its products. But Kraft plays games with the language, just as everybody else does. A more recent television advertisement goes like this: "Kraft Singles, every single time. Made with Kraft cheddars and other fine natural cheeses, Kraft singles have over 25 percent more natural cheese than government standards require. . . . Kraft singles: taste the *natural* cheese inside."

It certainly does sound *natural*, although the antennae of an alert consumer might prick up over the mention of "25 percent more natural cheese" and wonder why one had to look "inside" to get the "natural" taste. An examination of Kraft Singles outside the fantasy land of the advertisement, on the quasi-neutral territory of the label and of government regulations, shows that the product cannot even legally be called just "cheese" (which explains why it is named "Kraft singles"). It is *pasteurized process cheese food*, which, according to the U.S. Code of Federal Regulations, means "the food prepared by commingling and mixing, with the aid of heat, one or more . . . optional cheese ingredients . . . with one or more . . . optional dairy ingredients . . . into a homogenous plastic mass." The cheese ingredients are real—that is, *really* natural—cheeses, such as cheddar or colby, and they must make up at least 51 percent of the total weight of the product. (Presumably, then, Kraft was saying that its product was at least 63.8 percent real cheese, or less than 36.2 percent something else. Indeed, a company spokesman confirmed that the product was "significantly more than 63.8 percent natural cheese.") The optional dairy ingredients are cream, milk, skim milk, buttermilk, cheese whey, and others. Other optional ingredients are allowed, including water, salt, "harmless artificial coloring," spices or flavorings, mold inhibitors, lecithin as an antisticking agent in packages of slices, an acidifying agent, and an emulsifying agent. That last can consist of one or a mixture of thirteen chemical phosphates, citrates, and tartrates. A real cheese, on the other hand, such as cheddar, is made from milk and a clotting enzyme such as rennet, and may contain artificial coloring and a mold inhibitor.

Similar problems with the language of the marketplace may be anticipated in any of the areas in which food manufacturers seek to supply consumers' perceived needs and desires. No- and low-salt foods are a recent example. A consumer who purchased a can of Redpack No Salt Added Tomato Puree—who obviously was interested in his salt intake—discovered that while the label contained nutritional information in some detail, it said nothing about sodium. Federal regulations currently in effect make declarations of food's sodium content voluntary, but they state that when an assertion is made, as it was on the Redpack label, the package must list the number of milligrams of sodium per 100 grams and per serving.

The consumer wrote California Canners and Growers, the distributors of the Redpack line, asking for the information. Two months later he got a form letter from someone in "consumer services" thanking him for his "recent letter regarding our nutritional information booklets" (his letter had said nothing of the sort) and enclosing some printed material that did not respond to his question. The consumer wrote again, restating his question, asking again for an answer, and politely suggesting a response that was a bit more prompt.

California Canners and Growers never answered his letter, and he still doesn't know how much sodium is in a can of Redpack No Salt Added Tomato Puree. The firm has since gone into bankruptcy. One of the arguments manufacturers make in opposing efforts at requiring more label information is that while most consumers don't really want more information, those who do can easily get it by corresponding with the company. In practice, this claim is almost universally hogwash, as the author confirmed on a number of occasions while preparing this book. Replies to consumer questions are at best all-purpose form letters that frequently fail to answer the queries and that apparently take inordinately long to write, despite the fact that most of them obviously are churned out by computers. The consumer's only defensive weapon against such arrogance, it would seem, is to not buy any more of the product.

Again, it should be pointed out that word-stretching and outright deception are not unique to those who manufacture and sell food. Consumers are lied to with alarming consistency by most portions of their society, from their organized religions to their various elected governments. In one notorious case a few years ago, the head of the New York City Department of Consumer Affairs (no longer there) was found to be larding broadcast spots on the department's good works with examples of enforcement efforts that did not exist. None of this excuses the deception that does go on in food selling, of course.

Food advertising that is published represents, among other things, printed promises that can be saved and judged and tested against reality by the consumer or interested regulatory agencies. But the sort of advertising that is broadcast, particularly by television, occupies quite a different category. Usually it offers little in the way of useful information, aiming instead at more subtle invasions of the watcher's emotions with promises of beauty, sexiness, and fulfillment. It is transitory, its claims are more imagery than facts, and it does little to help a consumer reach an informed decision. This is particularly dangerous with food advertising aimed at children, who, it has been shown, spend several years watching television before they learn that it cannot be trusted.

Enormous sums of money are involved in food advertising. The industry uses more national media advertising than any other American industry—in 1978, an estimated $2.5 billion was spent by manufacturers, retailers, and food service companies, and another $3 billion was spent advertising nonfood items commonly found in grocery stores. The shopper pays these bills; advertising takes about 4 cents out of every dollar consumers spend on food at home.

About 90 percent of the total food advertising revenues went to television, giving that medium 22 percent of its total take from ads. A great percentage of the products advertised are highly processed, packaged, and differentiated.

All this is profoundly disturbing, for big-time advertising is a device for increasing concentration and a means by which big and successful companies can erect barriers to entry in front of smaller potential competitors, with the potential goal of higher prices. Some of the more liberal agricultural economists think there should be a public discussion on the possibility that food advertising should be regulated.

That advertising creates barriers was borne out in a discussion with Henry Girodo, the food broker, although he sees the obstacle not as a threat but as a natural component of the American enterprise system. Girodo was asked what would happen if a small manufacturer approached his brokerage firm with an idea for a better mousetrap, or perhaps a better tortilla chip or canned stew.

"He would get a hearing with us," replied the executive, "and he would get a hearing with other brokers, but he'd have to pretty much convince the broker that first of all, he had the financial background to perpetuate that product. If you were a big supermarket chain, and Joe Zilch came in with his new product and a broker, the first question they'd ask would be, 'How are you going to get this message to the consumer? We can put it on our shelf, but it's going to be on a shelf next to ten thousand other items. How are you going to get the message before the public?'

"He may say, 'I don't have any money to do that.' If that's the case, he's got to do some thinking."

Another form of selling in the food business is much more subtle than national advertising but still quite effective. It might be called "editorial promotion"—the pushing of specific products or categories of foods in environments the lay person doesn't usually associate with advertising. It's likely that few Americans know that many, perhaps most, of the recipes and photographs that appear in newspaper "food sections," the inserts that are published on heavy supermarket advertising days, come from manufacturers and advertising agencies and are gratefully accepted by the editors. This helps explain why so many of the recipes call for "one 16-oz. can bean sprouts, drained" and "one 2-oz. can sliced mushrooms" rather than their fresh counterparts. The newspapers that do this (there are some proud exceptions) apparently have no ethical qualms about running promotional material submitted by parties who have financial interests (and who might be advertisers). The bean sprout and mushroom growers are not the ones furnishing the recipes and graphics.

The sellers of fruits and vegetables proudly report that some 64 million people hear their pitches for fresh produce monthly on radio and TV "public service announcements," which are not classified as paid advertising and usually promote nonprofit causes like the March of Dimes. And there are hustlers who specialize in getting food products—a bottle of your ketchup, a six-pack of your beer—into motion pictures and television shows.

Many of the women's and shelter magazines are enthusiastic participants in this free advertising. One of the more blatant examples was a 1977 announcement by *Seventeen* magazine that it was "launching a major new food program intended to meet the rising demand of teenage girls for solid, basic information on food, food preparation, and meal planning." The major new program, continued the announcement, consisted of a "new three-page editorial feature called 'Now You're Cooking' . . . as well as a major supporting merchandising effort."

The "merchandising effort" was to include "supermarket promotions" that incorporated recipes from the magazine's advertisers, "in-school demonstrations . . . in major market cities of supermarkets participating in *Seventeen*'s promotions," other attempts to rope faculty members in on the campaign, and cooking demonstrations "to be franchised to one department store per trading area."

*   *   *

Several of the forms of food selling involve the consumer directly, but none takes the shopper as straight to the supermarket door as do coupons. There were about 90 billion cents-off coupons of all sorts (for food and nonfood items) distributed by manufacturers and retailers in 1980, up by 80 billion since 1965. Coupons have become the nation's most rapidly growing form of food advertising. USDA economists Anthony Gallo, Larry Hamm, and James A. Zeller recently did a thorough study of what the industry calls "couponing," and they came up with these additional facts:

■ About 60 percent of the coupons redeemed in grocery stores were for food, and they had a total value of close to $900 million.

■ Only about one out of twenty coupons issued is redeemed. The average face value of coupons is 23.5 cents. Lower-income consumers use fewer coupons than other income groups.

■ About 3.3 cents of every $10 the consumer spends for food goes to cover the cost of coupons. People who don't use coupons subsidize those who do.

■ Coupons are primarily used for "storable, branded items instead of less processed, perishable products." The more concentrated a segment of the industry is, the more likely it is to engage in intense "coupon dropping," as the industry expression puts it.

Coupons are a rich source of income for thieves. One recent estimate was that "misredemption," the industry euphemism for cashing in coupons without buying the product, costs $200 million a year. Stores and store employees and others, not individual consumers, are usually the ones accused of misusing coupons. The *Chicago Tribune* conducted an investigation and found that coupons were counterfeited within hours of their appearance in the newspaper, and another investigation disclosed that when 25-cents-off coupons for a make-believe detergent named "Breen" were printed once in three newspapers in New York and New Jersey, more than two thousand stores in forty states tried to redeem them.

Whatever the means, method, or manner, food is sold to American consumers—about $350 billion worth of it a year at latest count, and the bill keeps growing. And despite the seemingly limited ways in which people can purchase and use that food, the marketplace and the thousands of products in it keep changing. At the center of it all for the past several decades, and likely to remain in the premier position as food-seller to the American people, is the grocery store, represented for most of us by the supermarket. For better or for worse, for richer or for poorer, it is the major connection most of us have with the food system.

7

The $252 Billion Grocery Store

We love it and we despise it. It consumes far too much of our busy lives, but we look forward to it with something approximating pleasure. We curse the ever-increasing amounts of money we spend there, but on the next week or the next day we go back and spend more. The place is part of our emotional makeup: We've been going there since we were kids, and when we become grownups we take our own children along on our visits. We start them when they're infants, wheeling them along in front of us in specially built carriages and imprinting on yet another generation of the species the physical and mental sensations of the place where food comes from. For very nearly all Americans and a lot of other people around the world, the grocery store is a very important part of life. It is, after all, one of the places where we get the things that make continued life possible, and much of the time comfortable, and sometimes even delightful.

The manifestation of the grocery store that is familiar to most Americans is the supermarket, which typically is a large one-room building where customers walk past shelved displays of food, picking out what they want among the 10,000 or so items on display and putting their choices in a cart or basket and then paying for them on the way out at one of several cashiers' stands.

The idea of a one-stop grocery store evolved in the late 1890s from the shops operated by the big tea merchants, but the stores remained tiny and sold their wares from behind the counter until 1916, when the Atlantic and Pacific Company introduced self-service as a cost-cutting idea. The modern name did not appear until 1933, when the Albers Supermarket opened in Cincinnati in a building specially constructed for it. Since then, supermarkets have grown with the nation, undergoing very rapid expansion during the suburban boom that followed World War II.

The statistics easily bear out the importance of this segment of the food chain. The important trade publication *Progressive Grocer*, in its April, 1983, fiftieth annual report on the grocery industry, reported that grocery stores were responsible for $252 billion in sales in 1982. Some 72 percent of those sales were rung up in supermarkets (which the magazine defines as stores with gross annual sales of $2 million or more), while almost half came from chain stores.

Progressive Grocer said there were 162,000 groceries in the nation, of which 28,950 were supermarkets. The average size of a chain store was 25,964 square feet; of an independently operated store, 17,715 square feet. Groceries stock around 10,000 items each, and the food retailing business provides direct employment for around 2.5 million people.

Food retailers are no more immune to the temptations of differentiation than any other part of the business. But with them, diversity is more likely to be an economic necessity than a calculated way to make the same old thing look like ten NEW! things. With the nation's population growth and mobility settling down a bit, and with the costs of energy remaining so high—and on top of that with the punishing effects of the national and worldwide recession of the early eighties—food retailers have been forced to retrench and seek newer and better ways to make a buck—or, in a business where volume is king, to make a penny one hundred times.

Out of the economic and sociodemographic change of the last decade or so, then, have come several new forms of food retailing. One scholar is said to have found ninety-seven varieties of food store on the American scene. Of these, the conventional supermarket still is the food seller to be reckoned with; but the others, which are essentially outgrowths of or variations on the supermarket, are becoming increasingly important. These are some of the identifying characteristics of the major forms of retail stores:

The conventional *supermarket* sells mostly foods but some nonfood items. Around 10,000 self-service items may be stocked. The store is 15,000 to 30,000 square feet in size.

The *super store* covers perhaps 30,000 square feet, has 15,000 items, has specialized departments (such as delicatessen and meats), and offers more general merchandise than do supermarkets.

A *combination store* is even larger—50,000 square feet—and carries 25,000 items. Its chief characteristic is that while it remains a food store, it contains another store as well, usually a pharmacy.

The *hypermarket* (an Americanization of the French *hypermarche*, which is a Europeanization of the American *supermarket*) is very large, at about 100,000 square feet, and has around 40,000 items. Many of those items are not food at all; they can include lawn mowers, furniture, tools, and housewares.

On slightly different tracks, but still close relatives of the great American supermarket, are two other forms of retail store which are quite familiar to millions of Americans: the *convenience store* and the *warehouse store*.

C-stores, as the industry calls them, are thought of as recent additions to the food-selling environment, but actually they've been around for quite some time. By one account, they were begun in 1927 by the Southland Ice Company, forerunner of the Southland Corporation, which operates the 7-Eleven chain. Convenience stores are small—about 2,400 square feet—and although they carry a relatively complete line of grocery staples, the number of brands and package sizes is limited. Many sell gasoline. Much of what they sell is sold in smaller quantities than supermarkets—a pack of cigarettes instead of a carton, a can of beer rather than a six-pack—and they are further distinguishable from supermarkets by the fact that their prices are much higher, in some cases outrageously so. The fact that their customers are willing to pay them is an indication of the premium that many people place on convenience.

The warehouse store, as its name implies, is a large, barn-like facility, very plain in appearance (sometimes by careful design), often selling its goods from bare metal shelving or straight from the shipping cartons to eliminate as much labor and as many frills as possible and to pass at least some of the savings along to the shopper. These stores, which started appearing in the late seventies, may run around 25,000 square feet, and their offerings are confined to 5,000 or fewer products and a limited selection of brands, sizes, and flavors.

A close relative of the warehouse store, and often lumped with it in descriptions of the retail market, is the *limited assortment store*, also known as a "box store." It can be much smaller than most supermarkets, with only 400 to 1,000 separate items, and may have no perishables at all. In return for what often are the lowest retail food prices in town, the store cuts back on some of the things the shopper may have come to expect: evening hours, check-cashing, variety in brands and sizes.

Regardless of its size, shape, and selection, the American supermarket traditionally has settled on an image to lay before the public—a device called by the business its "unique selling proposition." Two researchers from Purdue University, in a paper written several years ago on the subject of consumer loyalty to food stores, explained what that proposition is based upon: A food store, said R. L. Kohls and John Britney, "does not simply sell food but rather merchandises a complex attitude mix made up of various components which have had different values to different people." The three most important such components, they said, had to do with the consumer's feelings about the food products being sold, about convenience, and about the behavior and integrity of the store itself.

The elements have not changed through the years, and it is still possible to identify, from a store's advertising or its ambiance, whether it wishes its customers and potential customers to think of it as primarily a place where money can be saved, where convenience and service are supreme, or where quality is the highest consideration.

Many stores want people to think they offer everything—Kroger's, in Buena Vista, Virginia, says it offers "the best of everything including the price," and Safeway in suburban Washington claims "fresh, quality produce at super low prices"—although this is not possible, given the economic climate of the food business. Almost always the store assigns one of its claims a priority much higher than the others, and it is often possible to discern from its advertisements the specific image the retailer wants to project.

As with most everything else in the food business, a consumer who spends a few moments studying the situation and seeking the real meanings behind the claims can gather information that might be valuable. The shopper who is unimpressed with high-tech graphics, a full-scale delicatessen operation in the store, and cheerful employees who help load the family station wagon with the week's haul, for instance, might save money by patronizing a store that stresses economy in its ads and keeps the frills to a minimum.

If consumers are often lax about evaluating a store's unique selling proposition, they are even sloppier about perceiving the physical geography of the store itself—while nevertheless responding to it and being deftly guided by it in choices and purchases. The interior of a modern supermarket is a cornucopia not only of food, but also of devices and tricks of the trade—gimmicks and rules of thumb that have been learned by retailers through generations of trial and error and not a little scientific and quasi-scientific research, much of which has been financed by the consumers themselves. The tricks of the trade wouldn't work nearly as well as they do if it were not for the fact that such a high percentage of supermarket purchases is the result of impulsive decisions and the fact that most shoppers don't make lists of what they want before they enter the food marketplace. They—we—are even better than sitting ducks: We are ducks who move slowly down the aisles, pushing very large baskets on wheels, and filling those containers with things we didn't really know we wanted.

The inside of the supermarket may seem comfortable, clean, and well lighted, or it may be frenetic and dirty, but the chances are overwhelming that it was laid out according to a specific plan to promote the highest possible level of spending. The shopper who is aware of the care that goes into this planned store geography is likely to be a shopper who has control over his food expenditures. If this sounds like another way of saying "forewarned is forearmed," that's because it is. Some people, to be sure, don't *want* to be too prepared when they visit the supermarket or any other retail store. But everybody should be aware that the store is quite forewarned on the subject of its customers and the habits and desires that influence their spending of money.

"Understand that the goal of any business is profit," said Howard Tisch, the executive secretary of the Greater New York Metropolitan Food Council, in an interview. "Any business that doesn't make a profit goes out of business under the capitalist system." (Well, not *all* businesses. There is selective socialism and involuntary taxpayer support, courtesy of government subsidies, loans, and tariff regulations, for a growing cadre of firms, including the manufacturers of Chrysler automobiles, Harley-Davidson motorcycles, sugar, munitions and armaments, tobacco, luxury hotels built on urban development land, and corporations that fail to clean up their toxic waste dumps.)

"The supermarket people are not saints," continued Tisch, "and they're not on a mission. They are here to run a business and to make money."

Store design is part of that money-making process, he explained. "Stores are laid out, generally, quite scientifically to encourage sales. That's the name of the game: sales. So you find that staple items tend to be on the bottom shelf. Impulse items tend to be at eye level. Why? Obviously it's because if you're going to buy flour, you're going to go *looking* to buy flour, and you will find it wherever it is. You know it's in there somewhere, and you say, 'I'm going to buy some flour.'

"But if you want something that's not a staple, that's different." Tisch's visitor fancifully suggested a product with cinnamon 'n' apples with peanut butter chunks, and Tisch made a face and said, "Right. That kind of thing. You're never going to look for that, because you don't even know it's there unless we show it to you. So we're going to put it someplace special —in an end-aisle space, on an eye-level shelf, someplace like that.

"We want you to traverse the store, and we want you to see

our wares. So we're going to lay out our store in such a way as to attract you, in the course of your travels through our various sections, to see what we want you to see.

"One of the reasons the refrigeration unit, with the milk and cheese, tends to be on the outer perimeter of the store is because obviously that's where the electricity is. And I'm going to need my meat counter against the back room because I don't want to carry my meat all the way across the store from the cutters to its case. But it also performs another function, and that is that if I've got my dairy case against the rear wall, and I know that generally people who go to supermarkets are going to buy milk, cream, eggs, and butter, then I know that they're going to go through my store in order to get those things. And by going through my store they're going to see the products that I have available for them, that I want to show them. The things where I want to say, 'Hey, try this product.'"

Most, quite likely all, of the geography of the store is designed in conjunction with the principles Tisch outlined, or, as the text *Food Merchandising* puts it, the rule that "the rate of exposure is directly related to the rate of sales of merchandise." To that end, research has been done on shoppers' habits and traffic patterns in stores, and much of it has been done not by the industry itself but at taxpayer expense by an agency that is supposed to work for everyone, the United States Department of Agriculture.

The studies have produced elaborate schematic pictures of what goes on inside a store, as well as some conclusions that have become accepted by much of the supermarket business, among them the belief that the greatest percentage of the customers entering a store will circulate around its periphery. Therefore, a store is likely to have its most profitable items along the edges. These include meat and produce.

Another rule is that a store should display items that are likely to be bought on impulse in places where most shoppers will see them while on their way to get items they have planned to purchase. Fruits and vegetables fall into the impulse category. So do frozen foods. Both departments are often encountered "on the way" to the meat or dairy sections. Stores also like to figure out which aisle (usually one along a wall) is the "first" one for most shoppers, and to place goods there that will amplify the image the store wants to project. For stores that want the customer to think more about "quality" and less about price, the produce department might be in the number-one position.

Everybody agrees on the importance of end-aisle displays. As mentioned before, it is a prime spot for selling merchandise. "That space," said Larry Hamm, "is so effective in selling products that the companies that gain access to it have a comparative advantage over their competitors."

The reasons for this are well known inside the industry. Many shoppers believe, perhaps unconsciously, that merchandise stacked up at the end of a supermarket aisle is always on sale at reduced prices. Frequently it is. In fact, a store that wants to project an image of lower prices often uses end-aisles extensively as reminders to the public. But the industry also has found the spaces to be excellent locations for products it wants people to *think* are on sale. This can mean overstocked and slow-moving products, things that move well on impulse, and advertised specials; it can include seasonal items, such as stuffed Easter rabbits, holiday nut assortments, or midsummer iced tea mixes, that don't have much or any regular shelf space assigned to them. Whatever the consumer's beliefs about the products that occupy the ends of the aisles, it is the storekeeper's experience that they are great money-making territory.

Often, sale and advertised products wind up in the middle of an aisle, not at the end. This is not some mistake on the part of the shopkeeper, but rather a tipoff to the alert consumer that the grocer wants to draw her or him past other (and invariably higher-profit) products on the way to anticipated savings.

Grocers give special attention to the last part of the store the customer visits—the "front end," known to the shopper as the checkout line. This is the place where the financial reckoning comes, where the customer slows to a stop and, in those moments before the cashier adds up the cost, adds up in his mind the things he has bought. No better time exists for a few other, seemingly inexpensive impulse purchases.

"The checkout," proclaimed a trade publication a few years ago, "is the hottest piece of real estate in the supermarket today." "Hottest," in this case, means not only the vast numbers of flashlight batteries, packages of chewing gum, photographic film, razor blades, magazines, and tabloid publications of the "Killer Bees Cure Cancer" variety that get bought, but also the profit margin that goes with them. In a supermarket as a whole, as will be discussed shortly, there is a gross margin of profit of around 22 percent—that is, on average for every $1 the store pays for merchandise it collects $1.22. At the front end, margins run around 30 or 35 percent, and in some cases they average 45 percent.

Over the years the supermarket business has produced a rich vocabulary of terms that deal with the tools it uses to sell goods and with their placement within the store's geography. One of the most important terms is the "facing." A facing is a column of identical products on a shelf—twelve boxes of Tide, stretching from the front edge of the shelf to the rear; eight bottles of pancake syrup. Three facings of a product means three columns, and appears to the shopper as three identical packages, side by side.

Since the sales of products are widely held to be directly

related to their degree of exposure to shoppers, manufacturers and brokers and salesmen want to get as many facings for their products as possible. But space in even a huge supermarket is limited. So grocers develop highly detailed plans for the allocation of their precious shelf space. These are sometimes called "plan-o-grams," and no admiral maps out a battle strategy more carefully than a food retailer with a plan-o-gram. A plan is a schematic map of the shelves, labeling the products, their brands, the sizes (16-ounce, 48-ounce, and so on), and the number of facings each product, brand, and size receives. Not only is the number of facings of crucial importance to the sale of an item, the product's vertical position among the shelves carries great significance as well. Shelves at the typical shopper's eye level are cherished as prime movers of merchandise. One expert in these matters has been quoted as having discovered in shoppers a "purchase visibility curve" that promises to squeeze even more sales out of products that are somehow tilted at slight angles toward the customer's eye.

Once set, a shelf plan is likely to stay in effect for six months or a year, when the store again will make a detailed assessment of what moves and what doesn't. A shopper who wants to be aware of the physical and emotional environments of the supermarket, of the traps that have been set along those brightly colored aisles, should never assume that products are just put on the shelves wherever they fit. They are where they are for a single purpose, and that purpose is to get sold.

Facing is important, said Jennifer Ohl, an employee of a Spartan supermarket in Lansing, Michigan, "because you have only so many linear feet for a particular category of food." Ohl, who is one of the relatively few women in higher positions in the retail food business, is responsible for coordination of pricing at the store. She walked through her store with a visitor and Larry Hamm not long ago, explaining displays and terminology along the way.

The store contained the usual number of special displays—piles of merchandise with banners over them, or particularly large or noticeable signs giving price information. Displays are often used in supermarkets to control customer behavior. A store that wants to project the image of a high-volume mover of merchandise, for example, can stack large quantities of baked beans up in a display and give the impression (true or not) that it made a special high-quantity purchase and is passing its savings along to the consumer. Attention-getting displays also can be used to lure customers into what grocers call the store's "dead areas," or, if they are placed strategically in an aisle, they can slow or stop traffic in front of high-profit or slow-moving items.

Displays come in many shapes and forms. Standard "gondolas" are the two-sided shelving modules seen in most modern supermarkets. The "coffin case" is a thigh-high, open-topped cold box that displays frozen products. A "cut-case display," usually used in end-aisle situations, sells the product directly from the case, without shelving. An "island display" is one that is open on all four sides. It, too, can be used to slow traffic, and of course it offers shoppers an opportunity to buy its offerings from four points of the compass, not just two as with ordinary gondola shelving. A "dump bin" is a bin or basket that fits into a store's shelving layout so employees can simply dump the merchandise in, rather than neatly stack it. Items such as baby food and bars of soap lend themselves to dumping. A "sore-thumb display" stands out like one.

Jennifer Ohl pointed to a colorful piece of paper, about the size of an index card, that projected from the edge of a shelf. "We call this a 'shelf talker,'" she said. Some shelf talkers are installed by representatives of the manufacturers, some are added by the store itself. Although it is widely known in the business that too many shelf talkers are self-defeating, a lot of stores decorate their shelves like Christmas trees. As with most displays inside a food store, there is no guarantee that a shelf talker, or its cousin the "shelf strip," which is a message fixed along the molding where the price tag is displayed, are actually advertising anything special. They may just be attention-getting devices, and the product they are pushing may not be on sale at all.

The term "cross-merchandising," said Ohl, refers to the practice of displaying together items that go together: wine with cheese (or, more likely, with expensive cheese, since many consumers like to think of wine as something for a "special" occasion) and crackers (again, the premium crackers, not the saltines); mint jelly with the lamb. In recent years cross-merchandising has invaded the air space over the meat department. Some clever merchandiser realized that was an ideal place to sell foil packages of marinades and products that make meat more tender. It is likely that there is no square inch of the modern American supermarket that has not been considered, and quite likely tried, for its possible utility as a place to sell more merchandise.

The one part of the supermarket where merchandise is not sold is the "back room." To the uninitiated, the storage room at a supermarket must be a cavernous place, full of cartons of food waiting to be stacked on the shelves. In reality, a successful supermarket needs a back room of minimal size; the one at the Spartan store in Lansing could almost be described as tiny, and most of it was given over to storage of empty bottles and cans waiting to be picked up in compliance with Michigan's container deposit law. On one side of the back room there was a large walk-in freezer and on the other there was a cold room for dairy products. Larry Hamm said, "Keeping this room empty is a secret of success."

"That's right," said Jennifer Ohl. "We try to keep it all out there on the floor." Food sitting in the back room rather than on the selling floor is money tied up in inventory. And a supermarket cannot survive for long with its money tied up anywhere.

*   *   *

One expression frequently heard among supermarket people is "better a fast nickel than a slow dime." It explains a lot of the business's economics. The Food Marketing Institute, the Washington-based trade representative of the America's retail grocers (and one of the more responsibly run lobbying groups in the food business), points out in several documents for its members and the public that, in the words of one of them, "low markup for the sake of high volume is the fundamental principle of mass merchandising operations, developed by the grocery business in the mid-1930s." By "low markup" the industry means its traditional gross margin—the difference between the amount the retailer pays for an item and the amount it charges the consumer—of about 22 percent. From that 22 percent markup the store must pay for labor, interest, rent, energy, advertising, and other operating expenses. When expenses are deducted, the store is left with a net profit of less than one cent on the dollar.

That does not mean the typical supermarket makes less than 1 percent profit, although the industry frequently tries to make it sound that way. It means that's the net profit on each item it sells, each time it sells it. If the store sells the same sort of item over and over, it makes more profit. And that's where volume comes in and why "turn" is so important. The faster the turnover, the more quickly merchandise moves through the back room and the less money has to be spent on financing that inventory. *Progressive Grocer* has counted as many as 27.9 annual turns in a sample of independent supermarkets grossing between $10 and $12 million a year; the average for all supermarkets is around twenty turns. Although retailers are not as poverty-stricken as some might have us believe, their profits are still below those enjoyed by many other segments of business.

How, the question might arise, is the industry able to make its gross margin hover around 22 percent? The answer lies in a phenomenon called "variable pricing," sometimes also known as "mixed-margin pricing." Essentially it is a system whereby different products are priced in different ways so that the overall average stays about the same. Economist Gerald Grinnell has explained the system this way in an article in the *National Food Review*:

Consumers are thought to be price-sensitive on about 300–500 items. These items may differ from market to market, but generally include most of the products that consumers buy most frequently, especially those at higher prices—and, therefore, account for a significant share of a store's total sales. Since price specials are as important as low prices, variable-price merchandising is noted for lowering prices of some products (and advertising these price changes) while quietly raising the prices of other products.

A firm that is especially successful at using variable-price merchandising may appear to consumers to have low prices when actually its overall price level is relatively high. The only accurate way to determine which store has high or low prices is to select a large enough list of products to measure overall price levels (this larger list of products may not be relevant to any one consumer). Since this is beyond the practical capabilities of most consumers, variable-price merchandising results in considerable confusion.

An example of variable pricing in action was offered not long ago by the president of a Santa Monica marketing firm who was advising retailers on ways to lure black customers into their stores. Lower prices on products that figure in blacks' menus, he said: "You can up allied items by a few cents to compensate. For instance, sell ribs cheap, but charge a little more for onions, barbecue sauce, et cetera."

Products which traditionally have the lowest gross margins are dry groceries generally, canned juices, coffee, baby foods, soaps and detergents, and oils. Those with the highest mark-ups usually include nonfood items such as housewares and health and beauty aids (even though they may be priced lower in the supermarket than in other stores, which reap even higher margins for them), produce, frozen foods, cookies and crackers, soft drinks and drink mixes, relishes, pickles, and olives, and candy and gum. Prices are variable within food categories, too: One survey found that the margin on canned sliced cling peaches was lower than the average for canned fruits, while that for canned sliced freestones was considerably higher.

With shelf space so valuable it is calculated in dollars per square inch, with end-aisle displays so important that they are matters of contractual obligation, and with profits measured in pennies and nickels, it is no surprise that powerful economic tensions exist among the leading actors of the marketplace, particularly between the retailer and the manufacturer.

There is a constant struggle going on in the food business for control in the selling of food. The manufacturers and the sellers agree on one major aim—they both want rapid turnover—but beyond that there are many differences. Some are as simple as package design. A manufacturer might feel its campaign for market share is aided by putting its product in unusual-sized boxes, while the distributor and retailer who have to deal with those packages might consider the product a big pain in the neck.

The competing ambitions exist in a rather precarious balance, one that each side is continuously trying to change. Retailers own the shelves on which the food is displayed, so they are the gatekeepers of the entire system. But manufacturers control the availability of the product to the retailer, as well as the availability of information about the product to the consumer—the advertising and promotion of it, the description of the product that the consumer is led to believe she will get if she buys it.

The rules of the game used to be simple, back when manufacturers were putting out mild variations on the same basic commodities. But then came differentiation. Manufacturers moved away from commodities as quickly as they could, creating separate identities for their cornflakes by adding sugar and cinnamon and dried apples to it. Competition was waged not with prices but with differentiation, packaging, coupon drops, and promotional deals to retailers. And, especially, with national advertising.

The result is that manufacturers now have not only a lot of control over their prices, but also over how, when, and where their products are sold at retail and in what quantities. Manufacturers now know they can produce great consumer demand for their products—"new" products, an old product in a new package, an old standby whose position seems to be slipping—by putting a few million 15-cents-off coupons in the mail or by running a few million dollars' worth of advertisements on prime-time television. And they know that retailers *must* have the product in stock, for the entire industry dreads the specter of consumer frustration if popular items are out of stock, even if temporarily and for whatever reason.

The manufacturers don't hold all the cards, however. The retailers have private labels and generics.

Private-label groceries have been around a long time. Also known in some cases as store brands or house brands, they are packaged foods (often canned, but also frozen and dry-packaged) that bear either a label that does not have a "national" ring to it (because it is not nationally advertised) or that is owned by the supermarket chain itself. Ann Page and Sultana are house brand names that have been used by the A&P chain, and the chain's Eight O'Clock Coffee goes back to the days when A&P really *was* the Great Atlantic & Pacific Tea Company. In some cases, including A&P, a chain has two or more house brands in a product category, representing different qualities and price levels.

The house brands (or the private label, in the case of a retailer that does not have its own label) are usually displayed in the store next to the nationally advertised brand or brands of the same product. Not haphazardly next to the brand names, though; often retailers will place their private labels to the right of the branded facings, so that most shoppers, if they are right-handed, would have to go to the trouble of reaching past the store's own product in order to get the advertised brand.

Private labels and store brands in a supermarket mean that store is less at the mercy of the national brands and their advertising and promotional campaigns. They also are profitable for the retailer. Private labels, in fact, have a higher profit margin than national brands, even though they sell for considerably less. According to one study, the margin for national brands runs around 20 to 25 percent, while it is 17 to 20 percent for private labels. The lower selling price is accounted for by the lack of expenses for advertising, research and development, and test marketing, and by the fact that such products are moved through the system in large quantities. The quality of a first-line private-label product is usually comparable with that of the nationally advertised brand, but it is lower in the second- and third-line private labels. Quality means different things to different people, however, and canned peas that are random sizes and cosmetically unattractive might be perfectly acceptable in a stew or a chicken pie.

Larry Hamm, who studied private labels extensively in connection with his dissertation at Michigan State, found that a firm that wants to produce a private-label product will approach a packer with a list of specifications that are based on an almost microscopic analysis of the product—often but not always a nationally advertised label—that is the leading seller in the firm's own marketing area. Hamm wrote:

Private label laboratories . . . will, for example, tear down a frozen meat pie; count the number of individual peas and corn kernels; determine the type of meat; weigh the amount and number of pieces; weigh the sauce and determine its viscosity; break down the components of the crust, etc. They will test packaging, cooking instructions, and shelf life. Through analysis, they attempt to know a product as well as its manufacturer does. Specifications will be written to try to duplicate the original exactly while generating the cost differential private label products need.

The quality control department might alter the private label product's specs in an attempt to lower the cost. They may, for example, authorize thinner aluminum dishes or reduce the amount of meat in each pie. They attempt to make these adjustments without noticeably altering the basic character of the product. The goal is to develop a product which is less expensive than the brand, but to do so in ways which will not cause the comparative shopper to forgo the distributor's brand alternative. If they fail to retain the basic character of the product, consumers will perceive the choice as a lower-quality product for a lower price.

In an interview, Hamm said that he had run across a ketchup "racing" machine in his investigations of private-label specifications. "Heinz has been selling their ketchup for years as the slowest ketchup in the West, and using terms like 'Anticipation' and all that, and I came across a private-label organization that had this little incline set up with little metric rulers on one side and a little gate at the top, and they put the ketchup bottles from the different private-label suppliers on this incline and lifted the gate. The ketchup would run down, and they would time it, and it had to be within so many seconds of Heinz's time. They told me all you had to do was add cornstarch to slow it up."

Some product categories, such as canned soups, baby foods, and disposable diapers, are so tightly controlled by a leading brand that most private-label invasions have been repulsed. And it is not true that all private labels and house brands are just national brands in different labels, although that is often the case. At the end of the assembly line in the Chef Pierre pie factory in Traverse City, Michigan, there are thick rolls of stick-on labels, some with the firm's own name on them, several others with the names of other organizations. The pies that receive those labels are identical. Land O Lakes, the dairy cooperative, runs ads in *Private Label* magazine saying, "With Land O Lakes on the inside of a package, you'll be proud to put your name on the outside." But many fruits and vegetables are canned by packers who deal in private labels alone.

More recently there has been another form of private label in the marketplace, and one that promises even more leverage for retailers in their constant tug of war with manufacturers: the generic, or "no-name," or "no frills," product.

Generics have been around since the invention of agriculture—an ear of corn is "generic" and a home grown tomato may boast of "no frills" but be infinitely more tasty than the branded version—but it was not until 1976 that a French firm started selling plain-wrapped packaged foods as generics. The midwestern chain Jewel introduced generics in the Chicago area in the following year, and since then the category has grown enormously.

There are arguments in the trade over just how lasting or how much of a fad generics are. The disputes have a lot to do with whose box is being gored. Clippings and documents in the "Generics" file at the library of the Advertising Research Foundation in New York City are remarkably consistent in their predictions that these strangely unadvertised products are mere flashes in the frying pan, while the file of the same name at the Food Marketing Institute in Washington brims with optimism about the future of generics. What is fairly clear is that stores sell generics at a lower gross margin—10 to

20 percent, according to some studies—and for lower prices—
15 to 44 percent below the prices of both private labels and
national brands.

It appears that generics, which frequently, are of much
lower quality than national or top house brands, are on their
way to replacing the second- and third-line private labels, and
that retailers are willing to make relatively little money on
them because they view the no-name items as devices to get
more people into the store. And when more people shop, they
spend more money.

Generics are also getting to be less generic than they used
to be. Several supermarket chains, driven by the food business's insatiable lust for differentiation, have already designed
their generics' labels so that they are less than the plain, black-
and-white statements they were at first. A&P has added two
shades of green to its generic labels, along with its logo, and
Grand Union prints "BASICS" in white on a red background
on the labels of its generic line. Soon, no doubt, the word
"NEW!" will start to creep onto the packaging. Or perhaps
the slogan "NOW!! WITH FIVE TIMES AS MANY FRILLS
AS THE LEADING GENERIC!!!"

Concentration of power is growing in food retailing, just as
it is in production and manufacturing, and the same economists and other observers of public policy who are concerned about concentration in breakfast cereals and
meatpacking are worried about cities with too few supermarket chains. High concentration leads to higher prices
throughout the industry, but it is felt intimately by the consumer at the retail level.

There is a significant relationship, researchers have found,
between the net profits of the large food chains, and the market concentration and the chains' share of the market. And the
number of highly concentrated markets is increasing. Econ-

omist Bruce Marion has estimated that in 1974 consumers paid about $660 million extra for food in metropolitan areas "because of noncompetitive retail markets."

Some of those markets are rather notorious. The one most frequently cited by economists (perhaps because many of them put in time at the Department of Agriculture head-quarters there) is Washington, D.C., and environs, which is dominated by two chains. Denver is usually named as an-other. Cedar Rapids is high, and so is Atlanta.

Metropolitan areas usually cited as having relatively low concentration intensities include Los Angeles, Detroit, Fresno, Columbus, Ohio, Oklahoma City, Topeka, and New York City, where there are many independents and small local chains to challenge the national groups.

A likely reason for increased concentration is heightened merger activity, particularly mergers involving large and con-glomerate organizations. Until 1975, the government had sev-eral policies in effect that tended to restrain or slow down such mergers, but they have since expired or been allowed to lapse. Russell A. Parker, who has studied retail grocery con-centration for the Federal Trade Commission, has noted that recent mergers by large food retailing firms increased despite economic conditions that usually work against such activity; with an improvement in the nation's economic environment, he said, even more mergers and concentration could be ex-pected.

Some of the conglomerate behavior, according to Bruce Marion, raises questions of possible antitrust activity. But the existing federal antitrust regulations, he writes, have had rela-tively little effect "on those issues that are of greatest concern for the future competitive viability" of the food retailing in-dustries.

A consumer might well be appalled to learn that the gov-ernment in Washington, with all its vast resources and obliga-tions for gathering information, passing and enforcing laws, writing regulations, and generally protecting its citizens, is doing little about the economic inequities of the food market-place. But antitrust activity is only one of many areas in which the federal government has eagerly served the mer-chants of the food system at the expense of the consumers.

8

The Other Additives

As we have seen, a lot happens to food on its way along the chain from earth or sea or orchard to the ultimate human consumer. A great portion of what happens to food is not seen at all, or at least not by the casual observer whose credentials in the food business are those of the consumer. Few lay persons have seen the inside of a supermarket back room, fewer still a giant distribution warehouse. Elementary schools routinely send their children on field trips to museums and zoos and seats of government, but only rarely do children get to see a place like the Hunt's Point Market in New York or the Eastern Terminal Market in Boston. And yet things happen continuously at these places, and at all the other points along the chain, that have immense bearing on the quality, quantity, and cost of the food we eat.

Some of those unseen events cause a great deal of apprehension among a lot of people who consider themselves advocates of nutrition, food safety, and consumer protection. They have (quite properly) raised a lot of fuss in recent years about the chemical additives that the industry, as it moves further from the basic, simple commodity, puts in our food in order to differentiate it, color it, endow it with a longer shelf life, and attempt to resurrect tastes that were annihilated in the processing, differentiating, coloring, and preserving. Once dismissed as faddists and worse by the industry and much of government, these advocates are now enjoying unprecedented support from the general public. The demonstration has been so strong that the industry recognizes this "fad" as a lasting and important one—one to be dealt with, if not by actually avoiding additives, as many manufacturers have done, at least by printing up labels and advertisements *claiming* to have avoided them, or by bamboozling the public with double-talk about how the natural fruit or vegetable is made up of chemical substances, so therefore the synthetic substitutes are just as good.

There are other "additives" that figure prominently in the food system as well. Like the chemical sort, these are not always additives that add something. Often they subtract from the food—reduce its nutritional value, damage its taste, lower its quality and quantity. Some of them are designed, at least, to raise quality and quantity, and some succeed at it, but many fail. Like their chemical counterparts, these additives almost always result in higher prices for food. There are countless such economic additives, but the ones that have the most profound effects on the food system are waste, crime, safety and contamination problems, and the changes that are wrought on food by the most powerful of all the presences that stand between the producer and the consumer, government.

No one knows how much food is really wasted, but that has not prevented speculation on the amount. The measurement of the loss of edible food can be attempted in terms of the decline in a product's weight as it moves through the system, or the decline in a product's nutrients, or its loss in dollar value.

In the late seventies the General Accounting Office undertook a study of food losses and concluded that in 1974, about 20 percent of the crops harvested in the nation, by weight, was "ultimately lost" to spoilage, damage, pests, spillage, and plate waste. The loss amounted to 137 million tons of crops, said the GAO, and represented $31 billion worth of food. (If that sum is converted to 1982 dollars, it becomes more than $54 billion.)

Households, said the report, wasted the most edible food, about $11.7 billion worth of the 1974 crop. One study on which the GAO relied was conducted by anthropologists at the University of Arizona at Tucson, who poked through household garbage and concluded that people wasted more than 10 percent of their household food purchases in 1974. They also found, said the GAO, that:

> The biggest food wasters are middle-income families, not the very rich or the very poor. The middle-income neighborhoods waste almost 25 percent.
>
> Over half of the food thrown out over a three-year period was not table scraps; it was straight waste—a half a loaf of bread, untouched fruits, half a bag of vegetables and, in some cases, unopened packages of food. . . .

It might seem strange, but neither the General Accounting Office's report nor most other documents on food loss mention something that everyone connected with the food system knows is of immense importance: crime. True, the network of crime and criminals, both petty and organized, who feed on the system probably does not remove much actual food from the chain. But it does account for a great and uncounted amount of economic loss. It is a loss that, once again, the consumer has to pay.

The business has a word for the disappearance of food—a clinical, almost neutral term—that manages to cover both the sorts of losses that are incurred by spoilage and those that stem from crime. It is "shrink." One explanation of the term is that it "refers to pilferage, loss in weight or spoilage, damage due to natural or handling causes, and markdowns or reductions in price below the original retail selling price.*

There are ample opportunities within the food system for what might be called "deliberate shrink." As it passes from the farmer and the fisher to the consumer, food is handled by many people. The trucking industry, which has a rich reputation for criminal activity, occupies a very important position in the food chain. So does the garbage-hauling business, which removes the leftovers at every level of the process. Individual businesses, retail and otherwise, are wide open to the husky-throated overtures of the protection racket. Since almost everybody buys food, and since food is sold and resold several times as it moves through the stages of production, processing, delivery, and wholesale and retail distribution, the bill for crime is spread over a very large population base, making it more difficult for an individual to claim successfully that he has been damaged. And finally and overwhelmingly, because food is a *business*, it remains virtually immune to the attention of law enforcement authorities, who tend to the belief that the business of business is business, and that problems within the industry will be worked out by the industry itself. Food lends itself very neatly to invasion by both petty and organized criminals, from the bakery route salesman who cheats every store on his run out of the price of a loaf of bread to the czars of organized crime.

Some spokesmen for the retail food industry have placed the amount of their stores' loss from theft at 2 percent of their gross sales, but others, including a self-proclaimed former

* Theodore W. Leed and Gene A. German, *Food Merchandising: Principles and Practices* (New York: Lehnar-Friedman, 1979).

thief named Jack Henry, who now advises retailers on their security problems, has said the figure might be more like 5 percent. Some of that loss comes, in supermarkets as in department stores and practically everywhere else, from shoplifting. Skilled shoplifters are said to be able to walk frozen turkeys out of stores by clenching them between their legs (the technique is called a "crotch job"). Amateurs often do their stealing by moving the hot merchandise past the cash register in a place even more resistant to investigation—their stomachs. This eating-while-you-shop method is known as "grazing."

Some stores are responding to the shoplifting threat by attaching electromagnetic labels to their food, just as clothing and other stores do with their merchandise, and setting alarms to ring if a clerk has not deactivated the label. The cost of this, of course, goes onto the price of the food that everyone buys. Another form of theft, and one that is not widely discussed publicly, probably adds even more to the consumer's bill. It is the stealing that is done by store employees themselves. Jack Henry, in an interview in the trade publication *Supermarket Business*, explained some of the ways. One way: An employee can take a large box of something—detergent or cereal—into the bathroom, empty its contents into the toilet, fill it with more expensive foods or other merchandise, reseal it, mark it, and replace on the shelf. Later, the employee can visit the store on his or her off time, purchase the box, and take it home.

Henry estimated that half of the dollar volume of a store's theft takes place at the cash register, where there are imaginative schemes for diverting some of the customers' money from the store to the clerk. Another ripe source of illegal income is tapped by vendors who charge stores for products that they don't actually deliver. A store that fails to check on incoming merchandise, said the former thief, can lose one-third of what it's supposed to be getting.

Various forms of extortion have long been observed in the

parts of the food industry that involve transportation, and the problem historically has been severe in the meat business. One example involves the widespread existence of people, known in the trade as "lumpers" or "swampers," who are on hand at the loading and unloading docks in many of the food industries, but particularly in meat, and who "help" the truck driver. The driver who rejects this offer (which often may be to do something that doesn't need to be done) may find himself delayed or with several slashed tires. Most drivers fork over a fee, which can run from $30 to $100.

The Federal Bureau of Investigation has been strangely reluctant to go after violations of this sort, as well as any others that hint of ties to organized crime. One exception involves the notorious Fulton Fish Market, New York City's waterfront distribution terminal for fresh and frozen seafood. Although city authorities have kept their hands off the market, the U.S. Attorney's office has conducted a thorough probe of the place that has resulted in several prison terms.

The fish market is a dramatic example of the heavy-handed sort of crime that characterizes some sectors of the industry. But it is likely that wrongdoing in the food business is most significantly represented by what white-collar people like to call white-collar crime.

A Federal Trade Commission judge ruled in 1981 that ITT Continental Baking Company, of Fresh Horizons and Wonder Bread fame and the world's largest baker, for a decade and a half had tried to monopolize the business by engaging in illegal price discrimination and other practices. The decision is now on appeal to the commission. Deceptions in advertising and other forms of merchandising are commonplace and are virtually impossible to correct or punish. Coupon fraud is widespread, as are allegations that firms that should be competing are actually fixing their prices. An institutionalized form of short-weighting—not the classic case of the butcher's thumb on the scale but far more damaging economically—is omnipresent.

New York City is one of the few jurisdictions that has tried to deal with this last form of economic crime, despite the fact that it occurs everywhere. In recent years the city has issued around 120,000 citations annually to grocers whom it accuses of violating the law on short-weighting. Most of the allegations concern foods packed and shipped by manufacturers elsewhere, but sold locally. Presumably, then, any city that wanted to enforce short-weight regulations would find the same widespread violations. There is good reason to believe that New York's main motive in enforcing the law is to raise revenue from fines.

The grocers say the shortages are caused by natural factors, the chief among them being the evaporation of water from the product after it has been packed. This hydroscopic weight loss, as it is called, affects all packaged and unpackaged foods to some extent, and the law takes this into consideration in two ways: The definition of a "pound" or "quart" has a little leeway, over and under; and the content weight of most foods is measured by the batch, not the individual container. As the Food Marketing Institute points out, much of the variation is in the customer's favor, and "you are at least twice as likely to get a container that is overweight as you are to get one that is underweight."

For some reason, however, the underweight ones keep popping up when New York City's inspectors visit the stores. To those who argue that the city is unfair, Bill Rattery, the assistant commissioner in charge of enforcement, weights and measures, had a simple reply: "If you have a package of bacon and it's short five-sixteenths of an ounce, and it's been short over the years and has been getting violations, just put another slice in the package. Very simple. We talk these days about automation of the food industry, and these guys can't put out a package that's full? Don't tell me it's all because of moisture, because it's not. Another cookie in the box will solve the problem." Another solution came in 1983, when the city reached a settlement with the grocers that allowed them to settle outstanding violations for about 2.5 cents on the dollar. This cast considerable doubt on the city's sincerity about short-weight crime.

Economic crimes seem to infect the milk business more than others. Again, New York City and its environs offer a glimpse at a situation that has national implications. New York State Attorney General Robert Abrams announced an agreement in the fall of 1982 in a conspiracy and price-fixing case involving twenty-five milk companies and untold millions of dollars that were ripped off consumers. The companies supply virtually all the milk drunk in New York City.

According to the attorney general, the companies acknowledged that they had divided up territories and fixed prices for more than a decade. The amount of their overcharge was not known, but the settlement called for a refund to consumers of $6.7 million and payment of a $500,000 fine to the state. The form the refund would take was not immediately worked out. At one point the publicity-minded attorney general announced, on a television interview show, that the guilty companies would print discount coupons on a scientifically determined sample of their milk cartons. This never took place.

Once America had become (or thought it had become) the master of food technology, with sanitary canning and freezing techniques and lots of laws on the books regulating the cleanliness and healthiness of the places where foods were grown, processed, and sold, the public tended to set aside any worries it might have had about food safety. Just as we and those who sold food to us could boast that we spent less of our income on food than most other nations, we also could claim that our food was probably the safest in the world. Of course, there were occasional problems with food-borne disease—a botulism scare here, traced to inadequate sealing of a batch of mushrooms or canned fish; a food-poisoning incident there. But by and large, we had little to worry about. Our biggest problem with food was that we endangered our lives by gorging ourselves on too much of it.

Now that situation seems to be changing, and the change appears to parallel what is happening with our supply of potable water. For decades we took the quality and quantity of our water for granted, assuming both that the available amount would always be infinite and that there were copious safeguards for what we drank, bathed in, fished in, and nourished our crops with. Now, however, we are finding that years of environmental abuse and increasing dependence on synthetic chemicals have taken their toll both on our surface waters and on the underground aquifers, which we had always thought to be as pure as the driven snow. And the driven snow and rain are turning out to be poisoned with acid.

As with the problems of water and toxic wastes, we are discovering that the patience of the planet, and the human body, for abuse and error in food is getting shorter. So in addition to the traditional problems of food safety, we now have a number of other difficulties that are much harder to deal with. These might be called food's environmental problems, and if we continue to ignore them we are courting a real crisis. Some examples include:

■ The Office of Technology Assessment, in a 1979 study for Congress, said that toxic substances in food posed a national problem of "ominous dimensions," made all the more ominous by the fact that the chemicals might not turn up in humans until years later.

■ A study by the Environmental Services Laboratory of New York City's Mount Sinai School of Medicine showed that an estimated 97 percent of all the residents of Michigan contained in their bodies traces of another toxic chemi-

cal, PBB, or polybrominated biphenyl. In the summer of
1973, from 1,000 to 2,000 pounds of PBBs were accidentally
mixed with food for Michigan farm animals, and by the
time the mixup was detected millions of chickens and cattle
had to be destroyed, some farms went into bankruptcy, and
an undetermined number of people had ingested the poison
when they ate meat.

■ Coffee manufacturers used trichlorethylene to make
decaffeinated coffee until 1975, when the Food and Drug
Administration determined that the chemical was a car-
cinogen. The manufacturers switched to methylene chlo-
ride, which research now indicates may cause cancer as
well.

■ In several cases, pesticides used on crops are turning
up in foods sold to consumers. Ethylene dibromide, a car-
cinogenic chemical also known as EDB, has been sprayed
on stored grain for twenty-five years, and now the poison is
showing up on grocery shelves in packages of brand-name
baking mixes and similar products.

One food safety problem that almost never comes up for
public discussion is contamination that occurs while food is
being transported. The problem is believed to be most severe
where railroad transportation is involved. The Office of Technology Assessment, in another of its reports to Congress,
called food sanitation a "top priority" item, and said:

> The basic problem is that much of the nation's food, which
> moves by rail, is held in unsanitary conditions during trans-
> portation. Boxcars may be infested with rodents and insects
> and may contain microbiological and chemical contamination.
> There are documented cases of pets dying from pet foods
> whose ingredients were contaminated with toxic substances
> during shipment. Food ingredients are frequently rejected by
> the processor because they have become contaminated during

shipment. Users frequently reject railcars or must decontaminate them before use.

Contaminated railcars, spoiled produce, purloined potato chips, payoffs to unnecessary "helpers," and chronic short-weighting are more than just annoyances to those of us who must cope daily with the American food system. Although they are rarely discussed in the media or tackled by the regulators or the industry itself, these are powerful economic additives—uncalculated extras that make our food budgets far larger than they need or ought to be.

9

The Errant Guardian

There is an entity charged with dealing with all of the economic additives we have discussed (and with the chemical ones, as well); it is widely believed to cope expertly with everything from contaminated boxcars to loading-dock extortion to short-weighting to the nutritional composition of the foods offered in the school lunch program. This entity is the government—or, more correctly, *governments*, although the one headquartered in Washington is the one with the most authority and money to do all these jobs.

What the government in Washington does is staggering in its ability to affect the quantity, quality, and variety of food Americans eat. One count by a government agency has found a total of 359 federal programs that are related to food, agriculture, and nutrition. Nobody knows the total number of rules and regulations. Among the most noticeable of the government's obligations are these:

It collects and publishes statistics which are used by the industry and by all sorts of governmental and private agencies as the justifications and bases for all kinds of programs.

It writes and issues regulations that have far-reaching effects.

It performs and financially supports research into thousands of areas related to food, from the production of new strains of plants and animals to studies of farm efficiency and new forms of fuel.

It tries to keep the production of various commodities orderly and secure by regulating production and producers' income. It endows the dairy and fisheries industries with enormous support. More than $8 million of the taxpayers' money, for example, has been poured into the effort to rename "trash fish" so the public will buy and eat them.

It controls not only food that flows across its own frontiers but also the food that enters global commerce. Often it uses food as an element of foreign policy.

Not the least of its undertakings has been its role in the nutrition of the most vulnerable Americans—the young, the elderly, and the impoverished.

Sometimes the government has even engaged in rather deep thinking about what the structure and future of the agricultural system should be. But more often the involvement by government is at the intricately detailed level, for example, as in what used to be known as the Food and Drug Administration's "filth guidelines." Now designated "natural and unavoidable natural defect guidelines," they set the limits of filth that manufacturers can allow into the nation's food supply. The guidelines are violated, for example, by the presence of more than thirty aphids, thrips, and/or mites per 100 grams of frozen broccoli; more than five *Drosophila* (fruit fly) and other eggs, or more than one maggot, per 250 milliliters of canned fruit juice; more than an average of *either* ten fly eggs, or five fly eggs and one maggot, or two maggots

per 100 grams of tomato juice; and more than five milligrams
of "mammalian excreta" per pound of sesame seeds.

The government carries on all this involvement through a
number of agencies, the chief of which is the U.S. Department of Agriculture. USDA occupies considerable physical
and political territory in Washington, with its base in the
massive, solid-looking South Building that anchors one side of
the Mall. Inside, and in satellite buildings around the nation,
there are offices that collect economic statistics, forecast the
world food outlook, study nutrition and food safety, regulate
and promote agricultural marketing, inspect plants, grains,
and animals, regulate transportation, study agricultural science, stabilize and conserve land and farmers, insure crops,
assist farmers in getting electricity, telephones, and homes,
run the Forest Service, and operate the Soil Conservation Service. In fiscal year 1981, USDA had a budget of $26 billion.

The Food and Drug Administration, which is part of the
Department of Health and Human Services, is another powerful agency. Its activities, according to the *United States
Government Manual*, "are directed toward protecting the
health of the nation against impure and unsafe foods, drugs
and cosmetics, and other potential hazards." The agency was
created in 1906, at a time when, according to a Senate committee report written six years previously, "The adulteration
of prepared or manufactured foods is very extensively practiced and in many cases to the great discredit of our manufacturers."

The Federal Trade Commission is charged with overseeing
the marketplace for food and other products, in some cases in
coordination with the Justice Department's antitrust division.
Its main objective, says the *Government Manual*, "is the
maintenance of strongly competitive enterprise as the key-
stone of the American economic system. . . . In brief, the

Commission is charged with keeping competition both free and fair."

One of the most important of the government's functions is not carried out by any one agency, but rather by a number of them. That is the dissemination of information on food to the public. In pamphlets, reports, and graphic media, consumers have traditionally been informed by their central government about food's safety and availability; about how to select, store, and cook it; and about that most important of topics, nutrition.

A lot of the information has come from USDA itself, and consumers have been able to purchase it from the Government Printing Office or, in many cases, get it free from schools or their members of Congress. A great deal of informative material flows, too, from a variety of other sources, a few examples of which are:

A publication named *Foodborne Disease Surveillance*, published by the Centers for Disease Control; the *National Food Review*, which comes from USDA's Economics Research Service; the *Family Economics Review*, a quarterly published by USDA "on research relating to economic aspects of family living"; documents commissioned by the National Science Foundation; massive one-time reports such as the *Global 2000 Report to the President*; USDA's annual *Yearbook of Statistics* and *Yearbook of Agriculture*; a series of thick bibliographies on food topics issued by the U.S. General Accounting Office; GAO reports and audits on subjects ranging from why food costs so much in the U.S. Virgin Islands to how efficiently the Senate restaurant is being run to the issues of nitrites in bacon; hearing records and reports from a number of congressional committees; and, voluminous documents published by quite a few of the agricultural states, most notably California.

✳   ✳   ✳

Government has always been more responsive to the most influential elements of the food chain, the manufacturers and processors and chemical companies, than to the consumers in the chain, just as it has always treated the manufacturers of munitions with more respect than the foot soldiers and the lumber magnates more politely than the trees. The better-off food businessmen have always had easy access to government, and they have always helped make policy; the two wealthiest members of the Senate are believed to be John C. Danforth, Republican of Missouri and scion of the Ralston-Purina fortune, and John Heinz, Republican of Pennsylvania, of the ketchup and pickle Heinzes. Lobbyists from food industries are prominent among those in Washington who influence and often actually write legislation, and the revolving door beckons constantly to government regulators who would like to switch to better-paying employment among the people they have been regulating. (Many government professionals, it should be remembered, are quite dedicated in their work and in their belief that they should serve the people, and it is our great fortune that they resist these very powerful temptations.)

The food industry is benefited in many ways by the actions and inactions of government at all levels, but the greatest payoff comes from agricultural research. Under the system that exists today, the government uses the taxpayers' money to subsidize research that benefits private industry—through developing new and more marketable strains of plants and animals—and that actually penalizes the public itself by raising food's price and lowering its quality.

Agricultural research has been supported by government since the Department of Agriculture was created, and now the total bill has reached well over $400 million a year. Research money is funneled through six agencies of USDA, fifty-five state agricultural experiment stations, fifteen schools of forestry, sixteen land-grant colleges established for black students, and Tuskegee Institute in Alabama. The General Accounting Office has determined that these organizations do about 95 percent of all agricultural research supported by the public. An uncounted amount of related research is done by agencies not directly connected with agriculture, such as the Defense Department and the various spy organizations. Much of what we know today about food packaging and preservation, for example, is the outgrowth of work done on military combat rations in World War II.

Research is supposed to make contributions not only to the agricultural *business*, but also to solving the broader problems of agriculture, to elevating rural life, and to improving the welfare of the consumer. And there are many within or just outside the research establishment who think it serves the consumer nicely. "We figure that part of our function is to be part of the education system," said Robert Learson, the deputy director of the technology laboratory of the National Marine Fisheries Service. And Michigan State economist James Shaffer bristled at the suggestion that government research benefits industry more than the public. "I think that's a terrible mistake in terms of view," he said. "The Department of Agriculture and the state departments of agriculture should have been known as 'departments of consumer benefits.' The bulk of their emphases has been in terms of improving the supply of food, which has benefited mostly the consumers. The research and the know-how have increased the average yield of corn about one bushel per acre per year for fifty years. That is a tremendous contribution. Who benefits? That hasn't made a lot of farmers rich, but that's made relatively inexpensive meat."

Research does not, however, do nearly enough either to educate consumers or to ease their financial burden. Much of the work done by the Gloucester fisheries laboratory seeks to bolster up a fishing industry that is disintegrating because of its own inefficiencies, and a lot of the consumer education consists of working on new ways to mince, extrude, and otherwise compromise the quality of fish that consumers eat. And it is by no means certain that increased yields are always beneficial for the consumer.

When researchers at the University of California at Davis, the largest and richest agricultural experiment station in the nation, used public money to perfect both a machine to harvest tomatoes and a succession of genetically engineered tomatoes that fit the machine (UC-82, one of the latest, is thick-skinned, juiceless, and square, and therefore perfect for everything but eating), the rationale was that the cost of labor would be reduced and the savings would be passed along to the consumer. This has not occurred. Elizabeth Martin, the director of the Davis-based California Agrarian Action Project, said her organization kept its eye on prices and found that in the first fifteen years since the machine was introduced in California agriculture, "tomato prices had risen 111 percent to the consumer. No other fruit or vegetable had even gotten close to that rise in price." Another payoff for the consumer, of course, was a tomato that tasted more than ever before like a damp roll of paper towels.

"The university is not gearing its research toward a consumer constituency," said Martin, who is a fifth-generation Californian with a degree from Davis in environmental policy analysis. "Rather, it gears its research toward wherever it can get grant money. It will follow the leadership of the people giving the money. And the people giving them the grant money are almost entirely the chemical industry and the big machinery companies.

"There's a lot of very *good* stuff happening at the university, also. But the greatest amount of innovation is coming out of the sections of the university that are doing research off large business grants and catering to large business needs." Privately supported research subsidized by the taxpayers, according to the California auditor general's office, has benefited such firms as the James Dole Corporation, 3M Company, Hunt-Wesson, the Pet Food Institute, the Monsanto Fund, Heinz, and the Pistachio Association.

Not only did the University of California's researchers use federal and state money to subsidize food and chemical conglomerates, they also meekly let the industry call the shots. One letter from a private company, with names withheld by the auditor general, made the relationship clear:

> [Company] wishes to award a gift for the amount of $20,024 to cover the total project cost of construction of a prefabricated greenhouse unit. It is agreed by [company] that the greenhouse facility will be the property of the Regents of the University of California and will be managed by and assigned to the [university department] upon completion of construction. Further, it is agreed that the [company] representative, [name of a company employee], will have a courtesy university appointment and in general will use the greenhouse for three years in conjunction with the [department] with provision for extension of use by [company] for an additional two years in cooperation with [department's] use.

The audit reported that the company got its employee his appointment while keeping him on its payroll; he did his research, which "centered around a specific interest of his employer"; the company gave money to the experiment station; and the taxpayers' university continued to do the work of industry.

Late in 1982, partly because of information disseminated by the Agrarian Action Project, the university system started examining its professors' ties to corporations that sponsored their academic research; some warnings were issued and one faculty member was officially reprimanded. But the California Fair Political Practices Commission, which oversees the conflict-of-interest law, has noted that it is faculty members themselves who do the examining.

Elizabeth Martin's side seemed for a moment in 1979 to have won a decisive battle. Bob Bergland, the Carter administration's agriculture secretary, was asked at a meeting in Fresno about mechanized farming. The subject is a hot one in California, and it is at the heart of the debate over publicly sponsored research. The university-built tomato picker and the university-built tomato put a lot of farm laborers out of work, and Elizabeth Martin's organization is one of several plaintiffs in a lawsuit attacking the regents of the University of California on that issue.

Bergland's spontaneous reply to the question was shocking to the academic entrepreneurs: "I do not think that federal funding of labor-saving devices is a proper use of federal money," he said. "This is something to be left to private enterprise and to the state universities. . . . But I will not put federal money into any project that results in the saving of farm labor. The economic incentives in the marketplace should be powerful enough so that that kind of research work can be done by private enterprise."

When Bergland got back to Washington and thought about it, he rephrased his position some to lessen the shock, but he stuck by his major point: "I do not believe a federally financed research effort ought to benefit a small number of individuals, corporations, or narrow interest groups to such an extent and in such a way as to make it possible, in time, for the beneficiaries to gain control of the farm-to-market structure, monopolize the sources of finance at every step, and increase their profits by selling what may well be an inferior product at a price that is insulated from competition."

But then the issue evanesced into talk about studying the matter more. In any event, the election of 1980 made Bergland and his boss private citizens again, and a new, pro-agribusiness and pro-industry president was in the White House. Ronald Reagan had, in fact, been governor of California during part of the time industry was getting such nice subsidies from its state university system and American tax-payers. And a prominent member of the university's board of regents at the time, as well as a director of Blue Goose Grow-ers, which owns agricultural land and eleven packing houses in California and elsewhere, was Reagan's friend William French Smith.

William French Smith went on to become, in 1981, Ronald Reagan's Attorney General. As director of the Justice De-partment, he had a strong hand in formulating the nation's policy on the issues of the good marketplace. This helps to explain why the government in Washington, which always has been the most tenuous of the consumer's friends even in the best of times, now often acts like an avowed enemy.

One year after Ronald Reagan became President, a coali-tion of seven national consumer organizations issued a joint report condemning the President's policies as "devastating" in areas such as food, safety, health, and energy. A press spokes-man for Reagan commented that his boss "believes that much federal regulation is wasteful and unnecessary and that the consumer's best protection is not a growing federal bu-reaucracy, but a free and competitive economy."

Of course, the consumer organizations were not asking for a growing bureaucracy but rather a government that was com-mitted to doing its job. In any event, Reagan's ideas about how to foster a "free and competitive economy" were il-luminated by the appointments he made to federal offices that are concerned with food and other consumer issues. There were many parallels in these appointments to the patently pro-polluter ones Reagan made in the environmental area. He filled many positions in the Department of Agriculture and other departments with people who knew and cared little about consumers, much less consumerism; they were people who represented the world of business, who felt comfortable with the business way of thinking, who saw nothing wrong with the way business had been conducting itself. These were not people who were disturbed when they heard the word "conglomerate"; some had worked for conglomerates themselves. The word that bothered them most was "regulation."

Reagan named John R. Block, a hog farmer and Illinois director of agriculture, to head the U.S. Department of Agriculture. Before he was sworn in, Block delivered himself of one of those unintelligent statements that seem to characterize official Washington. Food, he said, should be used "as a weapon" of foreign policy. Later he tried to beat his sword into "a tool for peace," but he had made his point. Block quickly broadcast his pro-business attitudes in a series of interviews, many of them carried by the trade press.

He wanted to spend more money on agricultural research, he said, while spending less on food stamps, school lunches, and nutrition, because "consumers need to be concerned about keeping research up so that this agricultural plant can be in a position to continue to serve them in future years with an abundant supply of food and fiber at a reasonable price." Block and Reagan installed C. W. McMillan, a lobbyist for the National Cattlemen's Association, as Assistant Secretary of Agriculture for Marketing and Transportation, and Richard Lyng, the executive director of the American Meat Institute, as Deputy Secretary.

James C. Miller III, a resident scholar at the conservative American Enterprise Institute and one of those who formulated the new administration's plans for chopping regulations everywhere, became the new head of the Federal Trade Commission. The commission's own literature, in circulation at the time the new administration arrived, had stated that its "regional offices carry out the bulk of FTC law enforcement." The Reagan administration closed four of the regional offices.

For his head of the Justice Department's antitrust division, Reagan chose William F. Baxter. While a law professor at

Stanford University, Baxter had performed research partly funded by International Business Machines, and had served as a consultant to the immense corporation. Once he was in the Justice Department, he went to Europe to lobby the European Economic Commission to go easy on IBM in an antitrust case pending before it. Back in Washington, Baxter killed the thirteen-year-old antitrust case the United States government had brought against the giant corporation, on the grounds that he thought it was "without merit." He stoutly denied that his support for an old benefactor was a conflict of interest. (Baxter resigned his post in late 1983, saying that he was "burned out.")

Virginia Knauer, Reagan's Director of the U.S. Department of Consumer Affairs, promised she would "not be intervening" in the administration's regulatory policies but rather would pursue sweet reason and work behind the scenes to convince business to do the right thing by the consumer—a line of thinking that was quite similar to that employed by Reagan's failed choices to run the Environmental Protection Agency's gentle little campaign against toxic polluters.

It did not take the new team long to get to work implementing the new administration's policy on discarding, defusing, and rewriting regulations and policies. The changes since January, 1981, have been many and they have been frequent, and all of them have injured consumers economically, nutritionally, and in most other ways, while enriching the larger members of the industry. What follows is only a brief sample.

In matters of food safety, the nation had moved by 1980 into an era in which both government and many consumers were beginning to understand that reasonable prices might have to be paid for unrestrained increased productivity, convenience, and availability, and that it was worthwhile in the long run, and probably in the short run, to assess the safety of

such wonders as pesticides, herbicides, and mechanized processing techniques. This newfound understanding of the system as it really existed extended to fears about what we were
doing to the soil, the groundwater, and the food we eat by
using ever-increasing amounts of synthetic chemicals in the
production of crops. "Organic" farming, once thought of as
some hippie aberration, started being practiced by ordinary,
clear-headed farmers.

The Department of Agriculture, which never had paid
much attention, through research or otherwise, to organic
farming, conducted a comprehensive study of it. The outcome, and that of another study commissioned by the
National Science Foundation, was shocking to those who had
always dismissed the technique: Farmers who practiced conventional, chemical-heavy agriculture got somewhat better
income from their yields, but the organic farmers had lower
expenses, particularly for energy. The USDA researchers
urged "strongly" that USDA should pay more attention to
organic farming and farmers. The department did, indeed,
establish a staff position to pull together research on the subject.

All that happened as the Reagan administration was becoming installed in Washington. Once the installation was
complete, the administration abolished the staffer's job. Richard Lyng, the Assistant Secretary of Agriculture and former
meat promoter, was asked by Daniel Zwerdling of National
Public Radio why the administration had scuttled the report
and its advice.

"Well," replied Lyng, "it doesn't deserve very much money,
because it is not an economically viable alternative. We don't
think it works on a commercially acceptable basis." Zwerdling
asked if Lyng, whose own agency had produced a study saying organic farming *did* work, could produce any evidence
that it didn't.

"No," said Lyng, "but just common sense tells us, those of
us who have had anything to do with agriculture, that when

you try to grow apples without treating them with insecticide, you get worms."

Sanitation in the meatpacking industry has long been a problem area, as has the quality of the inspections carried on in the industry by the federal and state officials who are supposed to enforce the law. Although millions of Americans might think a "USDA Inspected" stamp on a cut of beef or a package of pork chops is assurance that the meat was processed under the cleanest of conditions, several investigations have found this to be not true. In one of them, a 1981 study by the General Accounting Office, the auditors made surprise visits to sixty-two meat and poultry slaughterhouses in six states. They found sixteen of the plants "were not in compliance with one or more of the six basic inspection program requirements."

Another survey was conducted, quietly this time, by USDA, and it showed that in 32 percent of the 272 plants checked it was likely that meat products didn't meet USDA standards—even though USDA inspectors were giving the plants "satisfactory" ratings. That information had to be pried out of the department in 1982 by the *Kansas City Times*, using the Freedom of Information Act. In some cases, said the newspaper, meat that was approved by inspectors was contaminated with fecal material.

Against such a background, the Reagan administration announced that it wanted to cut in half the number of meat and poultry inspectors, leaving more of the responsibility to the plant managers. And the inspectors who remained would be expected to do their work faster: Chickens, for instance, would pass by the inspectors' eyes at the rate of 105 each minute. Under such circumstances, "inspection" becomes worse than meaningless, for consumers continue to believe that if their government certifies something as inspected, it has been inspected.

❃   ❃   ❃

In nutrition, the government before Reagan took office had been moving, too, toward a new role: that of helpful adviser to the public. Washington had always been good for pamphlets urging people to consume the basic, important foods, but more recently it had begun exploring matters that raised the hackles of the meat, chemical, and dairy lobbyists.

The explorations grew out of the publication, in February, 1977, of *Dietary Goals for the United States*, a document aimed at consumers that represented the judgment of the Senate Select Committee on Nutrition and Human Needs on the best existing thinking on human diet. The report included suggested dietary goals, among them consumption of more fruits and vegetables and whole grains and less refined and processed sugars, saturated fats, fatty meats, whole milk, eggs and other sources of high cholesterol, and salt. The Senate report, while reflecting the prevailing thought of moderate-minded nutritionists, thus managed to strike at virtually every high-powered pressure group in the food industry.

As the eighties began, several government agencies were spreading the word of the new guidelines to the citizens. The Food and Drug Administration's publication *FDA Consumer* carried lively and sometimes provocative articles on such subjects as vegetarianism ("vegetarians as a group may be a whole lot healthier than the rest of us"), vitamins, and roughage. USDA moved to implement some of the guidelines through its school lunch and breakfast programs; it demanded a lower percentage of fat in its ground beef, lighter syrup in its canned fruit, less salt in its canned meats, and restricted access to junk foods.

The biggest bombshell came, however, with the publication of a number of informative booklets by USDA's Human Nutrition Center putting the guidelines into terms consumers could really use—recipes and menus. One magazine-format publication, titled *Food*, was a particularly attractive and helpful departure from the standard fare of government pamphlets that showed smiling cartoon families in clothes from the 1940s gathering around Mom in her apron at the dinner table.

Another publication, almost pocket-size and named *Nutrition and Your Health: Dietary Guidelines for Americans*, offered condensed information and spread the government's message succinctly on its cover: "1. Eat a Variety of Foods. 2. Maintain Ideal Weight. 3. Avoid Too Much Fat, Saturated Fat, and Cholesterol. 4. Eat Foods with Adequate Starch and Fiber. 5. Avoid Too Much Sugar. 6. Avoid Too Much Sodium. 7. If You Drink Alcohol, Do So in Moderation."

"These are fairly conservative guidelines, relative to what *some* people wish had been said about some of these things," said Betty Peterkin back in early 1981. She was a scientist at the USDA Human Nutrition Center in Hyattsville, Maryland, and was proud of her role in getting the guidelines before the public. She handed her visitor a copy of the pamphlet and suggested that he take good care of it. "This is going to become a collector's item very fast," she said, "because the new administration is probably not going to reprint it."

She was right. Not only did the pamphlet not get reprinted; the new Administration team, assembled from industry, proceeded to dismantle the Human Nutrition Institute and to undertake other efforts to make sure that nutrition would not rear its ugly head in Washington again. The Reagan-Block-Lyng forces attempted to change beef grading regulations to please the meat lobby; to cut nutrition programs for low-income pregnant women, infants, and young children; and to rewrite the rules for the school lunch program. They had to back down a few times, once as a result of the public outcry over a USDA official's ruling that ketchup and pickle relish be counted as "vegetables" in school lunch programs.

And they tried to destroy the guidelines, or at least the public's access to them.

In a truly shabby display, Secretary Block flip-flopped several times on the subject of *Food/2*, the second publication in USDA's planned series on the guidelines and menus for implementing them. At first there was speculation that the new agriculture secretary and his boss wouldn't publish the document at all. Block countered this with the announcement that the department would, after all, publish it. Then the meat lobby's man in USDA, Richard Lyng, said the magazine would not be published. Then Lyng's superior, Block, said it would not be published. Then there was some talk about letting the American Dietetic Association publish it, but without the subversive material on fat and cholesterol. Later it looked as if the private group would screw up its courage and publish the magazine in toto.

In the meantime, the Center for Science in the Public Interest obtained a copy of the offending material. When the secret document was spread in the sunlight of public inquiry, it seemed decidedly uninflammatory. Like the others that had issued from the Human Nutrition Center before it was destroyed by the Reagan administration, it counseled moderation. Moderation apparently was not good enough for the President and the cholesterol lobby.

Government's newfound callousness toward the consumers of food has manifested itself in dozens of other ways. A clear signal went out that Washington no longer was interested in pursuing antitrust cases in the food industry or elsewhere; the new administration quickly dismissed pending cases involving not only IBM but also five soft drink manufacturers, chicken salesman Frank Perdue, eight large oil companies, and, in a celebrated signal to the more concentrated portions of the food business, America's three largest breakfast cereal manufacturers. The FTC staff had accused the cereal outfits of operating a "shared monopoly" among themselves.

Information has been another victim. Within its first eleven months, the Reagan administration eliminated more than nine hundred publications that had been distributed by government agencies. Some of them were worthy candidates for termination, but many—including those that advised the public about health, nutrition, and good food habits—deserved to live. A lot of publications that had been issued free of charge by agencies such as USDA now could be obtained only through the Government Printing Office, and only there at prices that were by any measure outrageous. Some publications remained on the free list. A consumer who wrote to USDA requesting copies of sixteen different folders explaining how to shop for various foods got ten of them, three months later.

The *Federal Register*, used by serious students of government to keep track of regulations proposed and passed (and rescinded) by various agencies, went up in price from $75 to $300 a year. Periodicals that had been issued by agencies free to those who were sufficiently interested to request them went under the Government Printing Office wing, too. Then not only did their prices start sharp rises, but the GPO managed to mail them out consistently late, if at all. Ralph Nader, the consumer advocate, called the government's new policies "a new form of secrecy."

And John Block, in an obvious bid to become the Earl Butz of the Reagan administration, explained to Congress why he didn't think people needed much nutritional information from their government:

"Hogs are like people. You can provide protein and grain to a hog and he will balance his ration. People are surely as smart as hogs. I am not so sure the government needs to get so deeply into telling people what they should or should not eat."

The Federal Trade Commission, sharing Block's philosophy, dropped its proposal for a federal standard to govern the use of the term "natural" on foods, and so the consumer lost another piece of valuable information. And the Agriculture Department moved to allow meat processors to sell the public products such as hot dogs, sausages, bologna, meat stew, and meatballs that are adulterated with as much as 3 percent ground bone.

The bone, mixed with the meat during a mechanical processing technique, has been allowed since 1978, but the regulations required that the product be labeled as containing "powdered bone," which is something that few noncanine consumers in their right minds would want to buy and eat. The Reagan administration apparently wanted to euphemize "bone" into "calcium" in the ingredients list.

As Carol Tucker Foreman has pointed out, the powdered bone issue is one that goes far beyond consumers' personal feelings about gnawing on bones. If the bone is allowed without proper warning to the prospective customer, an important economic question is raised. "The value of the raw materials going into the product is less when it has powdered bone in it than when it's made out of all meat, and the consumer ought to be able to know that," she said. "Only when that 'powdered bone' is on that label will that product be sold for less than the all-meat product."

Much of what the administration has done has been predicated on the idea—which has some basis in fact—that the nation is overburdened with regulations, and the further idea —which has no basis in fact at all—that a healthy, competitive food industry can and will regulate itself. There is overwhelming evidence already in hand that when the food industry is left to its own devices, as it pretty well has been in meatpacking, enough of its members will take every possible liberty with the credulity, safety, health, and even lives of the consuming public to make regulation of the entire industry by the public mandatory.

It appears, at least in the mid-1980s, that the government in Washington has absolutely no intention of being on the consumer's side in the vast, confusing marketplace of food, and is, in fact, arrayed with those portions of the industry who see the consumer as no more than an endlessly exploitable source of money. Just as we no longer can sensibly assume that "they wouldn't let them say that if it weren't true" in advertising, we no longer are safe in believing that our government is going to protect us from harm or deception in the food we eat. The government that we have now is a government that withholds vital information from us that our tax dollars have already purchased; that uses our money to subsidize food packers in growing tomatoes that are too awful to eat and chemical companies in perfecting pesticides that may make us sterile and our children lame; that helped out the fishing industry, when the swordfish started turning up with unacceptable levels of mercury in them, by rewriting the rules to make more mercury acceptable. And it is a government that perhaps is best symbolized as the outfit that wants to adulterate our hot dogs with ground-up bone and serve them to school children with ketchup that it classifies as a vegetable.

Carol Tucker Foreman, who was most responsible for USDA's promoting the dietary guidelines in ways the consuming public could understand and use, was asked in 1982, after she had been out of office for some time, if she felt it was proper to simply write off the federal government as a source of consumer information on matters such as nutrition.

"No," she replied immediately. "I think that the public should *demand* that the government do its job. People have got to take it on themselves to make the government do what it should be doing."

That is a tall order, of course, and one that many a consumer and even organization of consumers has failed at. It may be that most of us are simply not prepared to try to *make* the government do something. We lack the time, the energy, the money, and—certainly where food issues are concerned, for, as we have seen, the business of food is a complex one—the very information we need to do the job, particularly when the government is suppressing that information.

While we should never cease demanding that our government be responsive to us as well as to the meat, junk food, and chemical manufacturers, we will have to adopt other strategies, too. We will have to figure out how to develop our own resources for dealing with the business of food, and then calculate how to use them to get what we want and need and deserve. An understanding of the basic structure and operations of the business, such as that offered in this book so far, is one helpful component of our strategy. But there are some active things we can do as well to insure for ourselves something approaching a more equitable break when we walk in that supermarket door.

10

A Strategy for the Consumer

The forces within the American food system are enormous; when taken together, as they must be, they can be quite overpowering. No one, least of all the consumer, can ever hope to control them, particularly at a time when the national government is unwilling to help. Nevertheless, there are things that can be done that will make the system more responsive to the people who support it with their billions of constantly flowing dollars and millions of continually emptying stomachs. There is no reason why the system cannot be made to work more efficiently for consumers as well as for shippers, canners, processors, manufacturers, brokers, ad writers, wholesalers, route salespeople, retailers, and garbage collectors. These middle links in the system—the people and institutions who stand between the consumer and the producer—ought to share a little more of the system's benefits with the people who pay for them.

The things that can be done are not exactly simple things, and for that reason a lot of people won't be interested in trying them. They may not require a whole rearrangement of one's life, but they do demand more of our precious time than we have been allocating up until now. Nor are the results that can be expected immediate or overly dramatic.

The things that can be done are neither instantaneous nor magical, and they aren't NEW!! Many are obvious, and they are time-tested, and most people are already aware of many of them. Taken together with a rough knowledge of how the system works, though, they can make a difference to the consumer who is less than satisfied with things the way they are. Some of the components of this strategy for consumers involve action—getting out and doing something specific—and others are more cerebral. The first and most vital need, which this book should have made abundantly clear by now, is for an understanding that very little happens in the food system just by chance. Everything is planned, and everything is planned for economic motives.

That is not the world's most shocking bit of information. But it is very easy for us who consume food, and who know so little about what happens to the stuff between the producers and our plates, to slip into childhood feelings about food as something that just arrives on our plates; something that is so vital to life that its *not* arriving on our plates would be unthinkable. We know, many of us, just how close to "free" it is to grow a delicious tomato or a prodigious supply of zucchini in a tiny backyard plot or even a large windowbox. And *that* chain between producer and consumer is exquisitely short: We pluck the tomato from the vine, rinse it, slice it, and eat it. When we buy a similar item from a retail store, we may tend to forget all the other steps, cumulatively very expensive and often harmful, that are involved in getting it from the farmer to us.

Another thing to remember is that while everything is

planned, it isn't necessarily planned by some mischievous central force, as part of an evil conspiracy.

There is no big, all-encompassing conspiracy afoot in the food business. It would explain a lot of things if there were, and it would be comforting to a lot of people who don't like the system the way it is, but unfortunately there just isn't any convenient conspiracy. There are plenty of *specific* conspiracies, to be sure: agreements by milk distributors to set territories and prices; nasty little deals by bakeries to do the same thing; examples of extraordinary "cooperation" among other elements of the business, from soft drink bottlers to fish merchants.

At the higher, more economically powerful levels there are forces that work like conspiracies, but that under the law (as it is interpreted by whoever is in the White House at the moment) may be as American as apple pie. Concentration, as we have seen, exists at many levels of the business, and it produces effects that are little different from the more crudely arranged conspiracies. But even these unspoken intrigues fail to take in the system as a whole.

A really good, old-fashioned conspiracy requires a great deal of cooperation, and if it is to work properly it also requires that the conspirators subordinate, at least temporarily, their own individual desires and aims to the main goal. This doesn't happen on a system-wide basis, and it rarely happens within broad sections of the system. There is still too much competition for that.

And that is another thing the consumer should remember when formulating a strategy for the food marketplace. There really is competition. Not enough, perhaps; not always in the right places and at the right times; not of sufficient intensity to make the consumer feel he's really being benefited; certainly not increasing. But competition nevertheless, and a lot more of it than in most of the other marketplaces that affect our lives. So it would be to the consumer's great advantage to

develop ways to recognize and make the best uses of the
competition that does exist.

   Another set of childhood experiences has gone into what
each of us perceives as the *definition* of food or particular
foods—the rules of taste, texture, and appearance that must
be followed by, say, a hamburger or chicken or stalk of celery
if it is to meet our own personal standards for that food. We
must remember that the definitions of food are always changing, not always for the better and rarely for motives that are
worthy.
   Part of the change comes from differing methods of preparation. To a person now in her seventies, the definition of
"pancake" may be a food that is prepared by mixing together
flour, salt, sugar, baking powder, eggs, shortening, and milk,
then cooking the mixture on a griddle. To that person's son, a
"pancake" may be something that is created by mixing together a flourlike substance from a box with an egg and some
milk, then cooking. And to her granddaughter, a "pancake"
may be the frozen product that is poured from a waxed cardboard box onto a griddle, or perhaps a flat frozen object that is
put into a toaster. To some members of the family, a "pancake" may be obtained only by visiting an eating place that
advertises itself as specializing in the food.
   Each of the people may have a different definition of "pancake," and each of them may place one of the other's definitions somewhere along a range that extends from quaint to
revolting. But the fact is that each of them still has the option
of trying out the others' definitions: The grandmother can
buy a "modern," "convenient" fabricated pancake, and the
granddaughter can try her hand at making flapjacks from
scratch. The essential, traditional recipe for "pancakes" remains, ready for anyone to use as long as flour, eggs, milk, and
the other "scratch" ingredients remain pretty much un-
changed.

In some cases, those more fundamental definitions have been fooled around with, as well. Chicken now doesn't taste the way chicken tasted thirty years ago, because the food business has changed the bird's very formula by altering the creature's eating and living habits. The taste of eggs is influenced, too, by what the modern bird eats. Changing growing practices have also altered the taste and texture definitions of such foods as beef, pork, fish grown on fish farms, and, of course, our old friend and all-purpose example, *Tomato commercialis horridis*. An enormous amount of irreparable damage to foods' definitions is done by the fast-food-junk-food industry, which hypnotizes its prey while they are young and impressionable with misleading definitions for things like "hamburgers," "french fries," "chicken," "fish," and "shakes."

To correct these inequities, we must engage in long-range efforts at persuasion, or perhaps a little heavy-handed boycotting, but there are also some fairly benign ways we can help protect the integrity of many other food definitions. These are the definitions that are perverted not by generations of hybridization but rather by simple differentiation. Our definition of "strawberries with whipped cream" may be grievously assaulted by the currently popular simulation of whipped cream, a chemical concoction that sprays out of a can and that looks like just the thing for inflating flattened automobile tires. But we can solve the problem quickly and effortlessly by not buying the differentiated impostor at all—by banning its very possibility from our minds—and by using instead whipped cream that we make ourselves. If our definition of "soup" is something that does not come out of a can, we can easily make our own without the can, saving money and avoiding a lot of unneeded salt in the process—or, more correctly, in the lack of process. If, however, we are among those millions whose definition of "soup" is something that most assuredly does come from a can, we can avoid the stuff that comes in a foil envelope and that seems even saltier, not to mention decidedly dehydrated-tasting.

Obviously, then, an important component of the strategy is to avoid as much as possible the highly processed foods. In that one simple step we will have achieved several aims: We will get food that is much closer to its traditional definition, closer to the definition on which it won its reputation as "food"; we will avoid several layers of middlemen who otherwise would have taken their cumulatively enormous profits; and we almost certainly will feel better about the whole thing.

We also will be forced to invest a little extra time in preparing the food, and this is a price that many people are unwilling to pay. They would rather spend more, get less, and save time, which is understandable in an era in which it is clearer than ever before that time equals money. That has to be a personal choice, but it need not be an irrevocable one. Someone who must value time more than money and taste during the week may survive, after a fashion, on frozen microwave entrées and Tang, but make amends on the weekends with homemade moussaka, bread baked from scratch, and freshly squeezed papaya juice.

We also may devote more time to trying to find the undifferentiated items. It is becoming increasingly difficult to discover on the supermarket shelves products that are not highly processed (remember, the more processed they are the more profit they are likely to bring for both manufacturer and retailer). The dollar value of processed food that is sold to Americans has increased steadily over the years and is expected to go on increasing. One estimate is that in 1983, Americans will buy $175 billion worth of processed foods, or about $50 billion more than in 1981.

Another lesson of overriding importance is also depressingly negative: The modern consumer must learn not to place so much trust in the food system.

It is not that the system is crooked or evil, or at least any more crooked or evil than it always has been or than society's other systems are. It's just that we have been far too trusting of the food business all along. We have put it on a pedestal that it doesn't deserve. Again, we are influenced by beliefs that flow from deep in our emotional backgrounds: *They wouldn't let them say it if it weren't true. Nobody would do anything* unsafe *with food, would he? The government will look out for us, won't it?* As economist Bruce Marion said, "There is a tendency for Americans to trust their institutions, trust their competitive system—to think that it's doing a good job and will take care of their interests. And I think it's important for them to lay aside a few of those trusts and to realize that these companies are in business to make money, and that although they may be food manufacturers and food retailers, they don't approach their mission as being one of providing nutrition for American people."

It would help to rearrange our food vocabularies. We should abandon faith in all selling words such as "natural," "new," "improved," and "fresh." These terms have been misused by the industry with such dedicated regularity that their very use is a tipoff that the advertiser is probably trying to make us believe something that isn't true. Terms such as "flavored" and "food," as in "orange-flavored drink" and "cheese food," are also danger signals. Their use does not necessarily mean the product thus described is bad or inferior; it just means it isn't what we're supposed to think it is. The terms should never be taken at face value, and, even better, they should serve to place us on our guard.

We need to mount an especial lookout for "new" variations on old standbys. Kraft's Philadelphia Brand Cream Cheese is close to a commodity in the minds of many consumers, so they might be tempted to purchase some NEW Whipped Philadelphia Brand Cream Cheese. Some might like the difference in taste and texture in the whipped product—the whipped version is thinner, wetter, and flabbier than the slightly chewy original. But there are other differences that may not be immediately apparent. The whipped cream cheese is filled with air. ("A special whipping process incorporates air into the product," wrote a company representative in a prompt reply to a query. "The whipping operation increases the volume of the finished product considerably, and accounts for the product's light, fluffy consistency.") But it costs more per ounce than the original. And while space was limited on the tiny 3-ounce package of the original, it managed to include a panel of nutritional data. The much larger whipped packaging provides none. Some consumers will like the aerated product and its inevitable sidekicks (Soft Philly with "real strawberry or pineapple, zesty olive pimento, flavorful chive with onion bits and toasted onion"), but no one should assume that it bears more than a merchandising relationship to the time-proven food.

We should examine advertising claims very carefully to weed out the ones that have no meaning or meanings that are not what the casual observer might think they are. With television advertising, that means weeding out just about everything. Virtually all food advertising on television is meaningless, except as a device to appeal to fears and emotions. Much print advertising is hardly better, but at least it can be examined in dispassionate detail. An ad for the seafood department of a New York City supermarket, for example, boasts of what it calls the "great taste of Dockside Freshness," and speaks of its "wide selection of the best seafood in season . . . rushed to the [store] in our own refrigerated trucks."

Its printed nature allows us to examine what that ad really says:

"Dockside Freshness," although it is endowed with capital letters, is never really explained, so the reader is left with the conclusion that the fish are as "fresh" as they are at "the dock," wherever that is. In the case of New York, it could mean the Fulton Fish Market, which has a dock, albeit one that is rarely used. Or it could mean the dock where the fish really come off the boat, which could be in Florida or Massachusetts or New Brunswick. Or it could mean a loading dock of any sort.

The "best seafood in season" means nothing, really, beyond the fact that the fish, considered "best" by some unnamed authority, were caught at the time of year when it is possible to catch them. That they are "rushed" means little except perhaps that the store's delivery people run red lights—hardly unusual for motorists in New York City, and certainly not occasion for taking out an ad in the *Times*. And it is scarcely remarkable that the fish are delivered in "refrigerated trucks." If they weren't, the store wouldn't need to run advertisements: People would know it was there from the smell.

In sum, the ad was used to convey little more than the idea of "freshness," which is something that is very important in the minds of people who want to eat fish. But no real information on the fish's freshness was offered.

Consumers would do well to learn to examine advertisements for what they don't say as well as what they do proclaim. As has been seen earlier, food coupons are an increasingly important form of advertising; a reader who is drawn to a Sunday-supplement coupon display because she wants to save money may spend some time reading the advertisements that go with the coupons. One such ad for Steakumm, "the 60-second sandwich steak" that "goes from freezer to frying pan without thawing and in just one minute [is] ready to eat," calms a reader's potential fears that this is another frozen, fabricated fugitive from the TV-dinner era with the statement that Steak-umms "are thinly sliced 100 percent pure beef with no added preservatives or salt."

The insistence on "100 percent" and "pure" should be a sufficient clue to the wary consumer that this product is not what it might appear to be. And sure enough, if the shopper were to examine the package closely in the store (or use a magnifying glass to check the tiny, faint lettering on the picture of the Steak-umm package that adorns the coupon), she would find that this 100 percent pure delight is actually flaked, chopped, and formed beef. In other words, "pure" and "with no added preservatives or salt," are perfectly within the letter of the law, but also extruded food and certainly not "steak" within the traditional meaning of the word.

It may be that the excesses of the very institution that spreads so much noninformation about food through its advertisements, television, ironically is helping to educate Americans not to trust what it tells them. A 1981 survey of American teenagers by the Simmons Market Research Bureau, Inc., found that of those surveyed—members of a generation that, more than any other, has taken television for granted as just another part of human existence—only 26 percent agreed with the statement that "advertising presents a true picture of products of well-known companies."

Nor should the consumer place much trust in government. While many people who work for government at all levels are quite dedicated, and all are consumers themselves, it must be remembered that government's first real loyalty, in food as in most other areas, is to business and industry. It is a shameful comment, but true: If the government says a certain food or process or additive is unsafe, the prudent consumer should believe the statement. If the government says it is safe, the consumer would do well to doubt the statement and question the agency's motive in making it.

Research continues, with the public footing the bill, into ways to enrich everyone in the food business *except* the consumer. Scientists at Cornell University in Ithaca, where New York's land-grant agricultural college is situated, recently announced that, in the words of a breathless press release, they were "using an obscure tomato strain from Brazil to improve the ability of American tomatoes to be stored dramatically longer than now possible." The writer of the handout then proceeded to equate the wretched mutant's staying power with freshness: "This could mean 'fresher' and tastier tomatoes for consumers."

Many consumers, concerned about the nutrition and safety implications of the processed foods they're subjected to in supermarkets, have shifted their loyalties to another sector of the marketplace, a small but prospering one: the "natural food" or "health food" store. But it would be wise to be cautious here, too; the retailers and the manufacturers who supply them seem to be scarcely more solicitous of the consumer's real well-being than the average supermarket. There have been charges of contamination in nutrition supplements. And in the summer of 1982 the Food and Drug Administration ruled that starch blockers, used by millions of people as a device for losing weight, were "unapproved new drugs" that may have produced adverse reactions. The distribution and sale of the products must be stopped, said the FDA, until the manufacturers had provided evidence that they worked and were safe. Later a federal district judge ordered the seven major manufacturers to destroy all the pills in their warehouses, commenting, "The human population of this country should not be used as guinea pigs by manufacturers attempting to cash in on so-called dietary weight control remedies."

Several "nutrition" and "health" food stores, including the large General Nutrition chain, ignored the ruling and continued to sell the pills, despite federal seizures. General Nutrition says it was not a party to the original litigation, and the chain maintains that starch blockers are a food, not a drug, and thus not subject to such control.

"Health" food stores are no place to save money on the food

budget, either. One Brooklyn importer of Middle Eastern foods, who operates his own retail store, once told the author that he was the source for brown rice for a number of "natural food" stores, one of which was situated less than two blocks from the importer's own store. The "natural food" store, which is no longer in business, was selling the rice as "organically grown" (the importer said he had no idea whether that was true) and for approximately twice as much as the importer was charging.

The case was not an isolated one. In January, 1983, the New York City Department of Consumer Affairs issued a report summarizing a four-month investigation into prices at "health" food stores. The department said it surveyed thirty food items and found the "health" food stores charged as much as 244 percent more than supermarkets for comparable foods. In one-third of the items, said the department, the specialty stores charged at least 100 percent more. And the agency said an independent laboratory analysis did not back up stores' claims that their "organic" foods had lower levels of pesticides than did conventionally grown foods.

The consumer might do well, in light of all this, to conclude that "health" and "natural" food stores, despite their advertised and perceived images, represent little more than successful and innovative merchandising gimmicks.

It would be wise, too, to adopt a skeptical attitude about restaurants and eating places in general. For a variety of reasons, almost all of them economic in nature, the food service industry is heading in the same direction as much of the food sold for home use: highly processed, prepared elsewhere, sealed in foil or plastic, frozen, "portion-controlled," minced, ground-up, extruded, flaked, formed, shaped, and contorted out of any semblance it might once have had to good-tasting, satisfying food. In the process, grievous damage is being done to the definition of food. Children who are forming their impressions of tastes today are getting totally warped ideas of what "fish" is (something that comes in uniform triangular shapes, has neither texture nor taste, and has a thick armor of bread), or what a "hamburger" tastes like (a frozen, equally tasteless, pablumized disk surrounded by red stuff and the precisely one and one-half slices of pickle that give it its only real flavor), or what "french fries" should taste like (salt).

Adults who spend hard-earned money on a night out at a white-tablecloth restaurant are more likely than ever before to eat "shrimp teriyaki" or "chicken Kiev" that was fabricated at some faraway place (but not Kyoto or Kiev), entombed in plastic, frozen, and shipped to the restaurant to await its crowning moments in a pot of boiling water or the microwave. "Home-baked bread" is actually a frozen material made in Anaheim, California, and the "house dressing" is more likely to come from a warehouse than the kitchen.

The "soup of the day"? It may well be one of Campbell's Chef's Kettle "food service pack soups," which, Campbell's tells the trade in an advertisement in *Restaurants and Institutions,* are so good "you'll want to call them your own." The soups "save money," says the ad, "because they save labor and energy. Just open a Chef's Kettle can, add water (milk with New England Clam Chowder), heat, and you're ready to serve soup that tastes like your own." For the profoundly thick-headed who might miss the message, Campbell's alludes twice more to the potential for fobbing off these products as a restaurant's own, including the promise that they are "made with all the special touches of premise-made."

The patron doesn't know most of this, of course, because there are no labels on restaurant foods, no ingredients list, no federally required terms such as "imitation" or "flaked and formed." There are certainly no rules that something must be identified as "premise-made."

There *are* menus, however, and a number of jurisdictions

have laws requiring a good deal of disclosure on those written documents. The theory behind this is that a menu should tell the truth, and that if it lies the public is being defrauded. But it is a rare menu that really tells the truth, and it is an even rarer municipal government that enforces such a law.

The District of Columbia got into the enforcement business in December, 1977, following a survey of food service places that showed widespread lying. "Menu disparities," as a district report put it, were found in 84.5 percent of the establishments checked.

Consumers were being deceived, the survey revealed, when they paid for "fresh-baked" and "homemade" bread products that actually came from commercial bakeries; "fresh" orange juice that was frozen; "Roquefort" cheese that was not from Roquefort; "cream" that was half and half; "roast sirloin beef" that was bottom round; "fresh" hamburger that was frozen; "baked ham" that was canned boiled ham; "chicken salad" that was commercial cooked turkey (quite a few of the restaurants used this one); numerous "fresh" fish and crustaceans that were frozen; "maple syrup" that wasn't maple syrup; and "Everglades frog legs" that were from India and "Louisiana frog legs" that had hopped all the way from Japan.

Part of the District of Columbia's enforcement plan includes releasing to the public lists of establishments that violate the law. After enforcement started, another survey was conducted and officials said they found the rate of compliance had risen markedly.

Without strong enforcement of menu honesty, the diner is at the mercy of a restaurateur who subscribes to the philosophy expressed a few years ago by a spokesman for the National Restaurant Association. Asked about the issue of truth-in-menu, he said the NRA didn't think menus should engage in "any direct misrepresentation," but he added, "We do not feel that a menu is a legal document." To explain in writing exactly what goes into the food, he said, would be "counterproductive." He added, "If somebody picked up that menu and were to read all the fine print about what goes into your cheese sandwich, they wouldn't be interested in buying the cheese sandwich." Precisely. (The association's present spokeswoman says a menu "should accurately describe what's there. But a menu is a menu; it is not a book." An excess of "minute detail," she said, might confuse the customer more than help him. The NRA furnishes its members with a document titled "Accuracy in Menu" that assists them in deciding how to advertise their products.)

There are a few things the consumer can do. If a quick look at the restaurant's physical plant reveals that after all the tables and ambiance are subtracted, there's very little room for a kitchen, then expect a very limited menu. If you get a menu that bristles with exotic-sounding dishes from the four corners of the earth, suspect microwave, boil-in-bag treachery. Particularly if the restaurant is not a well-known "fish house"—few cities, even large ones, have more than one of these anymore, and many have none—the diner may suspect that the promise of a large selection of fish, all labeled "fresh," is a bald lie.

There are some places that are not fish houses that go to great trouble to get fish and other foods that *are* fresh, and they hardly ever promise large selections. This is because it is very inefficient to have a refrigerator full of different fish species that, if they are not ordered and cooked immediately, must be discarded. The efficient alternative is freezing. There's nothing wrong with this, as long as the restaurant doesn't say, as many seem compelled to claim, that the fish are fresh.

Jovan Trboyevic is the proprietor of two eating places in Chicago, both of which offer what is known as the *nouvelle cuisine*, a menu characterized by great attention to taste and freshness, not meat-and-potatoes bulk, and (some critics say) by amazingly small portions and high prices. The owner goes

to considerable difficulty to obtain fresh, high-quality ingredients for his food: unpasteurized crabmeat from Maryland, crawfish from New Orleans, halibut from Boston,
mushrooms from Oregon. "Instead of going to the market," he
said in an interview not long ago, "I spend my time with air
schedules." Trboyevic was asked what advice he would offer
to a consumer upon entering a restaurant.

"First of all," he replied, "if you see it's a small restaurant
and a huge menu, then you know that something's wrong.
Something's got to give. If you see a list of six, seven fish on a
menu, you know they're all frozen. The fish list on a menu is a
very tricky thing.

"What else you look for on the menu is, is the restaurant
trying to do something unusual? And if they are, I would try
it certainly. The best policy for somebody going into the restaurant is to try to take the restaurant at its best. What do you
think they do best? What is easiest for them to do well?" By
this reasoning, said Trboyevic, he would feel better about
eating in a place that tried to do hamburgers very well than
one that boasted of accomplishments he knew were unlikely.

Some people, he acknowledged, would argue that such a
philosophy smacks of elitism. "They say, 'Who needs great
music all the time? Why not listen to some other music that's
not great?' I can listen to Muzak. Sometimes I have to. Would
I want to? Is it better than nothing? I think quiet air is better
than Muzak. I would rather have a piece of good bread and
a raw onion than to have a miserable concoction of something that's been done a thousand miles away three months
ago."

Only a small percentage of the American population can
afford to eat at restaurants such as Trboyevic's, and only the
rich can afford to eat there regularly (and relatively few can
get their hands on even good bread and a fine-tasting raw
onion). It is possible, however, for people who think of dining
out as a celebratory occasion (rather than as the necessity

that it may be for travelers and office workers) to skip a few trips to the small-kitchen, large-menu, microwave places, save their money, and splurge on a really great place every once in a while. It will have the effect, among others, of sharpening the diner's definitions of such foods as chicken, fish, and vegetables that don't come from a can or freezer.

In the past, a diner could enjoy at least even odds on getting decent, "premise-made" food by seeking out purveyors of regional favorites. Often situated behind unpretentious facades, these restaurants offered authentic, tasty food with no hint of microwave action (except for those Deep South places that boasted of their "radar ranges"). Sometimes the absolutely best places were cafeterias or no-tablecloth dining rooms that were open only for the noon rush-hour trade. The consumer's best bets were ethnic foods that hadn't yet been discovered by the mass merchandisers—biscuits and sausage-and-flour gravy in the Middle South, Tex-Mex foods throughout the Southwest and up through the upper Midwest and upper Pacific states (the restaurants followed the trails of chicano migrant workers, with the result that far better Mexican food may be eaten in Minneapolis than in New York City), fried catfish in the deepest of the South, amazingly good barbecue in eastern North Carolina, crabmeat on Maryland's Eastern Shore, imaginative salads in California, bagels in the large cities of the Northeast, and, for some odd reason, croissants in Washington.

Unfortunately, one's success with the exotic and semi-exotic foods is no longer guaranteed. Fast-food joints across the country offer a rubber imitation of "home-baked" breakfast biscuits, some of them stuffed with mucilage sausage; croissants have been defiled beyond belief; and food manufacturers, realizing that everyone who tries it likes the food of lower-income Mexico and the border, are in full production of products for sale in supermarkets and eating places that will do lasting damage to the definition of real Mexican food.

Del Monte, for example, started selling 5-ounce, individually packaged objects that in 1981, according to a vice-president, "accounted for more than half of the 56 percent growth rate in the frozen burrito segment." The executive was quoted in a trade publication as saying he thought the frozen burritos were popular for four reasons: "They are an excellent value; they are filling; they can be prepared quickly and easily; and children love them." There was no mention of the "segment's" taste.

It is an important part of the consumer's strategy to learn, and to remember, that regardless of what we may have grown up believing, the food business is just a business. Food may be sacred, but the food industry is not. It functions along the same lines of profit and loss that govern the steel industry, the textile business, and motion pictures. What we do with food when we get it can be exciting, delicious, glorious, or memorable. But while it is in the economic food chain it is simply a matter of selling it or smelling it. Once we have learned that, we have made an important step in our ability to cope with the business of food.

It also helps to know what foods are seasonal and when they are coming to market. This is one of those things, like walking, that is very basic but that Americans have gotten estranged from in recent years. Everyone knows that fresh corn is available starting late in the summer, but we tend to get hazy on other produce. It may be handy, for example, to know that if you live in Virginia and want to eat domestic apples, as opposed to those from Washington State that are kept in storage and released throughout the year except in midsummer, your local crop will be at its peak in the fall and will drop to practically nothing in the spring and early summer. Or that the majority of the apricots sold in the nation come to market in June, or that some produce is so widely grown or so popular—bananas, onions, and carrots among them—that each is in season all the time.

Some of this information is available on a regular basis in newspapers; two examples are the "Best Buys" feature in *The New York Times* food section and "The Produce Man," by Yas Matsui, in *The Sacramento Bee*. A detailed, month-by-month availability listing of sixty-five fruits and vegetables, titled "Supply Guide," can be purchased for 50 cents from the United Fresh Fruit and Vegetable Association, North Washington at Madison, Alexandria, Virginia, 22314.

An essential part of the consumer's strategy is an understanding of the geography of the marketplace itself—the reasons for end-aisle displays, the importance of variable-margin pricing, the causes of product proliferation. A shopper should spend a little time deciphering the messages the store is trying to send him and other consumers. Does the "unique selling proposition" mesh with the sort of buying the consumer wants to do? If not, perhaps she should do some shopping around.

Does the store seem to be trying to mislead its patrons? Some do, by advertising a sale price on a certain style of food—a canned tunafish, for instance—thus attracting people to the store, and then hiding it while putting a higher-priced version in the end-aisle display. There is a large supermarket near the author's home in Brooklyn that does this with some regularity; an excursion into the store, which has a multiplicity of other disadvantages as well, is always exciting and educational. (Why go at all, then? Because some of the store's bona fide sale items are worth the visit and ensuing search. Retailers refer to this despicable practice of shopping just for the specials, by the way, as "cherry picking.")

How does the store treat its house brands and generics? Does it make them readily available, or does it hide them behind a bushel of higher-priced national brands? All these can be helpful when the consumer sees them as what they are—distinct, deliberate, and important components of the retail foodselling operation, rather than just accidents of the marketplace.

There are few shopping aids, next to a clear head and a full stomach,* that are worth taking along on a supermarket shopping expedition, but three of them can be quite helpful: a pocket calculator for figuring out unit prices (even in stores that are required by law to post them, but often don't), a shopping list that's been prepared in advance, and a pocket-size Department of Agriculture publication titled *How to Buy Economically: A Food Buyer's Guide.*

The publication offers tips on purchasing meat and poultry, cutting up a chicken, buying eggs, and buying fruits and vegetables. (An abridged version of the United Fresh Fruit and Vegetable Association's seasonal "Supply Guide" is included.) And of particular usefulness is a guide to comparable prices for whole chickens and chicken parts.

The chart compares the price per pound for a whole fryer, weighing about 2¾ pounds, with the prices for parts. For example, if the whole price is 59 cents a pound, breast halves without ribs are an equally good buy at 80 cents a pound, thighs at 66 cents, thighs with drumsticks at 63 cents, drumsticks at 61 cents, and wings at 48 cents. For a whole chicken costing 79 cents a pound, the comparable prices for breast, thigh, thigh-drumstick, drumstick, and wing are $1.08, 88 cents, 85 cents, 81 cents, and 64 cents, respectively.

A similar chart calculates the prices of eggs by the pound. Small eggs costing 60 cents a pound, for example, are equal in price by weight to medium eggs at 70 cents, large eggs at 80 cents, and extra-large eggs at 90 cents.

---

* Economists say retailers adore people who shop on their way home from work. Hunger, they say, is one of the best promoters of impulse buying.

Until recently the booklet was free to the public from USDA. But the Reagan administration has put a stop to that and many other consumer benefits, and for a while it looked as if the booklet would simply disappear. That may yet happen, but as of the spring of 1983 it was available, at the outlandishly high price of $7, in a packet with four other pamphlets that used to be free, from the Government Printing Office. Wise consumers may want to check with the office of their Congressperson to see if copies have been printed for what is called "congressional use," which means free distribution by Representatives.

The shopping list is something that far from all shoppers carry into the store, and such lack of planning is felt by many experts to add directly to the food bill. Mary D. Zehner, an extension specialist in agricultural economics at Michigan State's Cooperative Extension Service, says, "The most effective strategy for controlling food costs" involves increasing "the amount of pre-planning prior to the main grocery trip, and knowing the current retail food price and supply situation."

The consumer can also try to determine, if only by simple observation and checking newspaper advertisements, the degree of concentration in retail stores in his hometown. If concentration is high, of course, there's not much the consumer can do to lower it.

"First of all," said economist John Connor jokingly, "move to a city that doesn't have high concentration. Washington is definitely a very poor city to live in.*

"So is Denver. Los Angeles, Chicago, New York are all good cities—very low concentrations of retail grocery store sales

* Connor left USDA in 1983 to teach at Purdue University, in West Lafayette, Indiana, where the four-firm retail concentration rate, according to a 1979 USDA-FTC survey, was almost as high as it was in Washington.

among the leading firms. Here in Washington the two leading
firms share about two-thirds of the market. Just *two firms*
have *two-thirds* of the market.

"I would then try to shop at an independently owned store,
but one that's still large enough to achieve economies of scale.
Clearly mom and pop stores, or stores that are very small in
size, are at an economy-of-scale disadvantage in comparison
to larger stores. So I would pick one of the nonleading chains
in the city because their prices would tend to be a few percentage points lower on average.

"Then I would adopt an experimental approach with respect to private-label and generic products. At least try them,
to see if I couldn't be satisfied with some of them. I'd certainly buy them more than once, because I think a lot of
people's reactions to these products is, 'It doesn't taste the
same as the leading brand.' Of course it doesn't taste the
same. It tastes 'off,' because the leading brand or the brand
you normally buy is the standard. You're always comparing
others to that standard. The other manufacturer may have a
slightly different standard—as good, in terms of quality of
ingredients or the quality of the process. But people become
habituated to their normal consumption curves, and anything
else tastes 'off.' It may not really be 'off' at all."

Larry Hamm of Michigan State was asked what—given his
detailed knowledge of the economics of the food business—he
kept in the front of his mind when he walked into a supermarket to shop.

"I always remember that I'm not buying food," he replied.
"I'm buying retail service. I'm buying the fact that somebody
else is putting together a whole series of products that I might
be interested in. And therefore I choose my stores, or where I
shop and what I shop for, by the combination of things that
are being provided.

"Any store can sell me Hellman's mayonnaise or Miracle
Whip or Velveeta or a head of lettuce or a chuck steak or a

A Strategy for the Consumer

Holly Farms chicken. What makes a *difference* to me is these other things which, for some reason, make me feel better or make me worry less. So I guess what I would recommend to consumers is that they explicitly recognize that those things are important to them, and that they consciously make the tradeoff between the prices and the quality of the food they're getting and these other retail services. And if they do that, they will be much better shoppers."

Once inside a grocery store, whether it be a modern super-market, a highway convenience store, or a neighborhood mom and pop operation, the consumer who is equipped with nei-ther shopping list, nor government chart, nor pocket cal-culator still has the most powerful ally of them all: the food label. That all-purpose block of type and graphics and color that appears prominently on a can, bottle, jar, box, or package of meat is the single most important communications device in the entire food system. It could be even more helpful. Labels could be used to convey a lot more information of value to the consumer, but also the consumer could learn a lot more from the labels now in use. Carol Tucker Foreman was a strong proponent of better labeling when she was Assistant Secretary of Agriculture. She says complete, understandable food labeling "gives the consumer the ability to walk into the marketplace and make a rational decision."

The rationale behind federal regulation of food labels was stated in the *Federal Register* back in 1979, when Foreman was in office, by the three government agencies most con-cerned with the matter—the Food and Drug Administration, what then was called USDA's Food Safety and Quality Service, and the Federal Trade Commission's Bureau of Consumer Protection. (Another agency, the Treasury De-partment's Bureau of Alcohol, Tobacco and Firearms, rather feebly regulates the labeling of alcoholic beverages.) The three agencies explained, in the course of proposing labeling changes (later upset by the Reagan administration):

> The purpose of food labeling is to enable consumers to select and use products that meet their individual needs and preferences. To achieve this purpose, labeling must provide sufficient information to enable the public to identify foods and their characteristics, including their ingredients and nutritional value. Effective labeling, moreover, must also present this information so that consumers can understand and use it in deciding what foods to buy.

The agencies agreed that discussions of labeling should be carried out with three major areas in mind. In public health, they said, "advances in technology have created more processed and fabricated foods, and . . . the relationship of nutrition to certain diseases is becoming better understood," making "accurate and informative labeling about a product's nutrient content and its other characteristics [of] even greater public health significance now than in the past."

The consumer's right to know was important because "innovations in food processing and packaging have made it increasingly difficult for consumers to judge a product's actual contents from its appearance, even for traditional foods." The third area was the economic impact of labeling regulations.

A handy "Consumer's Guide to Food Labels" was published in the June, 1977, issue of *FDA Consumer*, and has been reprinted as U.S. Department of Health and Human Services Publication No. (FDA) 77-2083, although its availability under the Reagan administration is uncertain. In brief, this is what food labels must have:

■ The name of the product. Even this must conform to certain rules. There must be a "common or usual" name that provides accurate information on what's inside the package. A manufacturer may color his package bright orange and employ various other devices to make you think there's orange juice inside, but if it's a tiny amount of orange juice with a lot of chemicals and water the name must say "orange drink" or something similar. If there's no juice at all inside, the label must state that fact.

Some foods must be labeled as "imitation." This is required when the product is not as nutritious as the one it replaces. If it *is* as nutritious, the manufacturer can give it a new name in order to avoid calling it "imitation." An example would be the egg substitute known as Egg Beaters. And if you want a one-cup, instant cream of chicken soup, check the product's name closely. It may say it is cream of chicken *flavored* soup, which means something else altogether and which calls for a close reading of the ingredients list. On some fabricated products the word "flavored" is very difficult to read, being printed in faint letters or a color that does not contrast with the rest of the package.

There are definitions for some traditional foods, such as peanut butter and ketchup, tomato paste and margarine, that are laid out, almost recipe-style, in the Code of Federal Regulations. For these products, detailed label information isn't required as long as they adhere to the standard.

For some products, regulations require specific quantities. A "high meat" baby food dinner must contain at least 26 percent meat; "lasagna with meat sauce" must contain at least 6 percent meat; something called "meat and vegetables" must be at least half meat; "chicken à la king" has to have at least 20 percent chicken. And "beef stroganoff," to mention one of the more properly maligned of the boil-in-bag, pseudo-gourmet, airline-food fabrications, must contain at least 45 percent fresh, uncooked beef or 30 percent cooked beef and one of the following: at least 10 percent sour cream; or a combination of at least 7.5 percent sour cream and 5 percent wine; or 9.5 percent whole milk, 2 percent sour cream, and 2.5 percent wine.

■ A statement of the net contents or net weight. This is the weight of everything inside the package.

■ The name and address of the manufacturer, packer, or distributor.

■ For foods that don't have a "standard of identity" such as peanut butter or margarine, a list of ingredients. This is probably the most important element of the label from the consumer's point of view: the place where he can learn if the product is loaded with salt, sugar, preservatives, or various bizarre chemicals that the consumer would just as soon not put in his mouth. And because the ingredients must be listed in order of prominence, by weight, with the largest amount first, the consumer can make valid comparisons between and among similar products. For one spaghetti sauce, the chief ingredient may be water, while in another, slightly more expensive, it may be tomatoes. Which is the better value?

Spices and colors and flavors, both artificial and derived from natural sources, are required to be listed on labels, but only by their general names ("spices," "flavorings," and "colorings"). The dairy lobby has seen to it that even artificial colors don't have to be listed on cheese, butter, and ice cream. One reason given for the lack of a requirement for specific labeling of flavors—and, when you think about it, a powerful argument *for* their listing—is that there are about 1,700 food flavors in existence, according to the government, and that as many as 125 of them can be used in a single processed food. The average number of flavors used in a processed food, excluding meat, poultry, and egg products, is about forty.

Precise definitions exist for those mysterious "poultry by-products" and "meat food products" that pop up from time to time in the ingredient lists of processed foods, particularly the junk varieties. "Meat food product," also known as "meat product," is "any food suitable for human consumption made from cattle, sheep, swine, or goats, containing more than 3 percent meat." "Poultry by-products" are "all edible parts of poultry other than sex glands and 'poultry meat'" ("poultry meat" is the stuff most normal people think of when they think of the meat of chickens and turkeys). And, for the meal's crowning touch, "poultry foods products" means "any food suitable for human consumption made from any domesticated bird, containing more than 2 percent poultry meat." And "vegetable (or plant) protein," be it textured or not, is just a highfalutin way of saying "soybeans."

The ingredients list is valuable, too, for learning the lessons of differentiation. Foods that are closer to the commodities they came from will have shorter lists (or none, because they are standard items), while the more differentiated, and more expensive, ones are likely to have longer lists and lists that are clogged with polysyllabic words from the chemical laboratory.

In any event, the ingredients list tells the consumer what he's really getting.* The list often serves as an effective antidote to the claims made by the manufacturer elsewhere on the packaging or in advertising.

■ Nutrition information, for foods to which nutrients have been added or for which nutritional claims have been made. These labels explain how many calories, protein,

---

* It will not, however, go very far toward explaining what those polysyllabic words mean in terms of safety and nutrition. For that, one needs a guide such as Michael F. Jacobson's *Eater's Digest: The Consumer's Factbook of Food Additives,* Updated Edition (Garden City, N.Y.: Anchor, 1976). Another helpful publication is *More Than You Ever Thought You Would Know About Food Additives,* by Phyllis Lehmann, and its accompanying "Additives Index," HHS Publication No. (FDA) 82-2160, published by the Department of Health and Human Services, 5600 Fishers Lane, Rockville, Maryland, 20857.

carbohydrate, and fat are in a serving of the product, and list the percentages of the national Recommended Daily Allowances of protein and seven key vitamins and minerals. Figures on other substances, such as sodium, may be displayed at the manufacturer's option.

The RDA information is not as useful as it could be, since nutritional needs differ according to the eater's age and size, and these differences are not taken into account on the label. And the "serving sizes" that are quoted are often confusing as well. The three regulatory agencies, in their 1979 document, agreed that "some manufacturers use overly large serving sizes to inflate the nutritional value of their products; others keep serving sizes rather small, to avoid giving the appearance that the foods contain large quantities of undesirable components. Different serving sizes within a product class, moreover, make product comparisons difficult." Still, useful nutritional labeling could be worked out if government and industry were interested and if consumers exerted sufficient pressure.

Another bit of information that may appear on food labels is a lot less useful to the consumer than it ought to be. That is the number or letter that denotes the food's *grade.*

Grading was originally developed as a language by which various members of the food chain (but not necessarily consumers) could refer to food they couldn't see. A grower in Harlingen, Texas, could describe her sweet peppers on the telephone as "some U.S. Fancy and some U.S. No. 1," and the broker or wholesaler in Boston would know that both batches were, in the words of the definition adopted by USDA, "mature green sweet peppers of similar varietal characteristics" which were firm and free from injuries caused by mechanical means, sunscald, sunburn, freezing, decay, scars, hail, disease, and insects. But the broker would further know that the Fancy peppers were "well shaped," while the No. 1s were only "fairly well shaped," and that the Fancies were at least 3 inches in diameter and length, while the others could be ½ inch smaller.

Although all this was of limited usefulness to the public, or that portion of it that does not carry around copies of *United States Standards for Grades* of vegetables and fruit, some merchandisers hit upon the idea of putting grades (when they sounded good) on their labels to give their products what sounded like a seal of federal approval. This has been especially true in the labeling of meat, where consumers may make spending choices based on whether a product is graded USDA Prime, Choice, or Good.

But the rules are so confusing as to limit their value tremendously, except as an agent of marketplace confusion. For one thing, a lot of shoppers confuse food grading with food inspection, with which it has no connection. Nor does grading offer any gauge of nutrition. "Nutritional aspects of a product are not currently part of any grade standard," said USDA in 1980. "In most instances, the nutritional value is the same for all grades within a specific product."

And confusion is rampant even when the consumer does know what grading is. U.S. No. 1 is the third grade in fresh apples, while U.S. No. 1 is the top grade in summer and fall pears. With carrots it's even more absurd: The top grade for *bunched* carrots is U.S. No. 1, while for *topped* carrots it is U.S. Extra No. 1, according to the federal standards in use recently at the Boston Terminal Market. For the time being, at least, food grades are more likely to confuse a consumer than to help.

For all its value to the consumer, labeling presents several other areas where great improvement is needed. In many cases, that improvement was begun by people such as Carol Tucker Foreman in the Carter administration, then abandoned as quickly as possible by their successors under Ronald Reagan.

The Federal Trade Commission was well on its way to clarifying the mess that surrounds the term "natural" with a rule that foods thus advertised could not contain synthetic or artificial ingredients and could not be more than "minimally processed." It was a reasonable enough regulation, but in the end the commission scuttled it, opening wide the doors to the false claims of "natural" that now ring through the market-place.

Some existing regulations simply aren't being enforced. Under FDA regulations, all ingredients added to raw agricultural products except pesticides—such as waxes and colors and chemicals to produce cosmetic effects—must be named on labels.* That means fruits and vegetables found in a greengrocer's or supermarket's produce department. Says the government: "If these commodities are shipped in a bulk container and the product is sold at retail from that container, the declaration must be visible to the purchaser. If the raw commodities are sold from a container other than the shipping box, then placards or signs must be used to convey information on colors, preservatives, and waxes." The shopper who sees such labeling is witnessing an extraordinary event indeed.

Dating of food products is another idea whose time has not yet come for the consumer. Although many packages have dates printed or embossed on them, often the dates are in code that is decipherable only to the manufacturer and distributor and—supposedly, but not always in practice—to the retailer. Even if they appeared *en clair* they might be confus-

---

* Fungicides, bactericides, growth regulators, chemicals that inhibit ripening, and dyes are sometimes mixed in with waxes and applied to a variety of fruits and vegetables, according to the FDA. The Center for Science in the Public Interest has estimated that about 50 percent of the fresh tomatoes, 75 percent of the cucumbers, and 35 to 40 percent of the fresh apples are waxed. Waxes, says FDA, usually are a combination of shellac, carnauba, polyethylene, or paraffin.

ing, inasmuch as some represent a date by which the product should be used, some the last date on which it is supposed to be sold, and some the date of manufacture. A careful shopper, knowing the codes, would be able to buy the freshest products, or at least to avoid the stale ones.

Little effort has been made to make the coded information available to the public, however, although several manufacturers have moved to print intelligible "use by" dates on their products, particularly processed meats. This is called "open dating," and advocates of consumer causes feel it is an important addition to the shopper's toolbox.

At least one attempt has been made to decode some of the numbers and to present them to the public, although it is limited by the fact that it includes information only from companies willing to cooperate. The pocket-size booklet *Blind Dates: How to Break the Codes on the Foods You Buy* is published by the New York State Consumer Protection Board, 99 Washington Avenue, Albany, New York, 12210, and is free for the asking. It also decodes the "establishment" or plant numbers that are required in New York State for dairy products.

11

Action

There are some actions that the typical consumer of food can take that are less passive than studying labels and learning the geography of the supermarket, as worthy as these strategies may be. There are actions that in many cases will provide immediate payoffs in terms of money, in the quality of food, more than likely in nutrition, and in satisfaction. That last benefit, although impossible to define or to translate into quantifiable results, is nonetheless a precious accomplishment. It reminds the consumer that she is something more than a *victim* of the food system, something more than just the willing (and bumbling, gullible, stereotypical television-commercial) recipient of whatever the system chooses, literally, to dish out.

It reminds her that she can call some of the shots. Not all of them, by any means, for there are very few of us remaining in these days of nine-digit zip codes who have anything approaching an adequate mastery of our own destinies. But some of the shots, with the promise of more.

Food people are constantly explaining what they are doing as a *reaction* to what the consumers are demanding. While far too frequently this is just an excuse for some of the excesses and wastes of the system, it also contains a measure of truth, as a look at the nearest produce market confirms. Consumers really do want tomatoes in February and strawberries in March, and as long as they are willing to pay the freight (and a number of middlemen at points along the freight line) there will be farmers, shippers, brokers, wholesalers, processors, manufacturers, and retailers willing and happy to sell them.

Steve Goldberg is the manager of the Boston branch of C.H. Robinson Company, a food brokerage that operates nationwide. It is a high-pressure job, with telephones constantly ringing and deals constantly being struck in matters of fresh produce that, in Goldberg's case, feeds much of the New England market. The broker was asked if it bothered him that a head of lettuce that was grown in California should travel 3,000 miles to a dining table in Boston. He replied without hesitation.

"If the product is good, if it tastes good and looks good and the consumer will *buy* it, why not?" he said. "If they can do it more efficiently, and the consumer will pay for the product, why not? If it's a good product, and the housewife can afford it, why not? It's fresh. We have Chilean grapes in February. Who is to say that it's wrong to have grapes in February? If you want it, what's wrong with cantaloupes in January? There's a market for it; what's wrong with it?

"The law of supply and demand holds forth as much in the produce industry as in any other industry. Because it's a perishable commodity. It's not a commodity that you can generally store for long periods of time like you store plastic. It's *alive*. And if you have x amount of apples, and you have a price on these apples, and if there are too many apples to warrant that price, then the price is going to go down, isn't it? The final answer to anything in regards to produce, whether it's too high or too cheap, is the consumer."

Goldberg's argument is a strong one. But some people worry about the costs of those consumer demands. They worry about the enormous expenditures of time and energy that are involved in shipping across the nation something that could be grown practically anywhere. They may understand the argument about grapes in February in the colder parts of the nation, but what about grapes in August when those regions have warmed up? Why do the horrid-tasting fruits still have to taste that way, come all that distance, during the local growing season as well? In the past few years these issues have become less matters of principle and more ones of practicality because energy is no longer inexpensive. It suddenly costs a lot of very real, tangible money to ship produce from California to Boston—$3,000 to $4,000 for a truckload, as a matter of fact.

Some people worry, too, about the supermarket phenomenon that produces both greater variety, in terms of sheer numbers of seemingly different products, and less real diversity. If everything is to be differentiated because the manufacturers have discovered their economic security lies in getting away from basic, commodity-type articles, then what will happen to those commodities? They probably won't disappear, but won't they become more difficult to find, and perhaps more costly because there's no competition over them?

We have every reason to fear that the economic future of the food business will be one of increasing concentration, declining competition, and—it goes without saying—higher prices and prices that are even less controlled by the public's willingness to pay. Steve Goldberg's version of the law of supply and demand in the produce business would not necessarily apply in the canned artichoke heart business if there were only one canner of artichoke hearts.

And some people worry about food's even more fundamental characteristics. They worry that all the signs point to a depressing decline in food's nutritional quality and in its flavor—the major reasons we eat the stuff to begin with.

There are many who share these concerns, but not everyone can attempt to do something about them. Changing a system—or, more likely, changing one's relationship to a system—cannot be accomplished by part-time tinkering. It takes effort and time, and these are two things most people don't have surpluses of. But there are many actions that do not require full-time commitments and that provide great satisfaction for the consumer.

There is, for example, a great deal of information about the food system that is free for the asking and that can result in savings of time and money. Although the federal government presently considers aiding the consumer too controversial an undertaking, some components of the industry itself make available basic and useful tips. The consumer just has to keep always in mind the fact that the authors of this information see as their main aim the selling of whatever it is they are selling.

Most frequently the shopper encounters this information in supermarkets, particularly at those run by chains that are pushing a strong image of public accountability. Some stores have elaborate kiosks filled with leaflets explaining various food processes, recipes, and storage tips, and often they even have bulletin boards that are open to the public. Some have resident home economists to answer specific questions. In California, the Albertson's chain makes a regular production out of these leaflets, with well-written, pithy information on everything from how to select wine and understanding the metric system to tips on ethnic cooking and standard recipes. Other leaflets are less ordinary: an explanation of the chain's

own first-, second-, and third-label house brands; a primer on
generics; recipes for meatless main dishes; details on a relatively new packaging technique that uses Cryovac plastic film
to protect cuts of meat that are larger than those consumers
are used to; and, wonder of wonders, a pamphlet describing
the same government-compiled dietary guidelines that the
Reagan administration tried to suppress. And many of the
recipes for ordinary foods offered by Albertson's do not call,
as does much industry literature, for processed ingredients
("Add one can green beans") but rather assume the cook will
be working from scratch.

The new meat packaging process, referred to in the trade as
"subprimal" meat, is explained by many supermarket bro-
chures around the country because the stores realize customers need education before they'll buy the product; the
oxygen-deprived meat looks strangely gray when the wrap-
ping is first removed. The Stop & Shop chain in New England
publishes a great deal of informative material that could
almost be labeled "consumerist" in tone. Supermarkets in
New York City generally ignore this opportunity to assist
their customers, just as the great majority of them ignore
other common-sense rules such as cleanliness, freedom from
aisle congestion, and courtesy. (Indeed, it could be specu-
lated that if New York City grocers had "courtesy desks," as
the information and check-cashing cubicles are called elsewhere, they would immediately change their name to "insult
centers.")

Many food experts feel that consumers can save a lot of
time, money, and aggravation by cooking meals ahead of time
—using less hectic moments such as weekends to make what
some call "on-purpose leftovers" for freezing or other storage
until later in the week, when time is shorter. The system lends
itself to certain sorts of food, such as spaghetti sauce or
cooked dried beans, some of which actually improve the second or third time around.

A subcategory of on-purpose leftovers is the home preparation of "convenience foods"—not the sorts of "convenience
foods" that more accurately could be labeled "junk foods" but
rather those represented by boil-in-bag frozen entrées and
others that promise savings in time and energy.

Two USDA staffers who studied this, Larry G. Traub and
Dianne D. Odland, looked at canned and frozen vegetables
and fruits, which many people think of as commodities, as
well as the more highly differentiated concoctions such as
frozen fried chicken and frozen, minced, extruded, breaded,
and prefried shrimp, which only masochists would prepare at
home. They found that the processed versions cost slightly
more, cost somewhat less when the cook's time and fuel were
figured in, and impressed a taste panel as having roughly the
same eating quality as the home-prepared items.

All of which sounds like a strong case for frozen entrées,
except for a few other findings. The cost results failed to take
into consideration the fact that most of the convenience foods
come in small portions, while their homemade counterparts
have a built-in leftover factor that greatly reduces their cost
and preparation time per serving. Furthermore, the convenience foods were stingy on important ingredients:
"Chicken meat accounted for 38 percent of the weight of
home-prepared chicken chow mein and only about 5 percent
of the weight of the frozen or canned product," wrote the
researchers. And "the majority of convenience products included in this study contained a number of additives" and
devices for puffing up the product's weight and bulk, such as
soy protein. Although several processors have announced
since the study was done that they were leaving preservatives
and other controversial additives out of many of their lines of
convenience foods, making it at home remains the best way to
control quality, taste, and what goes into the stuff one eats.

For many consumers, stocking up is a useful way to establish some control over their food expenditures. If they have

the shelf and freezer space, they can buy staple foods in case lots or bulk when the prices are low. And for millions of others, stocking up is something that's done each summer when the backyard harvest is in.

The government has paid little attention to home growing, no doubt because the avocation has few lobbyists in Washington. The 601-page official volume *Agricultural Statistics 1981* contains no references to home gardening, while it does manage to record the number of mountain goats, bighorn sheep, peccaries, and wild boar "harvested" on National Forest System land. It is believed, however, that about half of all U.S. households have some sort of fruit or vegetable gardens, and that the most popular vegetables are tomatoes, beans, cucumbers, peppers, radishes, scallions, lettuce, onions, carrots, and corn, and that the favorite fruits are strawberries and apples. Home gardens can exist practically anywhere, but they have been popping up in increasing numbers recently on the urban landscape—on rooftops, in brownstone window boxes, and in abandoned lots.

Urban agriculture is, in fact, just another manifestation of the fact that a consumer who wants to get the most out of his food system might well want to consider moving to the big city.

That suggestion is more than a bit facetious, since most people's occupations don't allow them all that much choice about where they live and since, for many, starving may be preferable to enduring some of the emotional and physical hardships of big-city living. But it does appear that residents of large, densely populated urban areas have quite a few advantages over their suburban and rural cousins when it comes to food.

In many cities, as has been seen, there is abundant competition among retail food dealers for the consumer's dollar, with the result that the evils of concentration are reduced and prices are often quite low.

There is also ethnic diversity, which means ethnic eating places (often ranging from inexpensive to extra-fancy) and the availability of foods that might have been ignored before. By the time the Szechwan style of spicy Chinese cooking was catching on in the smaller towns of the country, New York's jaded diners, who had cleared their sinuses on Szechwan years before, were moving into Hunan-style food, which is hotter. A small but important wave of immigration from India in recent years has turned a few blocks in two parts of Manhattan into neighborhoods of Indian condiment and spice shops and eating places, running from cafeteria to white-tablecloth. A truly elegant and expensive Indian restaurant is well established in midtown, and smaller, storefront operations are appearing in the other boroughs. It has been the same with every large wave of immigrants to the city.

Life in the city is a life in ferment, a life of abrasion, a life filled with crises and dangers and insults and struggles for breathing room. In such an environment, the issues surrounding food become very important. They are, very literally, gut issues.

The big-city residents, being deprived of cows, cornfields, and collards, are likely to attach a higher value to such things than those who take them for granted—just as it is urban people, not country people, who lead the fights to preserve wilderness. And so it should not be surprising that community gardens, which for many urban people are the equivalent of home growing, are powerful tools of community organizing, almost on a par with such issues as housing, sanitation, and the quality of education.

City folk have traditionally sought out vacant plots of land to cultivate in times of uncertainty. The payoffs were deliciously clear: vegetables and fruits that were essentially "free" in exchange for labor and a small investment in seed and fertilizer, and food that was a good deal fresher than the store-bought kind. Another payoff has been a heightened sense of community among the gardeners that has made life in the city considerably more bearable.

Gregory R. Stack is an extension adviser and special urban gardening project leader for the University of Illinois's Co-operative Extension Service, an agency that ordinarily is more at home in a heroic-sized soybean field than in fourteenth-floor offices of a building on South Wabash Avenue in downtown Chicago. The project assists community groups in finding and farming community gardens in odd places around the city—on vacant lots, on government property, along the Chicago Transit Authority's right-of-way, and on the roof of a senior citizen housing project. The average size of a garden, he said in an interview, was around 330 square feet (the average Illinois farm is a little under 12 million square feet). "And a lot of them," he said, "are long and narrow like a bowling alley."

A major concern of urban gardeners might be called "plant security"—the protection of their provender from the rampant criminality that is said to hold urban life in its clutches. But Stack and his colleagues surveyed urban gardeners in Chicago and found that the number-one problem was something else.

"Insects," he said. "Fifty-two percent said insects were their major problem. Forty-two percent said they had too much rain. Forty-*one* percent said there was not *enough* rain. Eighteen percent said vandalism was a major problem for them, which to me sounds like not a heck of a lot." Stack said he believed one reason vandalism was minimized was the gardeners' use of snow fencing, borrowed for the summer from the state highway department. The fencing would not keep even a dyspeptic vandal out of a garden, he said, but it did serve to define turf. "It says, 'This is mine, and this is yours, and stay away from mine.'"

Stack found that Chicagoans who get involved in community gardening tend to raise crops that are staples of their

ethnic backgrounds—greens in black neighborhoods, tomatoes and carrots in the better-off white sections—but some of
the harvests are surprising. Newly arrived Laotian refugees,
he said, for some reason planted a lot of mint, "just flat-out
mint." Several people grew hops, and Stack assumed they
were carrying on the midwestern tradition of brewing beer at
home.

There are multiple benefits to urban gardening, but Gregory Stack said he thought one of the best was related neither
to economics nor to the high quality and taste of food so fresh
it begs to be eaten on the way home from the garden. "We
find that gardening is therapeutic to people who live in the
city," he said. "It gives them something to do, it gives them a
sense of accomplishment. This is the biggest thing, I think:
the sense of accomplishment. Some of these neighborhoods
don't have so much more they can accomplish because they're
so run-down.

"So if someone can grow a nice, green garden here in the
midst of all this garbage, then they get a sense of accomplishment. I think it's something that'll be here for quite a long
time."

The Illinois extension service's interest in community gardening is an example of how government can help not only
those who produce and manufacture food but also those who
consume it and are willing to take action to improve their
position in the food chain. Unfortunately, such examples are
hard to find. Although the man who was Illinois's agricultural
commissioner went on to become the overseer of the entire
nation's agricultural policy in the Reagan administration,
government at the national level has shown only cursory interest in consumer food issues beyond basic matters of safety—
and, as we have seen before, is trying to modify even that
obligation.

There are some individuals and organizations that are very much on the consumer's side, however, and they function at all levels, be they local, state, regional, or national. Together, they make up a formidable collection of advocates for improvement in the American food system, and a consumer who wants to improve his situation would do well to listen to them. These partisans, who might fall into the general category of "food activists," operate out of a diversity of motives and with a variety of aims. Some concentrate on the problems of world hunger and the special obligation of the United States, as the wealthiest nation in that world, to exert a proportional amount of energy toward solving those problems. Some concentrate on issues of quality, some on economy, some on safety, quite a few on governmental food policy.

Most, however, are bothered by the fact that the system, as efficient and as competitive as it is, does not treat people as they should be treated. The feeling was expressed by John R. Peirce, who serves the California Church Council's Office of State Affairs as its food policy advocate. Like many others who advocate a variety of interests before the California state government, Peirce has an office alongside the spacious, palm-covered state capitol grounds in Sacramento. Unlike most lobbyists, he has his office in a church.

"There are basically some profound discrepancies in our society," said Peirce one day in that office, "not only in the distribution of resources but in the whole societal priority and food distribution system. They raise questions of how we are going to treat those people who are in positions of no power, the downtrodden and the needy and the poor. What we're trying to address, particularly those of us representing the religious community, are the fundamental issues of societal priorities.

"I believe that every person in this country and around the world has a fundamental right to an adequate diet. And in point of fact, the globe currently produces enough to adequately feed every person on it. So it's not a matter of production; it's a matter of distribution. That's part of what we're trying to address."

Frances Moore Lappé, an author and the director of the San Francisco–based Institute for Food and Development Policy, is one of the advocates who agrees strongly that it is not the stereotypical "world food shortage" that is to blame for many of the system's problems, but rather the economic system that controls what food is produced and what happens to it after it is harvested.

Lappé's books make the point, as she writes with Joseph Collins in *Food First: Beyond the Myth of Scarcity*, that*

> We need to build a movement . . . that lays bare the truth that it is a single system, supported by governments, corporations, and landed elites, that is undermining food security both in our country and abroad. The forces in the Third World that cut people out of the production process, and therefore out of consumption, turn out to be the same forces that have converted our food system into one of the most tightly controlled sectors of our own economy.

The typical manufacturer's claim that it is giving the public the foods it demands, said Lappé in an interview in San Francisco, isn't correct, since manufacturers control food advertising and thus limit the public's knowledge of food to what *they* want consumers to know. If the system really did seek the public's opinion, she said, it would find that consumers want cheaper food, fewer chemicals in their food, and higher-quality and better-tasting produce. Price, she said, would be high on the list.

Her overall goal, said Lappé, is to convince people that it is possible on a world scale to overcome the deficiencies of price

---

* Revised and updated edition (New York: Ballantine Books, 1978).

and quality. "The way I phrase it," she said, "is 'reuniting the production of food with human need.' Those have become totally separated in our system. Food is just like any other commodity, just like any other raw material which is manipulated in whatever way will bring the most profit to the processors. One part of the solution is the idea of reuniting the production with the basic human need for food. And that is happening in some societies. In a country like China, for example, everybody's basic food needs are guaranteed. There are differences in income and so forth, but nobody is allowed to starve."

What Lappé wants, she said, is a tall order: "totally rethinking and restructuring the economic ground rules." It is a restructuring that cannot be done halfway. "I don't think that you can take any one piece and find the solution," she said. "The answers will have to come in some form of democratic planning. 'Planning' is almost as scary a word to Americans as 'communism,' unfortunately. People think of a kind of gray Politburo sitting there handing down production quotas and telling people what to grow. Most Americans don't have experience with any form of group decision-making and planning on any level. In their workplaces they're not part of the planning for their company. So when we think of 'planning' our imaginations block, and all we think of are top-down models.

"What we're saying is that there *is* planning. A great deal of planning goes on in our country. It is a very antidemocratic planning. It's planning of a sort where those who have the most money can make their proportionate demands felt in the marketplace and they can skew production toward luxury items while basic needs are neglected. . . . What I'm saying is that we have to begin to experiment with other forms."

Some of the "other forms" Lappé suggests would curl the hair of most powerful elements of the food chain: a control on advertising; a national planning structure that decides what foods the nation needs and how much; protections against wrongful control of the land used in production. "It would mean," she said, "that we would have to get over all the mythology about the marketplace's being the best allocator of our resources. I don't think there's any need to totally do away with the marketplace. I think it's a very neat way to find out what people want. But I think we need some kind of a combination of relying on the marketplace while at the same time not being controlled by the market.

"So my mission is to somehow break through some of the myths and fears. I don't have a blueprint for what ought to be done. I just carry with me the notion that something new *is* possible under the sun. In other words, people haven't experimented with every possibility of how economic and political systems can be organized."

Lappé is a slender, almost shy person who says she came by her convictions on her own, just by "following my nose" and asking questions about how the system works and why it doesn't work better. She is in great demand as a lecturer, and she always reminds her audience that if an ordinary person like her can get interested in food policy and try to do something about inequities, anybody can. Asked if she thought her work was perceived as a threat by members of the system she seeks to change, she said she doubted it. "I really don't think that we're seen as very much of a threat," she said. Lappé's *Diet for a Small Planet*, however, has sold well over 2 million copies around the world. Somebody is listening.

The Basic and Traditional Food Association is another organization that seeks change in the food system. Its primary goal, says the Washington-based group, "is to educate the general public about food and nutrition, and to focus attention on those foods which are inherently delightful, nutritious, and safe." Those foods, as might be expected, are the ones the association defines as basic and traditional ones.

"Basic" foods, according to the group's literature, are "the products of nature. They are whole foods, unpartitioned and unrefined, and are the foundation of our nutritional well-being." They include fruits and vegetables, whole grains, nuts, milk, fish, poultry, beef, pork, lamb, and some others, such as herbs and spices, coffee and tea, and honey, that are valued for characteristics other than nutritional ones.

"Traditional" foods are defined as " 'made dishes,' the products of centuries of human creativity," and they include breads, cheeses, soups, sausages, candies, beer and wines, and other foods "made in traditional ways with traditional ingredients."

The association invites public memberships, but it also welcomes representatives of companies that make basic and traditional foods. Since it is situated in Washington, much of its work is aimed at influencing legislation on such matters as nutrition, labeling, and advertising directed at children. It also publishes an attractive and useful wall chart ranking dozens of foods and quasi-foods according to their "Nutrition Scores," which are determined by judging their nutrients against their calories. Turnip greens are at the top of the list, followed by parsley, bell peppers, and (no surprise to Popeye followers) spinach, while scores of zero were shared by white sugar, fats and oils, chewing gum, cola, and alcohol.

Another organization with unquestioned loyalty to the consumer of food and all other things is Consumers Union. The union, which has published the monthly magazine *Consumer Reports* since 1936, accepts no advertising. It tests products (which it buys with its own money, anonymously, at stores around the nation) and presents the results, often accompanied by detailed ratings, in thorough, consistently enlightening articles. In addition, the magazine serves as a general watchdog on consumer issues, and the union frequently testifies on consumer legislation.

Sample undertakings have included bologna, which the magazine called "an expensive provider of protein" that "doesn't deserve its popularity," and samples of which were found to be "bland" and "adhesive" and to have "caused mouth burn" or to sport a "distinct grayish-brown, yellow, or green color." Some of the frozen fried chicken CU tested had "juicy meat," but other brands had "slightly chalky" light meat. Frozen fish portions "didn't taste or smell enough like fresh fish. But they *are* convenient." One of the magazine's most damning indictments, and one that is handed down against an alarming number of processed foods, is that something has a "cardboard taste."

In many cases, when *Consumer Reports* presents an article on processed foods it supplies equivalent information, including recipes and prices per portion, on the same food prepared at home—*non*-frozen fried chicken, *un*-cardboardy fish, soups that *don't* have too much salt. The prices are almost always lower for the home-prepared version, leading a reader to suspect that CU's testing methods are more anchored on practicality than were those of the USDA researchers cited earlier. Over the years the magazine has tested and reported on cake mixes, turkeys, canned salmon, milk, fresh chicken, frozen pizza, hot dogs, canned vegetables, fresh potatoes, instant potatoes, yogurt, orange drink mixes, instant nonfat dry milk, and scores of others. It is the best single source of consistent, useful, practical information for a consumer who wants to know more about what she is eating and what can be done about it.

Robert Rodale is another of the advocates. Perhaps best known as a proponent of organic gardening and farming, his Rodale Press is the publisher of a number of magazines, including *Prevention*, which promote personal health. Rodale also presides over a farm that practices what he and his colleagues preach, and the whole operation is situated in Emmaus, Pennsylvania, in what the Rodale Press letterhead refers to as "Organic Park."

A few years ago Rodale started a new venture called the

Cornucopia Project. It was intended, he told those who responded to newspaper advertisements, to perform two functions: to provide information to consumers who want to do something about food prices and other problems, and "to generate information that might be useful to government agencies, planners, farmers, and companies that serve the food industry." Wrote Rodale in a series of articles in his publication *Organic Gardening:* "It is my conviction that America's vast natural resources can yet be turned into a veritable horn of plenty for centuries to come. But we need to unhook ourselves from the wasteful and destructive habits that have been so characteristic of our past." Rodale, like many others who have studied the food system, has not uncovered a convenient villain:

> My belief is that there is not a conspiracy to cause the destruction of that much land, or to give control of the food system to a few businessmen, or to contrive energy shortages to increase food prices. But I also believe that many important people are sitting on their hands and not doing much to prevent such happenings, figuring that their organizations will profit mightily when these factors cause a sellers' market in food to occur. That conspiracy could be somewhat passive, in the sense that the participants don't have a clear plan to make it occur. But the fact that saving our land for the production of food or decentralizing the control of our food system is not a high priority is clear evidence that there is at least a conspiracy of silence and inaction.

In its first couple of years the Cornucopia Project has produced a variety of information that is useful to the consumer who wants to take some action to improve his position in the food system. Its publications urge more home growing of food, advise manufacturers who want to prepare for an uncertain future, assess food situations in Maine and Pennsylvania, explain how one might conduct a similar assessment in his own home state, discuss growing foods in the city, and provide information on legislation affecting the system.

One of the most competent and aggressive of the consumer organizations is the Center for Science in the Public Interest, a nonprofit, tax-exempt group based in Washington that defines itself as "concerned with the impact of technology on society." Most of its work has been done on food and nutrition problems. Although the twelve-year-old organization is small by some standards, with a tiny staff and a membership of around 30,000, it turns out a constant stream of highly informative publications. It, too, produces wall charts, including a "Nutrition Scoreboard" listing hundreds of foods and a "Chef Pennypincher's Shopping Guide" that contains tips on how to save from 10 to 70 percent on food costs.

CSPI also publishes, ten times a year, *Nutrition Action*, a magazine containing articles on deceptive advertising and labeling practices, basic information on foods, recipes for nutritious vegetables and other foods, and examinations of institutions such as the dairy lobby, the diet pill industry, and the school lunch program. A "Food Porn" award is given each issue to products that CSPI feels are most obscene; winners have included Frito-Lay potato chips (for comparing 1 ounce of the product with 1 cup of milk and claiming the chips had fewer calories—but saying nothing about nutrients), Pillsbury's "Applesauce Spice Cake Mix" (with no applesauce), Nabisco's spray-can processed cheese spread, and Campbell's attempts to turn fresh mushrooms into a branded item.

Michael Jacobson is the center's executive director. An MIT-trained microbiologist who went to Washington in 1970 to work with Ralph Nader, Jacobson is an energetic and articulate writer, witness before congressional committees, and participant in television talk shows. He was interviewed not long ago at his desk, where he was finishing his lunch, a baked sweet potato without butter, salt, or Kraft Miniature Marshmallows.

"The ease with which processed foods can be prepared is sometimes less than what we're led to believe," he said. "Restaurant food's the same way. People say they have to go to restaurants because they don't have time to make a lunch. It clearly takes less time to make a lunch at home than to walk to a restaurant, wait for service, and so on—and then you pay through the nose. There are many natural foods that are extremely convenient. I put that sweet potato in the oven; forty-five minutes later I came back. And it tastes wonderful! Took no time; took me maybe a minute to shop for it; a minute to walk downstairs, turn on the oven, and come back upstairs; and then I ate it. It's one of the most nutritious foods you can get. You can't make it more convenient. And it's dirt cheap. It cost maybe a nickel.

"There's no encouragement to eat easy-to-prepare natural foods," Jacobson continued. "You never see an ad explaining how to make yogurt at home. Yogurt is a processed food: They take milk and turn it into milk, basically. They add some germs to it. You could do that at home, too. It takes maybe ten minutes to make a quart of yogurt.* But there are never any commercials for that because there's no profit in it."

Jacobson was asked why, then, so many people insisted on eating processed foods and patronizing restaurants at lunchtime. "I think it's laziness," he replied. "When I fixed that potato, I had to think: How do you cook a potato? What temperature should it be at, how long should it be in, what kind of a potato should I cook? There aren't any instructions on a

---

* "Chef Pennypincher's" recipe calls for heating a quart of milk to 140 degrees, cooling it to 110 degrees, adding a heaping tablespoon of plain yogurt (it contains the necessary active culture), stirring gently to dissolve, pouring it into 1-quart vacuum bottle, and allowing it to sit overnight. Then the yogurt is chilled before eating.

potato. There are instructions on a box that any idiot can follow that'll say, 'Add one cup of mashed potato flakes to three cups of boiling water and stir and wait five minutes.'

"Plus you go to McDonald's because you recognize it. It's familiar. And we're trained to be such sheep, so nonexperimental; such non-risk-takers."

Jacobson has problems, as do others, in finding villains, although his organization takes frequent potshots at people and organizations it thinks are doing wrong. The fault, he says, is that of "the rules of the game, and the rules of the game are skewed against the consumers."

How, then, he was asked, should the rules be changed?

"I don't think the rules are going to be greatly changed in the United States," he said. "The capitalistic economy is going to continue. Safeway is no way going to disappear, even though A&P is disappearing. McDonald's isn't going to go away. But it's possible to set up institutions that are devoted to consumers' interests. Consumer cooperatives are one example." The federal government could not be counted on for help, he said: "It's a disaster."

"But there are some thing consumers can do. You don't eat in restaurants. You cut down on highly processed food and eat more basic commodities. You buy supermarket house brands or generics rather than national brands. If you follow just that advice, you will save 60 percent on your food dollar. If consumers are interested in saving money on their food, and cutting out a lot of middlemen, they can make tremendous improvements with just modest effort."

Although CSPI's director had expressed pessimism about seeing changes in the rules of the food game, he said he felt very optimistic. "I don't think everybody's going to become a natural food nut," he said, "and start cooking at home for a group of friends instead of going to restaurants. But if you compare the way you think now to the way you thought in 1970, there's been a remarkable change.

"Back then, anybody who ate whole-wheat bread was considered a real nut. You couldn't *get* whole-wheat bread. There weren't any natural food restaurants. There were supermarket house brands, but not for nearly as many products.

"There weren't any of the concerns about salt, fat, sugar, cholesterol. Things have changed tremendously. And it takes a long time. There's tremendous inertia in the system. But more and more kids are taking consumer courses in grammar school, and they will grow up with that. They'll grow up with unit pricing. They know that brand names are a ripoff. They read *Diet for a Small Planet* or *Supermarket Handbook** and all that stuff that encourages people to make good, natural foods at home.

"And they are doing all that, more and more. So I'm pretty optimistic. I think things change very slowly. But in general, they're moving in the right direction."

* Nikki and David Goldbeck, *The Supermarket Handbook: Access to Whole Foods,* revised and expanded edition (New York: New American Library, 1976).

12

More Serious Action

Michael Jacobson, Frances Moore Lappé, and others among the food advocates are quick to speak of the advantages of consumer cooperatives as a means of changing the balance between the consumer and the food system. Like most of the options that a consumer can exercise to improve his lot, a co-op takes time and energy but provides easily measurable benefits. It is one of several actions the consumer can take that are more aggressive, less passive, and thus more likely to provide measurable results.

Co-ops come in different forms. For many Americans in their middle years or later, the term "food co-op" may provoke a vision of long-haired hippies, caparisoned in beards and granny gowns, ladling dried mung beans out of barrels. There are some natural foods co-ops that still look like that, but "co-op" also means something else these days. In Berkeley, California, the land of the hippies' nativity, there is a chain of cooperative supermarkets that is competitive with anything the corporate world has produced. In the centers of cities like Detroit and New York, there are smaller, neighborhood co-ops that serve both poor people and the middle class. In hundreds of communities around the nation, from medium-sized cities to small towns to rural enclaves, there are other co-ops that own no real estate but distribute food in church basements and community centers to families who are saving as much as 40 percent on their food bills.

Co-ops generally fall into one of two basic types: those that operate as retail stores, and those known as "pre-order" co-ops, in which members' orders are placed, gathered, and distributed on a set schedule, such as once a week or twice a month. Most co-ops are organized around what is called the Rochdale Principle, after a nineteenth-century cooperative of English weavers: Membership is open to anyone (although some organizations may set a maximum size limit); each member has one vote on the co-op's policies; the amount of money that is invested is limited, since the purpose of a co-op is not to make a profit for its members but to provide them with goods and services; profits are turned back to the members in ratio to the amount of food they purchase (in larger operations, dividends are paid once a year, while smaller ones can deliberately keep their prices so low as to barely break even); education of the members is considered an important part of the co-op's work; and co-ops seek to be cooperative among themselves through joint purchasing, warehousing, and delivery agreements that further lower their operating costs.

The flagship of American food co-ops of the retail store variety is the one Frances Moore Lappé shops at—the Berkeley Co-op, operated by the Consumers' Cooperative of Berkeley, which is a chain of a dozen supermarkets and affiliated operations (hardware, wilderness supply, pharmacy, wine and liquor, credit union, health plan, travel agent, legal services, bookstore, and burial society) in the San Francisco Bay Area.

To the uninitiated, the Berkeley Co-op may at first look like an ordinary supermarket—anyone may shop there; the members receive their dividends at the end of the year—but a closer examination of the shelves reveals some distinct differences. The "shelf talkers" are not the attention-grabbers of a corporate-run store, but rather informational messages that sometimes even warn consumers against buying a product that is on display. If a food is exceptionally high in sodium content, a sign may "advertise" that fact. Similarly, the caffeine content of soft drinks is likely to be posted near the drinks themselves. If the Co-op's members feel a manufacturer is the bad guy in a labor dispute or is "charged with antisocial or anti-environmental practices," as Co-op literature puts it, that goes on a sign, as well. Information of a more positive nature is offered, too: There are tips on how to read labels, thumbnail recipes for inexpensive substitutes for processed foods (The "Secret Fruit-Drink Recipe" is half a glass of grapefruit juice, half a glass of water, and one ice cube), explanations of marketplace terms such as "enriched flour" and "rolled oats," and proper storage practices (keep green pears in a paper bag at room temperature until they are ripe).

The Co-op maintains a staff of home economists who come up with this information and present it to the public, and who are available for in-person consultations. Other policies include promises not to use deceptive signs, to use end-aisle displays only for "sound consumer values," to adhere to strict unit pricing, to ban colored lights (which make meat and other products look better than they are), and to trim meat so as to leave no more than half an inch of external fat.

The Berkeley stores sell national brands, but precedence goes to the Co-op label of house brands, which are prepared by Universal Cooperatives, Incorporated, of Minnesota, a central purchasing, manufacturing, and merchandising operation for consumer cooperatives.

It would seem that the Berkeley operation is such an obvi-

ously needed alternative to the retail food environment of so
many Americans that replicas of it should be emerging all over
the country. This has not happened, and economists and others who have studied the situation are not exactly sure why
not. Some feel it is the particular population mix of the Bay
Area, and especially of the Berkeley side of the bay, that
makes such an undertaking a success. The Co-op's constituency includes not only college students who might be expected to share an anti-establishment attitude in matters of
food purchasing, along with very many representatives of the
California subculture that places great stock in minimally
processed "natural" foods, but also a good number of lower-
income people who need to save every penny they can.

For consumers elsewhere in the country who would like to
share in some of the Co-op's benefits, however, there is a way.
It is *The Berkeley Co-op Food Book: Eat Better and Spend
Less*, edited by Helen Black and published by Bull Publish-
ing Company, Palo Alto, California, 94302. The large-format,
soft-cover book is crammed with information about nutrition,
safety, storage, buying techniques, preparation, terminology,
and other valuable tips that Berkeley Co-op members get
every time they walk down an aisle.

Compared with the smooth, high-volume professionalism of
the Berkeley operation, pre-order co-ops might seem insignifi-
cant. But for unknown millions of Americans they are an
effective, efficient way to beat the food system. They can
flourish anywhere, in the midst of any sort of population mix.

The Seminary Food Co-op is in the Chelsea section of New
York City's Manhattan borough, and the mix *it* enjoys is about
half Episcopalian seminarians and half families from the
neighborhood. Pam Wolff, a Chelsea resident, mother, art-
isan, and building manager (she runs the cooperative apartment house her family lives in), is the sort of person who is so
competent and thorough at everything she does that she is

constantly chosen for jobs. She has held each of the positions at Seminary at least once. Wolff explained in an interview that the member whose turn it is to do the buying obtains food from wholesalers each week and the food is placed on display that night at the seminary. Members come and buy what they want; if they don't show up they are subject to fines. What's left over goes on a "surplus table," which is opened the following morning to any member of the public who knows about it.

Members of the co-op save money, said Wolff: "Butter, for instance, is a dollar a pound cheaper than at the supermarket. But that's not the main thing. It's kind of middle-class here. Everybody wants the best temple oranges and the best navel oranges and the best juice oranges. They're not looking for the bargain; they're looking for the quality."

For the members of the more than a dozen pre-order co-ops in rural Emmet County, Michigan, price *is* the object, and the operation is year-round. For some members, co-ops have totally supplanted the supermarket.

The proliferation of consumer cooperatives in a single county, tucked up high in the northern part of lower Michigan, is largely the result of work done in the late seventies by Julie Micheal, a county extension home economist with the Michigan State University Cooperative Extension Service, and by members of the service's offices on the East Lansing campus. Micheal was disturbed by the fact that many of the families she saw were being forced by inflation to make drastic cuts in their food budgets. "I was doing a little puppet show on nutrition for the children at the Head Start program in their school," she recalled, "and I realized that they hadn't even had breakfast." Knowing that nutrition education wouldn't help if people couldn't buy the food, the home economist looked into the possibility of purchasing foodstuffs in bulk—in essence, forming a cooperative. Until then, she had not known what a food cooperative was.

The idea caught on quickly, and within two years the

county had fourteen separate co-ops. The organizations employ a relatively new technique known as the "food bag approach." Each group sets the price it wants to pay for a bag of groceries— $25 would be typical—and then decides on the general makeup of the bag, prescribing its contents in terms of relative proportions of protein, fruits and vegetables, and staples. When they place their orders, members specify the number of bags they want—not the bags' individual contents. They pay for each bag's value, plus a markup of from 2 to 10 percent for the co-op's expenses.

Once the orders are in, the co-op's volunteer buyers make their purchases from wholesalers (by now the wholesalers are aware of the purchasing power of the cooperatives and they eagerly solicit the groups' business). Buyers have the freedom to shop for best buys, but they must follow the group's guidelines on the proportions of food groups.

On delivery day the foods are assembled by volunteers into bags, and members come to pick them up. As in Pam Wolff's co-op in New York, there is a surplus table for unwanted food. Somehow, everything gets used.

There are numerous advantages to the system that operates in Emmet County. Julie Micheal says members realize savings of from 30 to 40 percent of their former food bills. "I shop strictly with the co-op myself," she said. "And I've cut my food bill, I would say, in half."

The co-ops have made impulse shopping, of the sort that supermarkets count on, virtually impossible. And the use of the food bag system has brought a measurable improvement in family nutrition, according to Elizabeth Chase Scott, a Michigan State extension specialist in food policy.

There have been interesting spinoffs. Five of the co-ops formed a confederation to operate a depot and warehouse. Artisans who were members of one of the groups formed a craft cooperative. Two meat processing plants opened in response to the groups' needs. One co-op member started a bakery to supply bread to members. Farmers in the vicinity increased their planting in 1981 because co-ops had bought their entire vegetable harvests in 1980.

There have been other payoffs as well. In the late seventies, Elizabeth Scott spent much of her time away from the campus, meeting with groups in Emmet County that wanted to know more about forming co-ops or that had recently started theirs. "Some groups by the third meeting were ordering their food," she said, "and they were discovering that you have a certain type of power in a group that you don't have otherwise.

"This is the thing that people begin to realize when they go to a meeting and see all these other people there. Always before, they've gone into the supermarket and the supermarket made the rules. The rules were, if you don't like the price, you leave. That's not true when you're in a co-op. You have more control over the prices; you have more control over your food."

Julie Micheal sees the same changes. "People are telling me that they feel a sense of community and belonging that had been obliterated," she said, "but that now is returning. Now they know their neighbor who lives half a mile down the road.

"Another thing is that people have a real feeling that they can control their own decision-making—how they spend their money, where they live, whether they grow their own vegetable garden, if they want to burn wood rather than pay a large heating bill. All these kinds of decisions are being firmed up by the fact that they belong to the co-op. They realize that they can have a choice. They don't feel like they're at the mercy of the big-business person. They have a choice."

Micheal has watched another interesting development in the Emmet County co-ops, too: "They've learned that they have leadership, an ability within themselves to solve the problems and to take leadership roles. A lot of the people in the co-ops have gone to another step. We have people who were on food stamps and unemployed who now are running their own restaurant business. They've gone on to say, 'Hey, look; I can be productive. I can do something myself. I have the capabilities.' "

Food cooperatives are powerful tools for consumers to use in developing strategies of action. Another is direct marketing. It is perhaps the single most important strategy of them all, and it is one that produces immediate benefits. Not only does direct marketing eliminate the middlemen, it provides payoffs that span most of the areas of concern that consumers feel and that are at the heart of many of the current problems of the food business—the cost of food, nutrition, freshness, and flavor. As with cooperatives, this action requires the expenditure of some energy and time. But the expenses are tiny in comparison with the richness of high-quality food that results.

Direct marketing is just what its name says: a form of food selling that proceeds in a direct line from the producer to the consumer, with none of the middleman's "additives," be they the literal ones of chemicals, packaging, and other examples of dubious "value added"; the economic ones that take so much of the dollar we spend on food; or the less easily defined ones such as loss of quality because of time spent in transit. To millions of Americans, direct marketing means food that is for sale in urban farmers' markets that have been organized specifically for the purpose. For others, it is roadside stands along secondary highways, often on the property of the producers themselves.

Direct marketing also includes pick-your-own operations: one visits a farm, takes a basket into the fields, picks what one needs, and pays for what one picks. In California, it can mean a relatively recent phenomenon called "Rent-a-Tree," in which a lover of apples, say, or cherries or some other fruit that grows on a tree, can strike a deal at the beginning of the season with a farmer for the total produce of one or more specific trees. The farmer promises to maintain the tree and notify the absentee husbandman when the fruit is ripe. The customer pays a flat rate, usually in advance, and reaps the harvest with a borrowed ladder and gets a day in the country to boot.

Although subletting an apple tree sounds quintessentially modern as well as Californian, there is little else about direct marketing that could be called new. Buying food directly from the farmer is, after all, only slightly more newfangled than growing it all oneself. The only thing that is really new about direct marketing is that it seems to be undergoing a vigorous renaissance.

The resurgence serves several purposes, all of which are quite pertinent to the nation's current economic and social environments. It provides consumers with food—almost all of it fruit and vegetables, but in some cases meat, fish, and other staples such as eggs, honey, and baked goods—that is vastly fresher than that available through what have come to be the "regular" channels. Because it has undergone less deterioration since it was harvested, the food is of higher quality in terms of its vitamin and mineral content, as well as taste. And because the middle echelons of the food business are avoided, the food is almost always cheaper—from 10 to 20 percent less expensive on average, according to some of the experts.

The other chief beneficiary is the farmer, who sells his produce at a price approaching the one a supermarket would charge, but who gets to keep, in addition to his own usual margin, all the profits that ordinarily go to shippers, wholesalers, and distributors, as well as retailers. It is for the benefit of the farmers, in fact, that most of the formal direct marketing programs are mounted by state governments. State departments of agriculture, like others in the industry and government, find it currently fashionable to give lip service to those of us who *consume* food, but their guiding policies and philosophies are concerned almost exclusively with improving the lot of the farmers who are their constituents. This can mean assisting farmer groups (especially the more politically powerful ones) with setting up marketing orders. It can mean helping the most powerful groups (the dairy lobby is a premier example) establish monopoly positions. Often it means starting direct marketing programs to help local farmers sell their products. Several states have campaigns to label and advertise food as "Grown in New York" or "Grown in Massachusetts"; they serve, really, as uncritical promotional consultants who use the consumers' money to sell things to those same consumers. It is nearly coincidental that what they sell is almost by definition of higher quality than food that is processed and shipped great distances.

Agriculture in some states, particularly those that once were rural but that have undergone recent urbanization, needs all the help it can get. A particularly touching example of this is Maine, which has a reputation as a place of fiercely independent farmers who have managed to scratch their livings from inhospitable soil. At congressional hearings in 1978 on direct marketing, Maine's agriculture commissioner, Joseph N. Williams, described the change. A century ago, he said, "Maine was virtually self-sufficient in producing staple food stocks." But now, "we have lost our capacity to feed ourselves."

The affliction has struck formerly rich farming communities that are close to population centers and thus ideally situated for providing cheaper, better food. Long Island, which runs for about 100 miles to the east of New York City, once provided the city with a great part of its fresh vegetables, seafood, and other foods, including ducks. Now much of the farmland has been covered with condominiums and ruined by overapplication of chemicals, and governing bodies have become populated with people who think duck farms and cauliflower patches are unseemly, offensive intrusions into their styles of living.

As a consequence, New Yorkers get most of their produce from California and Florida. Even at the height of the local harvests, California's share of the New York metropolitan area market is close to 50 percent. Furthermore, when local producers *do* raise crops and try to sell them in the city through the regular channels, they are rebuffed. A 1982 study by the Center for the Biology of Natural Systems, at Queens College of the City University of New York, found that local farmers were consistently paid less for their produce at the city-run terminal at Hunt's Point than were the purveyors of produce from California.

Several states, and New York is prominently among them, have undertaken impressive and quite helpful campaigns to inform consumers of the whereabouts of direct marketing facilities. Because state government is very good at spending the public's money gathering and printing information but usually quite confused about how to share such data with that public, it often is not easy to get information about these campaigns. A postcard to the public affairs office of a state agriculture department ought to result in a publications list or bundle of folders, however.

Kentucky publishes a simple sheet—actually just a folded piece of legal-sized paper—listing roadside farmers' markets, but its authors also had the wisdom to include a table showing when eleven fruits and twenty-one vegetables are seasonably available. This is something that will benefit any consumer, particularly in a time when we are in such danger of losing our knowledge of what grows when, and assuming that strawberries in February are somehow "normal." Michigan publishes a *Country Carousel* booklet listing pick-your-own and roadside market places. Virginia calls its publication *Fresh Vegetable Guide*. Connecticut's well-done little booklet will fit neatly into the glove compartment of an automobile.

New York State's agricultural wealth is often overlooked,

but the state in 1981 was among the nation's top five in volume of some cheeses, apples, cabbage for sauerkraut, maple syrup, milk, ice cream, grapes, sweet corn for the fresh market, and various vegetables for processing. The state has a comprehensive series of publications and guides on direct marketing, a harvest calendar, and booklets promoting the state's major crops.

As might be expected, California has an equally impressive set of programs and campaigns to augment those run by the state's several marketing orders and trade associations. There is a toll-free number for information on direct marketing, directories of farmer-to-consumer enterprises, direct marketing shopping bags with distinctive logos, and group insurance for participants in farmers' markets.

Compared to its slavish attention to the needs and whims of other parts of the food business, government encouragement of direct marketing seems restricted largely to the promotional level. Like organic farming, direct marketing violates the "rules" of the marketplace and makes bureaucrats uneasy. Lindsey Jones, the former codirector of a direct marketing program named the Agricultural Marketing Project, which has its headquarters in Nashville, has testified to a congressional subcommittee, "Our own experience with state departments of agriculture and state extension services has been fraught with indifference, ambivalence and opposition. Through negotiation with extension [officials] at the state level, we have overcome most of our differences, but it is quite clear that some state agricultural agencies still feel quite threatened by the 'intrusion of non-experts' into the field of produce marketing."

In spite of such an unsupportive atmosphere, direct marketing has prospered. According to the federally backed research that has been done in a few states, only 1 or 2 percent of cash farm receipts could be attributed to direct farmer-to-consumer sales. But that is 1 or 2 percent of a lot of money—

of an estimated $84 billion in 1982. And many of the benefits are simply not capable of being reduced to the neatness of dollars and cents.

In and around Newport, Rhode Island, one of the most joyous days of summer is the one when word first spreads that "Chase corn is in." That means that the sweet corn Sam and Harry Chase have planted on 20 acres of their 35-acre farm in Portsmouth, Rhode Island, is starting to mature and the first burlap sacks of it are appearing at roadside stands, small groceries, and a few supermarkets whose corporate chain bureaucracies permit such disruptions to the orderly flow of California produce to a Rhode Island store. The corn is much in demand during the all-too-brief season from the end of July to the beginning of October.

"This is why our corn is fresh," explained Sam Chase one day. "We have regular customers who we call each year to tell them when the corn is ready. We call them the night before the day we're going to pick. So that night we know, by eight o'clock, that we're going to have to pick, say, sixty bags of corn for the next day. We go out at six in the morning and pick sixty bags of corn, deliver it by eleven o'clock, and that's it for the day. Next day we do it again. That's why it's fresh; we pick just what we need for the day."

As celebrated as Chase corn is, the brothers say they couldn't make a living selling it alone. Survival, they say, comes from the remaining 15 acres, where they grow flowers and plants for sale. Said Harry Chase: "If you're trying to make money in agriculture, it's either get bigger or get out."

Several hundred miles to the south, in Clinton, Maryland, close to the seat of the national government, Parker's Produce Farms advertises that it has "The Freshest You Can Get Because *You* Pick It Yourself!" Starting with strawberries and peas in May, and running into the fall with corn, tomatoes, lima beans, onions, squash, broccoli, okra, and collards, Parker's is a haven for pick-it-yourselfers. For those who want to

stalk specific elusive vegetables, there is a recorded telephone
message updating the seasonal listings.

"I'd say 75 percent of our customers come out of downtown
Washington," said Elizabeth Parker, a member of the family
that operates the farm. "And a lot of them come from the
South—the Carolinas, Georgia. They're people who grew up
on the farm and came to the big government town to get a
secure job. And when they get here it's just like being back
home. They come out here and they just *pick*."

What they talk about, she said, is how delighted they are at
finding fresh food. "They really appreciate what the land
produces. Most of them take very good care of the vegetables
when they're out there in the fields. A lot of times I go out
there to pick myself, and I don't tell them who I am, and I
listen to the conversations. They talk about how pretty it is,
and about how you feel like you're back home on the farm.
How good the food is when you can get it fresh. And they also
tell each other, 'Don't do that,' 'Watch out for this,' 'This is
how you pick.'" Sometimes, she said, people who have moved
to the big government city forget how to pick and have to be
reminded of the way things are done and used to be. "They
pick the blossom on the squash. Or the blossom on the okra.
They're so excited to have fresh okra that they get confused."

In hundreds of cities around the country, direct marketing
has been taken to the people themselves in the form of farmers' markets in public places. These markets recapture, sometimes on a once-a-week basis, sometimes continuously during
the entire growing season, the flavor and meaning of the old
city markets that used to bring producer and consumer together in the hearts of countless cities and small towns.

The markets vary in size, shape, and ambiance—in some,
the farmers sell directly off the tailgates of their trucks; others
employ permanent sheds and counters; the ritzy ones sell

produce beneath brightly striped, outdoor-wedding-sized tents. Some cities tuck the markets away on vacant lots in poverty neighborhoods. Some give them the use of a city park (at the central park in Davis, California, the Saturday-morning farmer's market is a mélange of traditional farmers, aging hippies, and youthful back-to-the-earth types, selling everything from organically grown almonds to homemade jellies to live catfish, swimming disconsolately in washbasins). Some, as in Springfield, Illinois, function in downtown blocks that have been set aside as malls. In Knoxville, one end of the pedestrian mall that unites the downtown business district is given over to direct marketing of vegetables, fruits, and flowers.

In New York City, there are many forms of direct marketing—men with furtive expressions sell fish on the street from the opened trunks of their automobiles; in black neighborhoods in Brooklyn gleaming tractor-trailers driven by swashbuckling black entrepreneurs from North Carolina park along main thoroughfares and sell collards and yams and black-eyed peas and melons and long snakes of unrefrigerated smoked sausage to those who are far from "home." But the *official* version is called the Greenmarkets—a number of open-air enterprises on vacant plots of land where, on designated days of the week, farmers who are certified as the actual growers of most of their produce sell directly to consumers. The Greenmarkets are operated as a quasi-municipal function by the Council on the Environment of New York City, a nonprofit, privately funded organization, to bring better produce to the city, support regional agriculture and conserve farmland, and revitalize city neighborhoods. The Greenmarkets were started in the summer of 1976 by a city planner named Barry Benepe largely because, he said, he deplored the fact that even during the height of the fruit-growing season in the New York region he couldn't find a good peach in a supermarket.

The Greenmarket program's chief value, said Benepe in an interview, "is that it strengthens the regional economy by keeping our farms alive. That's really what our effort is: to keep our dollars in the region so they don't travel three thousand miles away and strengthen the California economy."

As with most everything else in the city that calls itself the Big Apple, direct marketing is not easy. Labor, management, bureaucratic jealousies and shiftlessness, political arrogance, petty crime, organized crime—everything has an effect on any attempt to challenge the traditional ways of doing things, which invariably are the wasteful and costly ways and, in the case of food, the ways that work against quality, taste, and economy. There is a commercial fisher who sails from Montauk, on the eastern tip of Long Island, who says it costs almost as much for him to fly his catch to Los Angeles as it does to truck it to the Fulton Fish Market. Barry Benepe knows a large-scale farmer on Long Island whose trucks "drive right through the city and go down to Georgia and even Florida to sell their produce because they can get a better price there."

The problems are manifold. Benepe thinks the biggest single problem in the city is parked cars, which tend to block the streets the Greenmarkets are on, despite signs and even the occasional appearance of tow trucks. At the flagship market in Union Square, a celebrated old Manhattan park that is the headquarters for dozens of winos and a flourishing retail dope trade (and that is situated literally over one of the field headquarters of the city's subway police), an attempt to expand the market to two days a week met with stiff resistance from transit cops who feared it would interfere with their free parking.

When Greenmarkets sought to establish a selling center in White Plains, a Westchester County town that has turned into a prototype of the emerging phenomenon of deteriorating suburb, there was objection from a hotel (which thought its patrons should not be subjected to the visual indignities of naked squash and romaine and the rudely clothed country folk who sold them), florists (who dug up a restriction against the sale of flowers), and the city (which had an ordinance banning outdoor displaying, which demanded a $250 fee, and which required the permission of seven separate agencies before even the first scallion could change hands). After its first year, when Greenmarket proved itself no more of a menace than most enterprises, many of the foolish restrictions were amended.

The rules by which the Greenmarket merchants are expected to play are very firm on the subject of where the produce comes from. "All fruits and vegetables sold at Greenmarket must be home grown by farmer," said the 1982 regulations. "A farmer may also sell any one variety of fruit or vegetable or fruit or vegetable by-product purchased from the nearest farm or any farm within twenty miles of his/her own (e.g. cider)." The produce "must be harvested no earlier than the day before the market, with the exception of such storable crops as dry onions, winter squash, and root crops."

Although the Greenmarket staff, and often Benepe himself, pays visits to farms in upstate New York, New Jersey, Pennsylvania, and as far south as North Carolina, to insure compliance, Benepe says sometimes a farmer will "just get that little extra greediness where he wants to be a little supermarket all by himself." The ultimate insult that one Greenmarket merchant can hurl at another, said the director, "is that he gets his stuff from Hunt's Point."

The benefits in New York, as everywhere else that direct marketing has been tried, are multitudinous. Perhaps because retail food prices in New York generally are so competitive, the price advantage has not been as pronounced there as in other places. In the 1982 season, the Greenmarket staff surveyed prices and found the margin between what was charged in their markets and what was charged in the region's grocery stores was slimmer than ever before. Still, consumers could save 5 percent on sweet corn (an item that is, of course, incalculably fresher and better-tasting when it comes from the Greenmarket, which in New York is the closest thing there is to the cornfield itself), 4 percent on tomatoes, 15 percent on cucumbers, and 23 percent on lettuce.

"The dominant reason people go to Greenmarkets," said Barry Benepe, "is the quality of the food. Quality being these things: variety. There's an immense variety of food you just don't see elsewhere. There's a melon grower who comes in with seven kinds of melons. Egyptian onions. Or shallots, or white eggplant. And maturity. The Greenmarket farmers grow for maturity, which means better-tasting. Freshness. With a fresh item you can have more vitamins, more nutritious food, better taste. Often when people talk about 'nutrition' they never talk about taste or the relationships between the two."

The Greenmarkets are considered a financial success. Benepe said, after an assessment of the 1982 season, "We are doing a volume of about $4.3 million a year at seventeen different locations. Maybe 5 percent of the food that's sold in the region is sold through direct marketing. It would be wrong to think that because it deals with just 5 percent of the people, direct marketing is not significant. For those 5 percent of the people it is *very* significant. To keep two hundred farmers alive, rather than to have no farmers, is very important."

Benepe was asked if all the techniques of modern food distribution and merchandising didn't make direct marketing a sort of nostalgia item, not too different from the horse-drawn carriages that take tourists around the classier streets of Manhattan. He replied, "It is, to a certain extent, but sometimes nostalgia items can be very contemporary, very meaningful. We're sort of undermining the system as we know it, a system that is very elaborate and complex. We're sort of working outside the food distribution system. We're setting up a new system that's parallel to it."

Another successful experiment in direct marketing has been carried out in and around Nashville by the Agricultural Marketing Project, which grew out of concerns by students and others at Vanderbilt University in the mid-seventies, at a time when the margin between what farmers were getting for beef and what consumers were paying for it was especially high. John Vlcek, now the project's executive director, said in an interview: "That was when we really began to take a look at direct marketing as an important step toward assisting farmers and recognizing that the marketing function is really where farmers in particular are having the most problems."

The project organized what it called "food fairs," which were essentially farmers' markets, but which had strict rules requiring merchants to sell their own produce. Consumers in the Nashville area, said Vlcek, previously had patronized "farmers' markets" that were dominated by truckers who hauled produce in from other states and who, in some cases, were on their way to the big terminal markets of the North and just stopped in the Music City to dump what they could of their loads.

So one rule was farmers only. Another was that the markets should be decentralized, rather than confined to one downtown area. Churches were asked to provide space for food fairs once or twice a week.

"Churches were chosen as sites here," said Vlcek, "because in the South churches are particularly powerful. And they have very good parking lots. They have very good, accessible locations. And they really serve as community centers. Old people especially like to patronize them. They feel safe going to their local church, whereas they might not feel safe getting on a bus and riding downtown."

A third rule was that the farmers should control the markets. Once a market became established, the Agricultural Marketing Project would withdraw its direction. Vlcek said the markets thus created now were on their own and functioning well. "Whether they can stay alive over the long run, for ten or fifteen years, without either being done away with by colossal institutions or without becoming reactionary and exclusive themselves," he said, "I don't know."

The food fairs' obstacles have been similar to those faced by New York's Greenmarkets—largely bureaucratic ones, with relatively little opposition from retail food merchants. The biggest fights that come up each year in the farmers' organizations, says Vlcek, "are over whether they should set prices." The project director says another obstacle is less tangible. "People who *don't* shop at farmers' markets are essentially people my age—people twenty-one to thirty, maybe thirty-five. Young people, single, who don't have a history of cooking fresh produce, who have busy lives, who eat out a lot. We don't reach those people. We see a lot of old people at food fairs. When you ask if these ideas can survive, the answer is yes. But if the question is whether they will grow and really get people to support them, then you've got to begin to break ground with new groups of people." Promotional campaigns similar to those used for highly processed foods is one way to do that, he said; another is to encourage educational programs that reach both adults and children. The project has created several publications that do this.

As for benefits, Vlcek said a survey found prices at the markets to be around one-third lower than in retail stores, and as much as one-half less when produce is bought in bulk. There are the usual improvements in freshness, taste, and nutrition. And there are spiritual benefits as well. "One of the things people have told us at the farmers' markets," said Vlcek, "is that there's a whole sense of reinvigoration of the sense of community; that some people will go to these food fairs just to see other people. Particularly older people. That there's a sense of togetherness. If they get to be good markets, they become places where people go to hang out and talk to each other and talk to the farmers and look at the produce and get recipes from the farmers and that kind of thing. I think in our society we really overlook the value of community spaces where we can just talk to each other. You don't do that at the grocery store."

Both John Vlcek and Barry Benepe, and many others who have become involved with direct marketing and consumer cooperatives, speak of what they do as far more than just an effective tool for the consumer or the farmer for obtaining or disposing of food that is of higher quality and is less expensive than what normally runs through the system. It becomes a means of teaching both ends of the food chain that they don't have to exist at the mercy of the people in the middle. Some, of course, prefer it the way it is. Some producers are owned, themselves, by the middlemen—by the oil companies and holding companies and conglomerates that control so much of the mechanisms and mentality of the food marketplace and all the other marketplaces, too—and they do not complain. Some consumers are willing to sacrifice taste, nutrition, freshness, and economy for the sought-after qualities of convenience and speed. But for those who find this unsatisfying, there are great benefits to be had.

Direct marketing offers marvelous educational opportunities. These are perhaps best observed in the urban setting, where people who either never put their hands in dirt or who have been away from it too long suddenly find out what real food tastes like. There are social payoffs in New York as well as in Nashville. Barry Benepe said he had received a letter from a white resident of Brooklyn who said she had been afraid of black people until she started visiting her local

Greenmarket, which is situated at the intersection of several neighborhoods of varying ethnic makeup. "She said that since she mixed with them in the easy and friendly atmosphere at the market she really, for the first time, had given up that fear," said Benepe. "And I got a very poignant letter from an elderly person. She said Greenmarket day was the one day of the week when her loneliness is relieved."

Some see even longer-range goals and possible payoffs: an emboldening of the consumer, through beneficial experiences at farmers' markets, consumer cooperatives, and other strategies, to undertake even more piercing examinations of and challenges to the existing business of food. If people can realize the benefits obtained by eliminating four or five layers of middlemen and several thousand miles of needless transportation—and realize them fairly instantly, as when biting into a peach or a slice of tomato while simultaneously pocketing the substantial difference in price—could this not lead to challenges of conglomerate concentration, monopoly overcharge, government collusion with manufacturers at the expense of consumers and producers, deceptive packaging and advertising practices, needless adulteration of basic foods with chemicals and flavorings? Could it not lead, in fact, to a challenge to the whole system as it now exists?

"What we're trying to do," said John Vlcek in Nashville, "is to promote the fact that people need to control things that matter to them the most. For farmers, it's the markets. For consumers, it's what they eat. And the price of that involvement is having to make decisions, spending the time, and being a part of a political process. I think Americans, both traditionally and in terms of being more recently brainwashed, have been taught that it's best not to be political. But that's how the system will change."

13

Coping with the Future

Whatever strategies the consumer may adopt for coping with the business of food, one fact remains certain: Everything will have to be adjusted to take into consideration that most unknown of quantities, the future.

The processes that have been discussed in this book—those that go into the production of food, its manufacture, shaping, combining, alteration, packaging, advertisement, transportation, and sale—are anything but static and unchanging, as hidebound as some of the links of the food chain may seem. All are constantly being reformulated and reevaluated, changed, redefined, "improved" (in the minds of some, but not necessarily of consumers). They are in the constant process of evolving into the future of our food system. As is the case now and as has been the case in the immediate past, the American consumer is inadequately prepared for the changes that are on the way.

Consider, for example, some of the implications that are raised in just this brief discussion of "Future Developments in the Food Industry," prepared by a research contractor, Charles W. Williams, Inc., for the Federal Trade Commission in 1980:

The terms "all natural ingredients" and "no preservatives or additives" are more and more frequent in the food system. Future technologies will reinforce these trends, but the various mechanisms to achieve stable shelf life without traditional additives may be somewhat inconsistent with the term "natural" in the exact meaning of the word. Just how "natural" will corn be that has been genetically manipulated to retard the conversion of the plant's natural sugar to starch or to yield a stock which is "ideal" for conversion to biomass energy? . . .

Technical capabilities will exist by the end of this decade to produce "no calorie" food. This product will consist of bulk filling that provides the essential food satisfactions of taste and texture, but with neither calories nor, unfortunately, nutrients.* Such a concept will carry "food for fun" trends to their logical conclusion. . . .

Many traditional foods like sugar or caffeine are either habit forming or "addictive" in the loose sense of the term: one develops a form of dependency on them. Future technical developments will make possible the inclusion of ingredients especially designed to create a form of "addiction." The ingredients will have a highly differentiated capability to make the "addiction" to a given source—a brand or a store label. Such ingredients can be [administered] in very small dosages, build up over time, and can be very difficult to trace. . . .

One of the well-known by-products of modern understanding of human behavior, psychology and society is an increasing sophistication in advertising techniques. Clearly, the seller

* It is interesting to note that when Thomas H. Stanton, deputy director of the FTC under the Reagan administration, delivered a 1981 speech to the Canners League of California on "Developments in the Food Industry to 1990," he included this sentence, as if it were his own, and with one prominent change. Where the study said ". . . neither calories nor, unfortunately, nutrients," Stanton said ". . . neither calories nor, possibly, nutrients." Thus he put the administration's food policy in a one-word nutshell.

and advertiser are being supplied with whole new arsenals. Some of these techniques are well known, and their potential threat to consumers well understood. Included [are] such methods as subliminal advertising or advertising designed to influence the buying habits of children and create a pattern of consumption that will be carried into adulthood. The next generation of electronic media will give advertising much greater power for the dissemination of such techniques as well as more insight into how to tailor them to be more subtle. The behavioral sciences and technology are approaching a number of convergences in which the possibilities of covert "manipulation" or at least markedly influencing behavior are growing. . . .

Studies have now documented certain determinants to musical taste which allow for the possibility of drawing a psychographic profile of a market segment and then designing music to capture that profile's attention. Of more profound effect, detailed work has been accomplished demonstrating enough of a correlation between certain musical modes and mood to make it possible to produce taped programs with predetermined moods in the audience at specified times. The next step will be to musically find a mood that says "buy." While it sounds farfetched, such specificity is probably attainable.

What the report calls the "next generation of electronic media" is already exciting the interest of many in the industry, who are very alert to the possibilities inherent in cable television. With multichannel cable systems, individual selling messages can be designed for specific zip codes or neighborhoods, with the result that market segmentation will be increased drastically, as will the stereotyping and typecasting of that wonderful mass of diversity that is the American people. The affluent can get the urbane pitch for "natural" cereal, with Pachelbel's Canon in D in the background, while the not-so-affluent can be sold the same stuff to a disco beat.

Joseph Sullivan, the president of Swift & Company, is one

of those who see an exciting future in cable. In an interview in his office in Chicago, Sullivan noted that his firm, which is best known for its Butterball turkeys, has done "a rather considerable amount of work in the cable television area.

"We have built around what is going to make it easier and more satisfying in terms of a person's food preparation," he said. "A case in point: How do you prepare a turkey effectively? How can you use blue cheese in a variety of different ways? Why Sizzlean is indeed a value to you *vis-à-vis* bacon. These commercials—if you will, commercial messages, educational messages—will run anywhere from two to nine minutes. The industry has been a slave to the thirty-second commercial. It can't be any longer as we move into the eighties and the nineties."

Sullivan's proposed uses for such messages seem relatively harmless—and even helpful, since one of his colleagues explained that a lot of people who call the "Butterball Turkey Hotline" around Thanksgiving are asking how to cook their turkeys, even though complete instructions are printed on each bird's packaging. But what happens when food and other products are sold on interactive cable, the medium in which the customer can punch a few buttons and place an order on the spot? As the FTC document points out, most sales transactions now have built-in cooling-off periods between the time the pitch is made and the time when the customer can actually plunk down the money. With interactive cable, decisions will be made during the heat of impulsion.

Another example of cable's use to food merchandisers is being demonstrated in a number of test markets around the nation. Sandra Salmans, writing in the "Advertising" column of the *New York Times*, reported in 1981 that two companies were linking consumers with the sorts of food advertisements they received on cable. Differing kinds of commercials for the same products are beamed at two different test groups, and their effects on shoppers are measured by the supermarket scanner, which compares what was bought with the shoppers' identities. (Those participating in the research are given identification cards, which they present at the checkout counter and which are read, along with everything else, by the scanner.) By monitoring a family's spending habits, wrote Salmans, a food manufacturer can determine which commercial sells more of its product. A separate device tells whether a family's television set was turned on when the commercials were broadcast.

Intrusions into our heretofore private lives such as these cry out for counterinsurgency actions—sabotage of the intruders' systems by consumers who swap identification cards and devise other ways to damage the data that are being collected —and by the tried and proven technique of boycott.

The new rules of processing and merchandising will be exploited by bad guys—that is a certainty. But it also likely that even the "good" members of the food business will attempt to use the changes that are coming as devices to further degrade the definition of food and raise its cost, while withholding as much useful information from the consumer as possible. Extruded and minced and reformed chicken, beef, and fish are examples that unfortunately are already very much with us.

It would be prudent, then, for the consumer to avoid believing most of the claims made about the foods of the future, and to not believe *any* claims that "the savings will be passed along to the consumer." It should be quite clear by now that nothing happens in the food system that the consumer doesn't pay for. But while a thoroughly cynical attitude toward the future is the only healthy one, we ought to recognize that some of the newer processes have their beneficial sides. The trick is never to forget two wonderful clichés that serve us marvelously well in these days and times: that everything is a tradeoff and that there's no such thing as a free lunch.

An example of this is aquaculture. What the technocrats

stuffily call "waste heat utilization," which nowadays means simply finding environmentally harmless ways to get rid of the heretofore "waste" heat produced by power plants, may play an important part in tomorrow's food. Things need warmth to grow, and there have been experiments with piping this surplus heat into greenhouses, using it to warm soil, to dry crops, and to heat food processing plants. The heat, absorbed by water, is also being used in a number of tests to create comfortable environments in which fish can be "farmed" in pools and raceways. These aquaculture experiments are being carried on with oysters, mussels, clams, lobsters, shrimp, prawns, salmon, striped bass, catfish, eels, yellow perch, trout, and carp.

One such test which has proved successful is being conducted at the Gallatin Steam Plant of the Tennessee Valley Authority, near Gallatin, Tennessee, on the Cumberland River. The huge plant burns coal to produce steam, which then produces electricity, and one by-product is a lot of heated water. The water, which formerly was discharged back into the river, to the detriment of water quality, is now used to grow catfish and trout in outdoor raceways near the plant. Because they are raised scientifically, with the water temperature just right, their pellet-sized food precisely formulated, and their antibiotics carefully administered, the fish grow rapidly and take up little room. Charles Collins, the project leader at Gallatin, figures he gets 9.2 pounds of fish per cubic foot of water.

The benefits of aquaculture are several. Not only does it keep heated water from reentering the river and shocking aquatic life there, it also means fish can be grown year-round. They can be cultivated close to their markets, which helps solve the "sell them or smell them" problem. Tropical species can be grown in colder climates. And—this may be the most important reason of all as we are told increasingly horrible tales of what industry has been putting into our free-flowing bodies of water—a close watch can be kept on the quality of the water in which the fish are raised.

But there are tradeoffs. While catfish raised at Gallatin are delicious, as confirmed by the author's personal inspection of a statistically significant sample at a Gallatin restaurant that has an arrangement with Collins to feed his visiting scholars, they lack the essential taste of *catfish*.

Charles Collins says he can tell the difference between cultivated and wild catfish. "The difference is, the cultivated ones are much better," he said. "They don't have that 'fishy' taste." After reflecting a moment, he added: "Of course, some people *like* that taste."

Other bits and pieces of the future are already here. Many of them have to do with packaging techniques that do the necessary job of destroying and suppressing the activities of microorganisms, but that do them in newer ways than traditional canning. Ultra-high-temperature pasteurization, known in the trade as UHT, is a way of packaging milk and other liquids that eliminates the need for refrigeration. Retort pouching utilizes a laminated plastic-and-foil bag that holds vegetables and other foods as would a metal can, that withstands the temperatures of processing, and that can be used as a boil-in-bag device. A more controversial technique is irradiation, which sterilizes foods (fish would be one example) without heat and allows storage at room temperatures.

All these processes have among their benefits (from the industry's point of view) vastly increased storage life. UHT milk will keep on a kitchen or supermarket shelf for "several months," according to Congress's Office of Technology Assessment. Irradiated foods, says the agency, "can be stored at room temperature indefinitely."

What none of the experts seem to be discussing is what all this will do to the essential nature of the food thus preserved.

Will milk processed by UHT and stored for months be the same *milk* we drink today? Or will it be as markedly different (and, some would say, of as decreased quality) as today's milk is from the substance we had delivered to our doorsteps only a couple of decades ago, the icy bottles of unhomogenized milk with the collars of cream at the top? What are the problems, recognized and potential, of subjecting foods to irradiation? Irradiation, after all, means bombarding the food (and, quite likely, the people who process it) with gamma rays or electrons. And once unleashed, how far and wide will this process spread? In Europe, irradiation is already used to control the ripening of fruit and the sprouting of potatoes. Will the issues of irradiation be debated openly and freely before the public, or will they be resolved in corporate boardrooms and in lunchtime conferences, with campaign contributions made by lobbyists to government policymakers playing a role in the resolution?

In such a confusing situation the consumer needs help. And that help, we surely must acknowledge, is not very likely to come from government. After all, the federal government is actually bankrolling and conducting much of the research on future foods for the industry itself, and using our tax dollars to do it. A government that refuses even to enforce its own laws on informing the public about chemicals added to fruits and vegetables is unlikely to go out of its way to warn us about potatoes that have been doused with gamma rays. The consumer who places his faith in government for help out of the tangled thicket of the food business is little better off than the one who takes television commercials at face value. Help, meaningful help, will have to come from somewhere else.

It may be that one place the consumer should look for helpful friendship is the place where most people come into contact with the food system: the supermarket, of all places.

*　*　*

Such an alliance is not as bizarre as it may first sound. If, as everybody says, supermarkets make their profits on "turn" rather than high profit margins on each item, then being nicer to the consumer would do nothing to reduce volume and would almost certainly increase it. Shoppers, even in these cynical times when experts debate solemnly the "risk-benefit analyses" of various environmental perils (and thereby attempt to place a price sticker on the value of human life that used to be called "priceless"), respond to friendliness and honesty in the marketplace.

There is ample evidence that consumers want such help. A survey conducted for the Department of Agriculture in 1974 found, according to an internal document, that more than a third of the consumers questioned "said they were rarely or never satisfied with the reliability and truthfulness of advertising by food product manufacturers." The level of dissatisfaction is even higher now; a poll taken in the fall of 1982 by Louis Harris & Associates found consumers somewhat angry about the treatment they got in the marketplace generally. Asked to rate institutions on their dedication to consumer protection, the respondents gave Congress a 71 percent negative rating and the Reagan administration a 65 percent negative rating. Almost half found consumer leaders to be out of touch with the people, and most felt they were getting a rawer deal in the marketplace now than they got a decade previously. Another survey by Harris a year before had found that 79 percent of the consumers polled would react positively to supermarkets that displayed cautionary labels on products believed to be unsafe, and that 61 percent wanted stores to provide them with information on health and nutrition.

Supermarkets, it could be argued without stretching one's imagination too far, could do an excellent job of stepping into the void between the consumer and the rest of the food business and serving as the consumer's advocate.

Some of them fill part of the void already, with campaigns to make nutrition information available in the store. A few go as far as the Stop & Shop chain in New England, which publishes a biweekly pamphlet called *Consumerisms* that contains information on storage, preparation, and values. In one issue, *Consumerisms* boosted the cause of locally grown produce and noted that in 1980, the chain had purchased more than $9 million worth of fruits and vegetables from more than a hundred local farmers.

The Berkeley Co-op has no parallels, however, in the strength and value of its efforts to inform customers of the contents and value of the food it sells, although any commercial chain that emulated the cooperative's techniques would surely gain instant customer loyalty. Few, if any, chains or big independents have taken up the challenge issued by several thoughtful students of labeling to provide shoppers with an in-store directory of additives and what they do and why they're in the food.

Such specific, highly pertinent information is sorely needed by people at the moment they are making food-buying decisions—few can manage to bring textbooks, calculators, and copies of the Code of Federal Regulations into the store, and the only people who can really read a label without these aids are biochemists—and an in-store display would fill a real need. If a supermarket really is dedicated to offering choice, and if it truly makes its profits on volume, then it needn't worry about scaring potential customers off the highly differentiated products with all the chemicals. Less-processed foods could serve as alternatives. Or the customers could gravitate toward commodities in the produce section, where the store makes one of its highest margins anyway.

Another obvious point where consumers and grocers can form an alliance is along the aisles where store-brand foods and generics are sold. Consumers can exploit the tensions between manufacturers and retailers, and save money in the process, by buying store brands and thus giving grocers more leverage. (What happens when they get *too much* leverage, however, is troublesome to contemplate.) With rare exceptions, supermarkets have done little to explain to their customers what generic, private-label, and store-brand foods really are.

Some observers of the food business think that despite some of its awkwardnesses in the communication field, the supermarket is already veering toward advocacy for the consumer. Carol Tucker Foreman believes retailers were surprised and impressed in the seventies when consumers reacted so strongly to changes in the price of beef that the result was an effective nationwide boycott of the meat. "People were mad at supermarkets," said Foreman, "because the prices had gone up a lot in a short period of time." Although supermarkets were hardly to blame for the increases, for most Americans they were the local, street-level representatives of the food system, and they took the brunt of the action, including picket lines and boycotts. "And the retailers pretty much made a decision then, I think," said Foreman, "that if there was a choice to be made between being a buying agent for the consumer and a selling agent for the processor, it was in their interests to be the buying agent for the consumer."

"Now," she quickly added, "the one exception to that is that supermarket concentration continues to grow." Foreman, like some economists, was worried about the effects of that concentration, but she added that chains may arrive at some sort of accommodation there—that they might agree to trade increased consumer information and lower prices for the security that comes from being one of the two or three leaders in a two- or three-chain town.

In Michael Jacobson's view, the supermarkets are currently at the pivot of the seesaw that holds the food manufacturers and the food consumers. "In a way," he said, "*they* are the consumers of the stuff vended by the big manufacturers. And there are some instances where they have made efforts to help consumers. In nutrition, several supermarket chains have encouraged customers to buy more nutritious rather than less nutritious foods. Some chains have put up good shelf labeling in terms of nutrition or unit pricing.

"But in general, supermarkets are trying to extract as much money from the consumer's pocket as possible. And they work hand in hand with the processed food companies. You have to go to the Berkeley Co-op to see the difference between a chain that's really consumer-oriented and the other stuff, which is mainly lip service."

Behind the elaborate facade of advertising and image are some indications that many in food retailing are not yet ready to comprehend or accept a role as partner with the consumer. Retailers, for example, display an inordinate sensitivity when such matters as their pricing techniques are discussed in public.

A number of food economists have conducted studies aimed at determining what happens when comparative food price information is collected and made available to the consumer. D. Grant Devine, of the University of Saskatchewan, and Bruce Marion, of the University of Wisconsin, reported on one such survey, in which comparative price data for major supermarkets in Ottawa were collected for twenty-eight weeks and published in daily newspapers for five weeks. They found that "the dispersion of prices across stores and chains narrowed, the average level of prices of the market dropped, and consumers satisfaction increased" in comparison with the satisfaction levels of a control group. Consumers also started shopping at the stores with the lower prices. And, reported the economists, "Within two weeks after the termination of the public information program, average retail food prices in the test market began to rise and increased 8.8 percent by the end of the research period."

When a Purdue economist, Joseph Uhl, undertook a similar study in Springfield, Missouri, and Erie, Pennsylvania, the supermarkets tried to keep his students from copying down the food prices. According to *Supermarket News*, the Springfield merchants disrupted the study after it began generating information on the widening price spread for a hundred-item shopping basket between the most and least expensive of the participating stores—from $5 in the first week to about $17 in the sixth week.

The stores had been allowing Uhl and his students to record the prices, and newspapers had been disseminating the price information to the public—a vital element of the experiment. But after some of the retailers banned note-taking and one newspaper backed out, Uhl used cash—from a USDA grant—to get his information by purchasing the items from the stores. The groceries, which cost from $1,100 to $1,500 a week, were given to charities.

Grocers could have done a much better job with scanning, too. Electronic scanning has been widely described as one of the most significant applications of modern technology to food retailing. It uses electronic devices, all but invisible beneath plates of glass embedded in the checkout line, to read the Universal Price Code that is imprinted on most foods and an increasing percentage of everything else. The code provides the store with a wealth of information, chiefly a description of the product and its package size. Once in the store's computer, the coded information that was brought to the checkout line by the shopper is compared with other information stored by the grocer—the price for that particular item, the time of day, the location of the checkout line. In much less time than it takes to tell, the current price is rung up on a cash register that is readable by the checkout clerk and the customer and an abbreviated description of the item and its price are printed on a somewhat more elaborate version of the traditional grocery-store cash register tape. A total is calculated, time of day imprinted, change figured, and complimentary close (something on the order of "Have a Nice Day") inscribed on the tape, and all the checker has to do is drag

boxes and cans across the scanner's eye and occasionally wipe
the blood from meat packages off the glass plate. Fully
automated front ends, as the industry refers to its highest-tech
scanner installations, also weigh produce and transfer the per-
pound and total prices to the tape. Some scanners now in
operation announce prices in simulated human voices as they
are rung up.

Scanning was introduced in 1974, but widespread use has
been retarded by the systems' high cost in a time of economic
chaos and by consumer resistance. Much of that opposition
can be traced to failures by retailers to deal with consumers'
quite reasonable and well-grounded fears that anything new
and "technological" that comes into the marketplace will
probably be used to screw them, particularly if it involves
computers. Anybody knows that who was around when department stores were trying to learn, at customer expense,
how to run their computers.

There are numerous ways the scanners can serve *both* consumers and retailers. But what appears to be a "we want it
all" attitude on the part of some grocers seems to have wasted
this opportunity to strengthen the consumer-retailer alliance.

Grocers who are installing scanners are quick to point out
the advantages that will accrue to consumers: They speed the
process of getting through the checkout line; they provide a
printed record of what was bought and what it cost; they are
more accurate than the old fingers-on-the-cash-register
method. Ancillary functions, such as check cashing and sorting of coupons and food stamps, can be combined into one
transaction.

But here, as elsewhere, there are tradeoffs. It is clear from
some of the language used by the industry to discuss the
promise of scanning that the electronic front end will be used,
among other things, to serve as a stopwatch on store employees—to set "goals" for number of items checked through
per hour (this can easily be translated into dollars collected),

and to punish those who don't meet the quotas. This has gone on, after a fashion, in many of the nation's assembly-line industries for decades, but those have remained out of sight and out of mind for the great majority of Americans. What will happen when every grocery shopper is exposed to the depressing and often inhuman rules of the assembly line? And, further, once the checkout process is speeded up, won't the logical next step be for managers to save money by closing down some of their checkout lines? And what business can resist the temptation of selling data gleaned by its computer —the information obtained, say, during the check-cashing process—to people who have no business using it but who nevertheless have the money to buy it?

The Food Marketing Institute, in a publication called *Checking Out Scanning: How It Helps Consumers,* says the detailed receipt "may be the most valuable feature of the scanning system for the consumer." Receipts, said FMI, "contain specific product information including brand name, as well as price, total, amount presented for payment, change, date and time. . . .

"The complete, itemized receipt provides a written record that can be used for budgeting, menu planning and future shopping lists. Comparison shopping is also simplified. Consumers can take the tape along when they check prices at other supermarkets."

An examination of typical tapes from a number of stores with scanners reveals, however, that the written record is less helpful than it could be. Some require advanced deciphering techniques, such as:

MC GROCERY	.40–
ENG MUFFN 6P	.55
BNQ CK BROTH	.42
GT FRNCH BRD	.75
A J LT SYRUP	1.67

After considerable thought, the shopper concluded that the first item referred to a manufacturer's coupon worth 40 cents; the second was not English muffins with English price attached but rather a "six-pack" of the things; and the next must mean Banquet brand chicken broth. "GT" in the next one undoubtedly referred to the house brand of something at the Giant supermarket, but the shopper to this day doesn't remember buying a French bird and would not be caught dead buying something called "French bread" in a supermarket. Nor does he find anything in his cupboard that could be properly referred to as "A J," even if it resides in light syrup.

Furthermore, a consumer who wants to use his receipt for comparison shopping and keeping track of costs over time will find that most stores do not print out the sizes and weights of packaged goods (although they could, easily, since they do record the information for their own use), so only the terribly meticulous shopper would be able to compare today's purchase of a 16-ounce can of peas and carrots with next week's purchase, at another store, of a 13-ounce can of the same thing.

Worst of all, as scanning is installed, supermarkets campaign to eliminate individual item pricing. This is the pricing that, under the traditional system, is affixed to each can or box in the store. Retailers regard item pricing as a needlessly costly expense—after all, *they* know what everything costs—and tend to forget that for shoppers, it is essential to making decisions. In some places where competition is low, such as Washington, D.C., stores have arrogantly gone ahead and eliminated item pricing when installing scanners. In some other places, such as New York, laws require complete or partial item pricing. The laws are under constant attack from retailers, and if consumers are not alert, easily manipulated legislators will repeal them. (In New York City, they have been effectively repealed by the city's unwillingness to enforce them.)

The store argument is that the current price is always marked on the shelf, and that errors are minimized by putting the prices into one central computer (that also makes it infinitely easier to change prices, and, as we have seen, except for sales and specials, grocery store prices almost always go up when they change). Some offer disgruntled shoppers grease pencils so they can mark shelf prices on cans and boxes themselves and comparison-shop within the store to judge the price of, say, a brand-name can of beans in an end-aisle display against that of the house-brand beans on Aisle 6 and to make sure the computer isn't cheating them.

Michigan is one of the states that require individual unit pricing, and the independent supermarket where Jennifer Ohl works, as the scanning coordinator, went to some pains to ease the transition into scanning. For two weeks the store maintained a scanner off to one side of the selling floor and encouraged its customers to play with it and ask questions of a demonstrator. Ohl discovered while on a personal trip to Houston, where item pricing is not required, that not all stores take the same care.

"What I found is that they are a lot more lackadaisical about making sure their shelf tag matches their [computer] file price," she said. "They don't have item pricing, and when I went shopping there I took my grease pencil and marked everything. And there was a difference—a penny's difference on some items, 20 cents on others. I took it to the store manager and he said, 'Oh, thanks for telling us'—and then he walked away! Here we could get a $250 fine. We make real sure that if a customer brings back an item, especially if it is higher in the computer file than it was marked, you say, 'Oh, thank you for letting us know; we want to give you a full refund of what you paid.'"

The fact of the matter is that if stores made proper use of this new technology, they wouldn't even need to resort to shortchanging the consumer on information and money. What are called the "soft benefits" of scanning are at least as important as the more obvious ones of saving labor at the checkstand or on individual pricing. Scanning offers enormous potential for making a store's inventory and ordering procedures more efficient in ways that can benefit both the store and its customers. The information being absorbed through that glass plate can show, among other things, when the store's slack hours are; sales by individual department; customer purchasing patterns; "zero product movement" lists revealing what products are "dead items" that don't sell in great enough quantity to earn their keep on the shelves or that might be out of stock and need to be reordered; how to best lay out shelves; how many facings to allot to products; how house labels stack up against national brands; how to judge national manufacturers' often inflated claims of product popularity against the reality of the store's own trading area; how to judge the appeal of "new" items; and proof that the store is living up to the terms of a "push" promotional deal made with a broker or manufacturer.

Plus: almost any combination of the above. One of the real wonders of computer technology is that seemingly endless mixtures of variables can be matched against each other in "what-if" situations. In a supermarket, this means various combinations of pricing structures and shelf placements can be tried out and assessed until the computer's printout shows a mixture that results in the sort of "turn" the store manager wants.

Scanning is illustrative of an issue that is growing in importance in the food industry as technology catches up with the marketplace. The issue, put in its simplest terms, is: Who will benefit? Will the marketplace reap all the rewards, and throw a few crumbs to the consumers (who, after all, pay for the technology and are required to deal intimately with it each time they go through the store), or will there be some reasonably equitable arrangement for sharing in the true benefits and savings? Must the relatively powerless consumer always be made to pay the bills, serve as the guinea pig, and absorb the abuse so that an already well-off system can prosper even more? Carol Tucker Foreman has noticed that every time the American business community finds itself in a squeeze for profits, "their first thought is, 'Let's get rid of health and safety regulations,' or 'Let's get rid of that information that benefits the consumer.'" The argument over individual item pricing, she says, is a clear manifestation of that sort of thinking.

In the case of electronic scanners, the stores may not be able to sell their crumbs much longer. Back when department stores were starting to use computers to confuse and infuriate their charge customers, many consumers were naive about the new technology and fell for the line that the computer was infallible (except for those occasions when something went wrong and it was "the computer's fault"). Now, with more and more Americans buying computers of their own, more consumers are finding that machines are mere donkeys that do the work given to them by their human drivers.

If the food retailers wanted to forge an alliance with consumers, there would be no better way to start than with the proper sharing of the technology, including scanning, that is bringing the future into the grocery store.

Other changes lie in wait for the consumer, too, less flashy than electronic scanners but just as important in defining what the American citizen's relationship will be with the industry that keeps us all alive.

There are the nagging questions of the definition of food and what will happen to it: how the changes will be made, who will make them, how or if consumers will learn the news that, for example, that "lobster Newberg" at the semifancy restaurant or in the boil-in-bag, home-prepared "gourmet entrée" is really what Food Industries Limited refers to as its "natural shellfish extract."

There will be an evolution of retail food stores, but nobody's quite sure into what. One USDA assessment is that "super stores" and "combination stores," the current heavyweights of the retailing business, "will become the dominant type of grocery store." But there is plenty of evidence from other quarters that no single sort of store will dominate the scene—that rather the market will undergo extreme segmentation. There will be stores for rich people, stores for people who are relatively well off, stores for the rest of us, stores for people in a hurry, stores for people who are not impressed by beige walls and color-coordinated shelving, stores for people who are willing to pay top dollar for "gourmet" takeout food. Poor people will get what's left over. As the eighties approach their midpoint, lots of retailers are gazing lustily at the sorts of stores they like to call "upscale," by which they mean stores that attract customers who don't mind paying a lot of money for foods, even traditional items, that are presented as "gourmet" products and offered in an atmosphere of service.

Stephen I. D'Agostino, the chief executive officer of the D'Agostino supermarket chain in the New York City area and the chairman of the Food Marketing Institute, left the business in 1982, when he was forty-eight years of age, and started a new career as a Coca-Cola bottler in Chattanooga. As he was leaving, he was asked in an interview what he would do if he were starting a supermarket chain from scratch.

He replied: "I would build a food store basically catering to people in the upper income levels who want variety in food and services—services being deli-bake, cosmetics, photo processing, maybe a pharmacy—along with produce and services that enhance the quality of food and the things that go with it. It would be upscale, not lowscale."

Asked why it would be for the more well-to-do, he said: "It

would be for the sort of person who's going to use the services, and my own style would not cause me to be into items that were inexpensive. I would more likely sell pasta and croissants than soft breads."

D'Agostino said his potential customers (who, in fact, appear to be similar to the clientele of the family chain he was leaving) were "the ones with the money in their pockets, who can spend it. They want variety, they want to be able to buy quality, they want to be able to buy value." They are the sort of people who like to be creative with food, he said. "They love to buy food, and they're looking for places that give them the self-satisfaction of buying food."

And the ones who were less well-to-do?

"They're going to shop somewhere else," he said.

The ones who have considerably less income may not have much choice of where the somewhere else is. In their pursuit of the upscale folks, chains are rapidly abandoning lower-income areas. A possible counter to this trend is another one which is noteworthy in the food business, and especially so in densely populated urban areas: Rarely does an abandoned supermarket remain empty long. Soon there is another tenant, flying a different set of banners, operating under a different name. Sometimes the name is new to the food business. Sometimes it belongs to a smaller chain that's trying to make it where the big one failed. There is apparently no end to the belief among food retailers that there's money out there, waiting to be made, if only the proper formula can be discovered.

As the evolution continues in food retailing, the situation is further confused, from the consumer's point of view and everybody else's, by the fact that all the major actors are trying desperately to become *something else,* and they don't really know what something else they want to become. If, as it appears, America's sharp population rises are of the past, the food business will not be able to enjoy the luxury of living off the nation's guaranteed growth. The sellers of food are going to have to do some scratching around for their profits. They're going to have to become adept at spotting trends and figuring out ways to exploit them. Everybody is aware by now of the parallel trends toward single-parent families, single-person households, women working outside the home, and two-income families. Food company executives can quote sales statistics on microwave ovens, the industry's universal symbol of fast food at home, and every manufacturer worth his monosodium glutamate has commissioned a glossy survey that proves the trends are real. But not everybody has come up with plans for taking advantage of those trends.

In the confusion, some silliness emerges. One of the upscale supermarkets that Stephen D'Agostino left took a full-page ad in the *New York Times* and spent a third of it announcing that it was selling "rich, ripe fruits & veggies out of their wraps," "stripped to show off every beautiful bit of the healthy dewy skin." Apparently the chain was trying to appeal to the "back to nature" segment of the food-buying public by offering produce that wasn't embalmed in heat-shrunk plastic—a treat the lowscalers had been enjoying all along.

A thinker at Stanford Research Institute has succeeded in identifying the "four clusters of values which will dominate the marketplace in the eighties," and they are "need-driven consumers," "belonger-oriented consumers," "achievement-oriented consumers," and "inner-directed consumers." The "inner-directed" among us are "active in vigorous outdoor sports like hang-gliding" and "seek inner revelation and understanding," and they "have a strong sense of the fitness of things—of foods, packaging, stores to fit the occasion." Their "interest in the occult may offer specialty opportunities for exotic foods and cooking styles, especially if tinged by Eastern tradition, as in cinnamon teas and Indian or Oriental dishes." Lurking uncomplainingly at the other end of the spectrum is the "belonger," who "seeks to become part of the group via his or her purchases," and wants meat-and-potatoes meals—"hearty, but hardly inspired." Probably not into hang-gliding.

Some stores solve the dilemma in the classical marketplace way by simply announcing things. A Northeastern supermarket made an effort to appeal to most everybody not long ago by hanging a sign from its ceiling advertising "Warehouse Prices" (i.e., prices identical to those at warehouse stores, a claim that hardly ever is valid except at the warehouse stores) and others offering grammar-school-level information about nutrition. What was on the shelves was similar in quality, variety, and price to what could be found in any supermarket, however.

And all over the nation, chains and independent supermarkets are trying to cash in on the "natural" phenomenon by setting aside shelves or whole sections for foods that claim to be "organic" and "natural" and that cost considerably more than their presumably "synthetic" and "unnatural" counterparts. The Kroger chain, according to the *Wall Street Journal*, in 1982 was opening departments in seven hundred of its stores "to sell carob drops, soybeans, sunflower seeds and the like." Carnation Company announced it was getting into the "health and nutrition" store business, with computerized analyses of customers' individual eating habits, advice on losing weight, and, of course, a full line of Carnation brand "health" foods and vitamins. Kroger, in addition to running "health" boutiques, started selling insurance, money market funds, and individual retirement accounts in one of its stores.

What is happening, quite obviously, is that the food retailing industry has realized, along with everybody else in the food manufacturing and merchandising chain, the great truth that there are only so many stomachs in the country. The grocery store, like Kraft and General Mills and Campbell, is trying to become differentiated—to offer something that appears to be a little different from the rest, in hopes of capturing a segment of the market and its loyalty.

The differentiating mode of choice, as this is written in the summer of 1983, is the sort of marketplace Stephen D'Agostino was describing: the "upscale" environment that takes advantage of the willingness of some consumers to spend money freely on what they perceive to be "quality" and the desire by many of them to use food not primarily as a means of staying alive, but rather as an entertainment device.

For some consumers and some stores, this means delivering "freshness" and "authenticity" on a scale that makes the 3,000-mile trip from the California cabbage patch to Boston look like a short hop. It must be tomatoes picked in Israel two days before; the sweetest little nectarines in all of Chile; delicious yellow peppers from Holland, the finest mesquite, shipped in from the Southwest, on which to cook the meal. It means self-consciously soignée department stores hanging copper pans from their hastily installed rafters and selling chili for $7 a pound and carrot cake for $3.50 a slice, and it means self-consciously soignée customers who are willing to pay for it. It means a mail-order outfit advertising, for "only $9.95," an unspecified number (there are actually four) of "Genuine hand-picked #1 Idaho Bakers Packed in real Idaho Wood Chips in a mahogany-lined box," "complete with owner's manual," at a time when other Idaho potatoes were selling in produce stores for about 30 cents a pound.

It means, in fact, the sort of marketplace Ernest Dichter has been dreaming about for a long time. Dichter, who now is in his seventies, is the founder of the Ernest Dichter Motivations, Inc., and he is widely known as the father of such probings into the behavior and motivations of people, particularly in their dealings with the marketplace. Dichter has helped a lot of companies sell a lot of things to a lot of people. The psychologist says that there are many changes on the way for food.

"We're going to rediscover the value of good food," he said not long ago in an interview. "The genuine, the natural, the real. Probably as a counterreaction against the plastic society. Everything *else* that we get is electronic; it's a wired society. I have a positive feeling about all these things of the plastic society. We want them, and they are going to free us to find more time to be creative. To paint, to cook, to do all sorts of things."

But because the desire for "value" will coexist with a demand for plastic "convenience," said Dichter, the marketplace will become a bipolar place. "I can imagine a supermarket of the future having several sections," he said. "One could be entitled 'In a hurry? Haven't got much time?' for the working woman, and another one could be called 'Feeling like being creative?' with all kinds of new ingredients or possible combinations, like 'Want to bake your own bread?' " And for those who answer positively to that last question, Dichter prescribes the Bisquick solution: "A half-finished product where *you* add the last touch." So the cook can enjoy a sense of fulfillment, he was asked? "Exactly," he replied.

"One of my dreams," the psychologist continued, "has been to have a supermarket which has psychologically labeled shelves. One shelf might be called—jokingly—'For honeymooners.' It might say, 'Well, maybe you're not too sure yet about your cooking ability and your new hubby needs a lot of strength. Here's a lot of vitamin-rich products that you can serve him.' Another might be, 'Getting bored with your wife's diet? Well, why not try cooking yourself?' It could be on a shelf addressed to men. Maybe for senior citizens."

Surely, Dichter was asked, one of his future shelves would have to be aimed at consumers who were suffering from the effects of too *much* food—those who are constantly on the prowl for painless ways to diet.

"Yes," he said. "But I also see a new possibility: keeping your weight. In other words, maybe an anti-guilt-feeling thing. 'So you're a little overweight? To heck with it; enjoy yourself. Most of the food we have on this shelf doesn't have too many calories. Of course it has *some*, but the most important thing is that it tastes good. So go ahead, grab it, put it in your basket. And enjoy yourself.' "

Much of Ernest Dichter's supermarket of the future is already in business. The Food Emporium, a spinoff of an ordinary chain in New York City, calls itself "more than a supermarket . . . an experience!" and carves its interior into boutique-like departments such as the "Better Living Center" and the "Country Dairy." Much of the presentation is style, however; the substance is that Arrid X-Dry deodorant is featured in the "Better Living Center" and the "Country Dairy" sells Velveeta.

Another chain based in the New York area, Grand Union, has put more effort behind its announcements that "shopping is no longer a chore and a bore at Grand Union." The chain is consciously trying to present food as entertainment and itself as a theater—a place where creativity and excitement can be found, along with generics for those who want them. "Our customers now experience the same personalized service, attention and variety they receive in neighborhood specialty stores," says a Grand Union description of the concept, "but at supermarket prices." Donald C. Vaillancourt, vice-president for corporate communications and consumer affairs, adds, "What we've tried to do in our new marketing philosophy is create within the store a 'theater of food.' The supermarket becomes a community meeting place, and we create activities within the store to interest people, to get them involved in the preparation of food, the selection of food, in working at ways to make food more nutritious for the family." To this end, Grand Union provides the usual boutiquey touches such as a seafood department named "Today's Catch," cookies baked on the premises, bulk vegetables and loose eggs, and an expanded "International Aisle." But it also has wooden benches in the front ends so the elderly, harried, and halt can catch their breath; there is a community bulletin board, and even a coffee pot for the customers. A Berkeley Co-op it is not, but it is a dramatic departure from what usually goes by the name of supermarket in New York City.

A genuine supermarket of the future already exists in Minneapolis. It is the five-store Byerly's chain, a set of stores that by conventional standards are very large, very plush, and very much plugged into all the most recently discovered trends. Articles that are written about Byerly's almost always focus on the exotic and usually high-ticket foods that are sold there—the buffalo steaks and truffles, the built-in chocolate shop, and the tanks containing live rainbow trout—but they often manage to overlook the chain's more significant contributions: those of information and of choice.

Shoppers who want to take advantage of the exotic variety that Byerly's provides are offered at every turn information on how to prepare, serve, and store. Kiosks are staffed by people offering free samples and free advice. There is nutritional information; there is help in understanding the complexities of labels, comprehending the definitions of foods. Not enough such help, but surely more than in most grocery stores.

Most important, there is choice of a sort that, far better than any simple image change and advertising campaign, serves the modern consumer—the person who may, as Ernest Dichter said, want "convenience" one day and "elegance" the next. This most significant part of Byerly's, as far as both food retailers and food consumers of the future are concerned, may be illustrated by a visit to its produce department.

Along one well-maintained and nicely lighted stretch of gently sloping display counter, there are the fresh carrots. On one side there are carrots that have been neatly julienned and packed in plastic—ready to be taken home and put on the table for a fancy occasion. The cost is high, reflecting the work that had to go into turning the homely but tasty commodity into a processed item. But there are some who would feel the price is a fair exchange for the work they would not have to do.

Next there are carrots that have been scraped and sliced in thicker strips—good for poking in a dip at a party. The person who is hurrying home from work to give a dinner party might feel they, too, are worth the extra cost. Then come the loose, whole, unscraped carrots, quite a bit cheaper. And finally, the cheapest carrots of all and ones that are closest to the true definition of "carrot": good, old-fashioned, generic, no-frills carrots with their feathery bright-green tops still on them, carrots to which nothing has been done beyond the essential act of pulling them from the ground and shaking the dirt away.

The consumer still has two precious commodities of his or her own: choice, and value.

Despite all the trends of the marketplace, all the seemingly inexorable tendencies of the food industry to limit choice, increase concentration, foster monopoly, suppress information, and confuse and distract by turning basic, cheap foods into differentiated luxuries, the consumer still has a wonderful degree of choice. Despite efforts by those in elected and appointed government positions to limit information, it is still possible to make halfway decent, informed decisions about the foods we buy and eat. It just takes a little more effort than we are used to expending when we go shopping for food.

Despite the immense complexity of the business of food, the intricate and byzantine structures of manufacture, delivery, and distribution that appear to be arrayed against the simple, confused, lone consumer, there is one thing that will bring the entire system to a sudden, shattering halt: people who decide not to buy the food.

Consumers tend to forget that fact, but the rest of the food chain doesn't. The industry spends millions of dollars a year trying to find out what consumers will sit still for, what they're dissatisfied about, what they will and won't buy. In discussions with dozens of people in the food industry during research for this book, fully half of them voluntarily mentioned the importance of what they perceive to be the power of consumers in the marketplace. Many referred, in unaccustomed tones of humility, to the consumer beef and coffee boycotts of several years ago. While the industry may treat consumers as laboratory animals who are easily induced not only to slurp up whatever is put before them but also to pay dearly for the experience, it also fears the power of consumers when they become fed up. Ordinary people may go to sleep with visions of sugar plums in their heads, but the food industry has recurring nightmares about what happens if consumers suddenly stop liking sugar plums.

Perhaps the best way to cope with the business of food these days is to let the industry know that our loyalty cannot be taken for granted—that we, too, can suddenly reverse a lifetime of habits and, when sufficiently provoked, cast about for alternatives to the current methods of nourishing our bodies. That we are not just a captive audience of loyal, uncritical stomachs. Then, perhaps, the awe that the food business has for the people who eat its products will turn into respect.

Index

Note: the word *food* has been omitted from items in the index such as *packaging* when it can be clearly inferred, and such items as basic foods, natural foods, for example, would be found under *b* and *n*.

Code of Federal Regulations, 111, 197
coffee, 92, 150
Coffee Holding Company, 92
Collins, Charles, 252–3
Collins, Joseph, 215
coloring, and labeling, 198
combination store, 120, 266
competition, 56–7, 93, 175–6; market concentration and, 58–9; price, 65, 67; perfect, 67–8; advertising and, 68, 105–7, 114, 134; distribution and, 92–3; various forms of, 134; FTC and, 154–5; declining, 206; in big cities, 210
composition of food, changes in, 57
computers, *see* technology
concentration of producers, production, 30–1, 58–62, 175, 193n; increase in, 60–1, 138–9, 206, 257; and advertising, 61, 113; low intensities of, 139; consumers and, 193–4; in big cities, 210; possible challenges to, 246
Condé Nast Publications, 97
conglomerates, 61–6; and cross-subsidization, 65–7; and mergers, 139; possible challenges to, 246
Congress, 25–6, 255
Connecticut, and direct marketing, 235
Connoisseur's Guide to Beer, 66n
Connor, John M., 50, 57, 63–5, 68, 99–100, 193–4, 193n
consumer franchise, 95–6
Consumerisms, 256
Consumer Reports, 218–19
"Consumer's Guide to Food Labels," 196
consumers, 52, 113, 128, 141, 143, 148, 206; and technology, 14, 264–265; and government, 15, 139–40, 156–8, 161, 166–73, 182, 213–14, 223, 254; and price, 16–18, 104–5, 117, 132, 148, 204–10, 221, 223; and marketing orders, 32, 35; and processing, 37, 44, 177–8, 183; and manufactured foods, 49–50; choice and power of, 50, 273–5; and natural foods, 52, 183; changing needs of, 53, 56; and concen-

tration, 58–9, 61, 138–9, 193–4; and advertising and promotion, 61, 99, 179–82, 255; loyalties and trustingness of, 63–4, 95, 122, 179, 183; and monopoly overcharge, 68, 246; shopping habits of, in NYC, 78; studies and surveys of, 95–7; and labels, 112, 195–203; and coupons, 116, 181; and evaluation of food stores, 122–3; and layout of store, 123–7; national organizations of, 161, 171; and safety, 163–165; and competition, 175–6; and definition of food, 176–8; and time-saving, 178, 208; and health food stores, 183–4; and restaurants and menus, 184–9; and seasonal food, 190–1; shopping aids, tips, and information for, 192–5, 207–10, 217–24, 227–8, 235–6, 256, 258–9, 273, *see also* and labels, *below;* and grading and dating, 200–3; possible actions by, 204–7, 220–1, 223, 225, 232, 251, 275, *see also* cooperatives, shopping aids, *etc., above, and specific types of action below;* and on-purpose leftovers, 208–9; stocking up by, 209–10; in urban areas, 210–12; advocates for, 214–25; and direct marketing, 226–33, 235, 237–8, 241–2, 244–6; and future, 247–51, 254, 265–8, 271, 273–5; rating of protection by, 255; and cable television, 250–1; and scanning, 260–1; belonger, 268–9; inner-directed, 268–9; deception and exploitation of, *see* advertising; packaging
Consumers' Cooperative of Berkeley, *see* Berkeley Co-op
Consumers Union (CU), 218–19
consumption, 19, 57, 70, 72, 75, 117; in NYC, 75, 78–9, 87; of fish, 96–7
contamination, 142, 149–51
convenience foods, 21–2, 51, 53, 209
convenience stores, 77, 121
cooperatives, consumer, 76, 83, 223, 225–32, 245–6; marketing, 31
corn, direct marketing of, 237
Cornell University, 182–3
Cornucopia Project, 74, 220

ABOUT THE AUTHOR

Fred Powledge is an author and journalist whose books cover a range that includes circus life, adoption, urban renewal, race relations, backpacking, and sailing. His magazine articles have appeared in *Audubon*, *The New Yorker*, *The Nation*, *Life*, *Esquire*, *Harper's*, and dozens of other publications. Before becoming a free-lance writer, he reported for the Associated Press, *The Atlanta Journal*, and *The New York Times*. Powledge lives with his wife in a restored brownstone in Brooklyn, New York, where he enjoys cooking, among other things, eastern North Carolina barbecue.